THE ILLUSTRATED HISTORY OF THE
VIETNAM WAR

THE ILLUSTRATED HISTORY OF THE
VIETNAM WAR

BRIAN BECKETT

BLANDFORD PRESS
POOLE, DORSET

This book was devised and produced by
Multimedia Publications (UK) Ltd

Editor: Jeff Groman
Production: Arnon Orbach
Design: John Strange
Picture Research: Picture Research,
Washington (Ellen Furneaux) and John
McClancy

First published in the UK 1985 by Blandford
Press, Link House, West Street, Poole,
Dorset BH15 1LL

British Library Cataloguing in
Publication Data
Beckett, Brian
    The Illustrated History of the Vietnam War
    1. Vietnamese Conflict, 1961-1975
    I. Title
    959.704'3   DS557.7

ISBN 0-7137-1790-4

Typeset by Flowery Typesetters Ltd
London
Origination by The Clifton Studio Ltd
London
Printed in Italy by Arnoldo Mondadori
Editore, Vicenza

Contents

INTRODUCTION

On April 30, 1975, tanks of the North Vietnamese Army rumbled into Saigon and brought to an end a war thirty years old. United States participation in that war was probably the most controversial episode in recent American history and certainly the most unpopular conflict in which this country has ever been involved. It was the longest war America has ever fought and arguably its only military defeat. It was not a military defeat in the obvious sense – the American Army in the field was never beaten in Vietnam and, on the contrary, won every major engagement it fought there – but a defeat in the hearts of the American people themselves. It was a war which nobody really wanted and one which – if it were possible to win at all – required a commitment that no one was willing to give. The United States wasn't driven out of Vietnam; it simply decided that staying on was no longer worth the price.

And the price had been high. The cost in American lives was over 50,000. The cost in money was untold billions of dollars. The cost, socially and politically, was to split the country and divide a generation. The war was fought to counter insurgency in South Vietnam and to show Moscow and Peking that Washington intended to back up its commitment to contain communist expansion around the world. If Vietnam fell, the reasoning went, the rest of Indochina would soon follow and, after that, all of Southeast Asia. It was better to fight the communists in Vietnam, President Johnson once argued, than in Hawaii, but he failed to convince the American public that the Saigon Government was worth saving or that its fall would ultimately endanger Hawaii or any other vital US interest.

Some of the statistics from Vietnam beggar the imagination. Someone worked out that the US Air Force dropped about two and a half million tons of bombs on Indochina between January 1969 and March 1971, compared to only just over two million tons in the *entirety* of World War II. Sometimes this figure is used to paint a picture of military inefficiency and futility since the enemy neither gave up nor went away, but it should be remembered that a large percentage of these bombs were dropped in order to save American lives by shifting the burden of US involvement to the Air Force rather than to the ground troops.

Even when Nixon sent the B-52s to Hanoi in late 1972, there was no real effort to cause the massive death and destruction visited on German and Japanese cities during World War II; much of the misery and devastation wrought by Nixon's B-52s occurred in remote villages in Laos, Cambodia, and Vietnam. Even so, ugly as it was, it wasn't the war's brutality that bothered the American public so much as it was the war's seeming pointlessness. People were willing to send their sons to battle when there was a worthwhile victory to be gained but, as the body bags began coming home across the United States, America rapidly became disillusioned with a war that had no clear-cut military objective.

Had it been politically possible for American forces to invade North Vietnam to force the issue, the US public might have given Washington more backing. But limited wars like Vietnam are fought for limited political objectives and there was little chance that the President would risk a wider conflict with the Soviet Union or China. So the war seemed purposeless to those who might have otherwise supported it and immoral to those who would have opposed it anyway. Towards the end, even the most hawkish Americans were more-or-less happy to settle for Nixon's "peace with honor." To many, the ultimate tragedy was the sheer waste of it all and the feeling that the South Vietnamese had been led down the garden path and then abandoned when things got too tough.

If there was a single obvious mistake, it was the ease with which successive administrations kept escalating the US commitment to Vietnam without having any real idea of how far they would have to go to defeat the Viet Cong and dissuade Hanoi from supporting the revolution in the South. There was also Washington's unfortunate public relations campaign which always tended to deal in morbid-sounding body counts or to paint overly optimistic pictures of an up-coming victory which was largely illusory; neither did Washington hesitate to bury its past mistakes and bad guesses.

When a Pentagon employee opposed to the war stole parts of an official file detailing the history of American involvement in Vietnam and gave it to the *New York Times*, Nixon did his best to suppress its publication. The Supreme Court, however, disagreed and, in one of the war's few enduring victories, ruled that if the American public were expected to send their sons to die from foreign shot and shell, they at least had the right to know the reasons why.

Previous pages November 1967. The USA's 173rd Airborne Brigade in war-shattered high forest near Dak To in the Central Highlands of Vietnam.

1 Seeds of Conflict

The historical background

Vietnam is a small country in Southeast Asia, not much bigger than New Mexico, but with a population as large as California, New York, and Pennsylvania (our three most heavily populated states) added together. It is an old country with a long and tortured history. For only about half of the 2,000 or so years of its existence has Vietnam been a free and independent nation; for the rest of the time it has been a colony dominated and exploited by various foreign powers. China ruled Vietnam for almost a thousand years; France for almost a hundred; the Japanese for barely five.

During the time of French rule were sown the seeds of what was to become one of the longest, costliest, and bloodiest wars in the history of mankind; a war which continues to this day, not only in terms of active combat, not only in the legions of dead and missing, but in the broken bodies and shattered spirits of the young men of many nations who fought and suffered there. It is a war that divided America, shook to the core her most fundamental values, and which remains even today a brooding sore on the national consciousness, far from healed.

French interest in Vietnam began as early as the 16th Century when her missionaries followed the silk and spice traders into the exotic lands of the Far East. The missionaries found fertile soil for their work in Vietnam which is why, even today, the country has a flourishing Catholic population and why certain Vietnamese splinter sects boast saints as diverse as Buddha, Jesus, and Joan of Arc. In the second half of the 19th Century, the French military landed in Vietnam mainly to protect the missionaries who by then had made themselves rather unpopular with certain of the native rulers. Various commercial interests followed the military and between them they soon carved out a vast colonial empire. By 1893, France laid claim to an Indochinese colony which included the complete territories of the countries now known as Laos, Cambodia, and Vietnam. For the next fifty years the French made many improvements to their colony. They built railroads, ports, schools, and hospitals; they increased rice production and planted rubber trees until, by the start of World War II, French Indochina was one of the richest colonies in the world – riches which were enjoyed mainly by French, French Colonials, and a small number of favored Vietnamese.

World War II was to change all this. In June 1940, Germany overran France, and without support from the mother country, French Indochina was left helpless in the face of Japanese advances in Southeast Asia. Three months after the fall of Paris, the Vichy French agreed to allow Japanese troops to occupy the northern parts of its Indochina empire without a fight, even though French forces in Indochina numbered some 50,000. The Japanese moved in and took power but permitted French officials to continue to administer the colony as before. Ten months later the puppet government in Paris agreed to allow the Japanese to occupy selected portions of Southern Indochina, again without a fight.

Opposite The Mekong Delta from the air. The Delta is Vietnam's major rice producing region and its lush jungle cover made it a main area of communist insurgency during the war.

Right Ho Chi Minh (circled) poses with other Far Eastern delegates at the International Congress of the Comintern held in Moscow between November and December 1922. Directed from Moscow, the Comintern was formed to foment communist-based revolutions throughout the world.

Through this bloodless conquest Japan secured what proved to be an invaluable base as her armed forces swept across Southeast Asia to conquer British-held Malaya and Singapore. Southeast Asia also became a vital source of raw materials for the expanding Japanese military machine, and French Indochina proved to be a willing and friendly business partner. Indeed, so smoothly had Paris been exchanged for Tokyo, that it took almost five years for the war to touch the life of the average French colonialist in Vietnam.

In August 1944, Paris was liberated and almost immediately the Free French government began scheming to regain its occupied colonies. In Indochina itself, sensing that the Japanese military defeat was not far away, the French colonial administration became increasingly less cooperative. Fearing that the French forces in Indochina might turn on them, Tokyo ordered a military coup. In March 1945, Japanese troops moved on the French garrisons, disarmed them, and placed them under arrest.

The French were taken totally by surprise and, for the most part, were disarmed without a struggle. There were notable exceptions in what was otherwise a French debacle; the heavily outnumbered French garrisons at Lang Son and Dang Dong near the Chinese border, for example, refused to surrender and were massacred to a man after inflicting heavy losses on waves of attacking Japanese. In the larger context of the Japanese takeover, however, such sacrifice was all but meaningless. Within days all resistance had ceased and three of France's Indochinese puppet princes – Sisavang Vong of Laos, Norodom Sihanouk of Cambodia, and Bao Dai of Annam (the area

covering most of what is now central Vietnam) proclaimed their "national" independence, revoked long-standing colonial treaties with Paris, and pledged themselves to Japan's "Greater East Asia Co-prosperity Sphere" – the Japanese euphemism for Japanese imperialism.

In the meantime, America was moving inexorably closer to the Japanese mainland as island by island her armed forces moved across the Pacific. She had been seeking local partisan and guerrilla support in advance of a possible landing somewhere in Southeast Asia. In Vietnam, America found support from various nationalist groups which had originally been set up to overthrow French rule but which, by coincidence were now the only effective force combating the occupying Japanese. One of these groups was to dominate the history of Indochina over the next thirty years. It was to become a name known around the world and, for a generation, the sworn enemy of America. It is one of history's curiosities, then, that this group was America's wartime friend and that the Viet Minh, as it was called, rose to power with the help and full blessing of the United States.

Our ally, Ho Chi Minh

On February 8, 1941, Nguyen Tat Thanh, a slightly built, fifty-one year old Vietnamese, crossed over the French Indochinese border from Southern China where he had been operating as an agent of the Moscow-based Comintern. It was the first time Thanh had set foot in his native land for thirty years. Since 1911 he had wandered the world alone, a solitary figure who worked as a seaman or at odd jobs in the many lands he visited. During

Far left Ho Chi Minh. Born in 1890, Ho left Vietnam in 1911 to travel the world. From his early days, he was a member of the Comintern and later the Indochinese Communist Party. During World War II, Ho worked closely with America's OSS in the fight against the Japanese. After the defeat of the Japanese in 1945, he became the leader of the newly independent country of North Vietnam and master-minded the war against the French and, later, against the Republic of South Vietnam. Ho Chi Minh died in 1969.

Left General Vo Nguyen Giap. Giap led the Viet Minh in the war against the French and later against the United States. Giap is best remembered for his victory at Dien Bien Phu in 1954 and is considered one of the great architects of revolutionary warfare and guerrilla tactics but he was always willing to accept massive casualties to achieve a major victory.

all those years Thanh had been a passionate believer in, and fighter for, the cause of Vietnamese independence. In his long career as soldier, scholar, writer, revolutionary, agent of the Comintern, and freedom fighter, Nguyen Tat Thanh was known by many names. The world knows him best as Ho Chi Minh.

On his return to Indochina, Ho established his headquarters in caves near the village of Pac Bo. His directive from the Comintern was simple – plan and create a revolution in French Indochina. Ho's power base was the Indochinese Communist Party (ICP) which he had formed in exile as long ago as 1930. To Ho Chi Minh, however, traditional Marxist ideas of class struggle were not as important as the immediate goal of liberating his country from the French and the Japanese. Acting under Ho's orders, the ICP deliberately played down its ideological aims in order to create a coalition of nationalist groups with as broad based an appeal as possible. Ultimately many disparate political factions were joined together under Ho's leadership. This coalition became known as the Vietnam Independence League – the Viet Minh.

The politics of wartime Indochina were complicated in the extreme. As an agent of the Comintern, Ho was the enemy of China's ruler, Generalissimo Chiang Kai-shek, and of the semi-independent warlords who ruled Southern China; Ho often found himself residing in Chinese jails when he crossed the border into that country. On the other hand, as an enemy of the Japanese, he was a useful ally who found himself receiving Chinese support. Chiang Kai-shek himself had designs on Indochina which he thought might give him a useful lever to pry the French out of Shanghai and other Chinese ports so Chiang,

although fighting for the Allies, was far from being committed to France's imperialist claims. To complicate matters further, Ho had the support of China's communist leader, Mao Tse Tung, who even then controlled large sections of China. Mao and Chiang were mortal enemies soon to be locked in a bitter and protracted civil war, but at that time they were in fragile alliance in the fight against the Japanese.

Into this caldron of intrigue, shifting allegiances, and political manipulation came the American Office of Strategic Services (OSS), the department in charge of special operations and the forerunner of the CIA. Gradually "Mr" or "General" Ho came to the attention of the OSS and, by 1945, Ho's Viet Minh was working actively with the United States. The extent of Ho's work with the OSS is still not clear, but it is known that the Viet Minh received large numbers of American weapons and cooperated with the Allies in setting up an intricate intelligence network throughout Indochina, as well as an air-rescue operation for downed pilots. Ho himself worked for a time in the psychological warfare department of the Chinese propaganda office in cooperation with the US Office of War Information. Intelligence passed on by the Viet Minh centered on Japanese troop movements, target data for Allied bombers, and information on various local Indochinese and French sympathetic to the Japanese. A few hit and run commando raids on Japanese positions were carried out as Joint OSS/Viet Minh operations.

Although the Viet Minh would probably have cooperated with anybody fighting the Japanese, America was in many ways an ideal ally. It was, after all, an ex-colony itself which had won its

Above French troops re-occupy a Viet Minh village in 1953. The village had been shelled and bombed before the troops moved in but sniper fire is still a danger.

Right French paratroopers charge Viet Minh positions at Na San on December 1, 1952. Viet Minh attacks the previous night had taken the hill and the guerrillas had dug themselves in.

freedom in a long and hard-fought guerrilla war. Not only that, but its leader, President Roosevelt, had made no secret about his dislike of European colonialism. After Roosevelt's death in 1945, Ho met several times with OSS officials in an effort to continue, and enlarge, US/Viet Minh cooperation. He seems to have sought no concession in return for his help other than an American commitment to support Vietnamese independence after the war. Such a commitment may well have been made by the OSS, but the OSS was a military organization making military decisions. Even as the war dragged to its end, the inescapable logic of geopolitics was slowly forcing America into an official diplomatic stance which, like it or not, would support France's efforts to hold onto its Indochinese possessions.

At the Potsdam summit in July 1945, Stalin, Attlee (who had just replaced Churchill as Britain's Prime Minister), and Truman began making plans for the post-war world. In order to disarm Japanese forces in Indochina, it was decided to divide the country along the 16th parallel; Britain would disarm the Japanese in the South; and China in the North. No one thought to consult the Vietnamese about these plans. On August 16th, the day after the Japanese unconditional surrender, representatives of various Vietnamese nationalist parties met in far humbler conditions in the small village of Tran Tao to discuss their future. They elected Ho Chi Minh their leader and resolved to pursue independence at any cost.

On September 2nd, the formal Japanese surrender was signed aboard the *USS Missouri* in Tokyo Bay, and the hopes of Vietnamese nationalists reached their peak. French authority had been shattered by the Japanese and now here were those same Japanese laying down their arms. For the first time in a

century there were no foreigners in charge of their country. Independence seemed to be so close that they could just reach out and take it. Milling crowds converged on Hanoi's Ba Dinh Square waving banners and placards in several languages – all celebrating national liberation. On the podium, Ho Chi Minh proclaimed Independence Day and the creation of the Democratic Republic of Vietnam. It was no accident that Ho made his appeal (and warning) to the world in phrases taken almost verbatim from the American Declaration of Independence and the French Declaration of the Rights of Man.

"The entire Vietnamese people," he said, "are determined to mobilise all their spiritual and material forces, to sacrifice their lives and property, in order to safeguard their right to liberty and independence . . . All men are created equal. The creator has given us certain inviolable Rights; the Right to life, the Right to be free, and the Right to achieve happiness." Banners in the crowd read, "Vietnam to the Vietnamese," "Independence or Death," and "Welcome to the Allies." In fact, Allied troops had not yet arrived in any great numbers at that time, but when they did come their welcome was to be short-lived.

In the South, in Saigon, Independence Day celebrations had been marred by rioting and looting as several different Vietnamese factions, including the Viet Minh, fought against each other and against French Colonials in the streets. A provisional Viet Minh government had declared independence in Saigon but the city was rife with rumors that the French residents were planning a takeover. Drunken looting by recently freed legionnaires further inflamed these rumors.

On September 13th, under the terms of the Potsdam agreement, General Gracey and 25,000 British troops arrived in

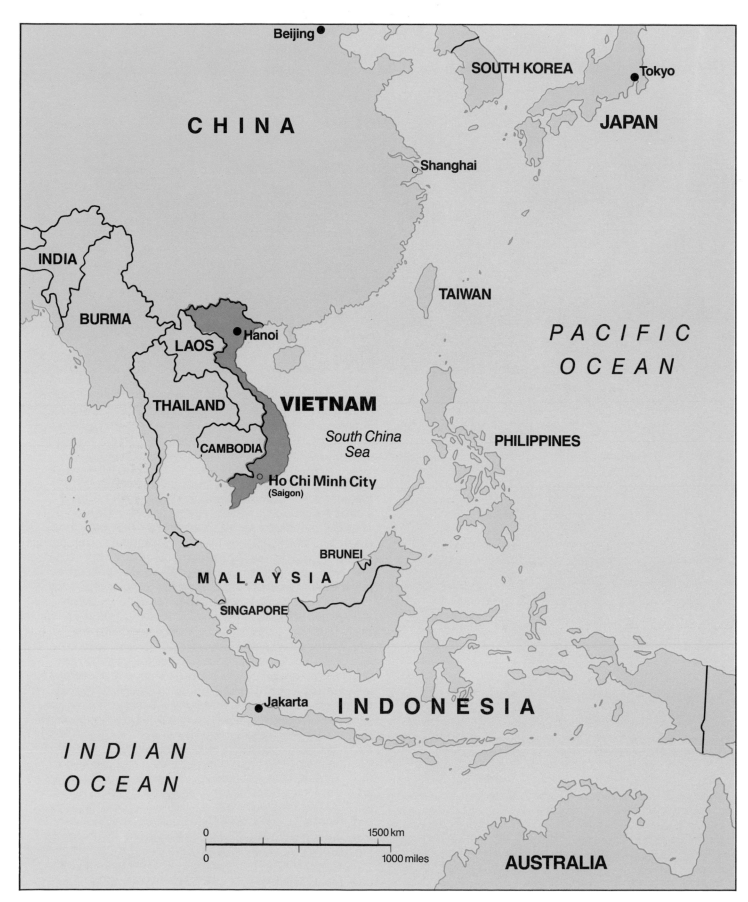

Left Southeast Asia today. Since the end of World War II the region has been one of the world's major battlegrounds, with communist insurgency movements in Indonesia, the Philippines, Malaysia, Burma, Laos, Cambodia and Vietnam.

Right A Viet Minh commando with a make-shift bomb. Charging his target, he will detonate the bomb and – more than likely – blow himself up along with it.

Below A French armored column clears a Viet Minh obstruction along the Nam Dinh Road. Blocking the roads not only slowed down French columns but it also made them vulnerable to sniper fire and hit-and-run attacks.

Saigon to disarm the Japanese. Gracey's orders were to avoid becoming entangled in Vietnamese internal affairs but it quickly became clear that, whatever his orders, Gracey personally favored the return of French rule and he went out of his way to accommodate French interests wherever he could.

On September 21st, Gracey declared martial law in Saigon. On the 22nd, with the tacit consent of the British, Saigon's French residents, reinforced by recently released POWs, carried out the coup threatened earlier in the month. They overran police stations, captured the radio station, and raised the Tricolor wherever they went. They attacked Saigon's city hall forcing the Viet Minh provisional government to flee for their lives. Other Vietnamese were not so lucky. Small bands of angry French locals roamed Saigon's streets beating Vietnamese of any age they could lay hands on. Viet Minh soldiers and officials were shot out of hand or put under arrest. Bodies littered the streets; some dead, some beaten too severely to move. This orgy of violence brought matters to a head in the rapidly escalating conflict between Vietnamese nationalists, French Colonialists, and a stubbornly prideful government in Paris. The British soon realised that they were caught in the middle and that the only way out for them was to be replaced by regular French troops as quickly as possible. An accord was swiftly reached between London and Paris giving the French full responsibility for the area below the 16th parallel. As soon as the French could take over, the British would go.

The Viet Minh was not slow in responding to the attempted coup by the French Colonialists. By September 25th, the Viet Minh had blockaded the roads leading into Saigon and no French dared leave. Talks and a fragile truce led nowhere. In early October, some 21,000 French troops under General LeClerc began arriving in Saigon. On the 16th of October these troops, supported by the British and, ironically enough, by re-armed Japanese soldiers, attacked Viet Minh positions in

Left French machine-gun position keeps a watch for Viet Minh guerrillas in the hills near the Chinese border with Vietnam.

Saigon. As the Viet Minh were slowly driven out of Saigon, the RAF and what was left of Japan's Air Force pressed home the attack. By February 1946, LeClerc was able to claim (optimistically) that the entire Mekong Delta region of South Vietnam was now under French control.

In the North, the Chinese troops of occupation which had arrived to disarm the Japanese, cooperated more or less fully with the Viet Minh provisional government there. The events in the South, however, increased Ho's fears that the French would invade the North in an attempt to regain their former colony. He was also aware that European residents in Hanoi were stockpiling arms in the hope of a return of French troops, or for a possible uprising against the Viet Minh.

In the circumstances, Ho thought the wisest course was diplomacy. After protracted talks with the French, Ho accepted a limited French presence in the North (25,000 troops for five years) in return for French recognition of Vietnam as a free state within the French Union. By this contrivance, Ho was able to rid the North of the Chinese whose presence he feared more than that of the French. French forces were landed in the port of Haiphong in the North and over the months that followed they patrolled the city in uneasy alliance with the Viet Minh.

Ho in the meanwhile went to Paris for further talks which, it was hoped, would result in a permanent settlement of the Vietnam problem – particularly about French attempts to set up a separate and "independent" republic in the South, to be called Cochinchina. Ho, of course, was bitterly opposed to any arrangements that would divide his country. Talks between Paris and the Viet Minh dragged on for months but, given the chronic political instability of French Governments of the time, the talks had little chance of success. And such proved to be the case. Ho returned to Hanoi in October 1946 with most of the major issues still unresolved.

In November, a squabble over who had the right to collect customs duties escalated into armed combat between French and Viet Minh troops in Haiphong. French forces seized the port's facilities and, in retaliation for Viet Minh attacks, shelled the Chinese part of the city. Some 6,000 civilians were killed with a further 19,000 casulties. For the next week, French troops battled the Viet Minh in the streets of Haiphong before gaining full control of the city.

Over the next few months the fighting spread to Hanoi and other urban centers. French troops gradually took control of the cities of Indochina, driving the Viet Minh into the jungle and countryside. From here, the Viet Minh was to wage its long-term campaign of guerrilla warfare. The French strategy was to hold the cities and the roadways linking them, then seek and destroy the Viet Minh in the countryside. Later in the war, the French commanders would try to "bleed" the Viet Minh into defeat by luring them into attacking heavily fortified positions from which the French could annihilate the attackers. There is something in the mentality of 20th Century French generals which finds this strategy appealing. It had worked to a point during World War I with the appalling slaughter at Verdun (but the long-running battle had weakened the French almost as much as the Germans). The idea of strategic fortifications also lay behind the building of the Maginot line and France's quick defeat in World War II. The impregnable fortress worked for a time in Vietnam too but it was to be put to rest for good at a place called Dien Bien Phu.

Right General Raoul Salan visiting French troops in the Tonkin Delta in May 1952. Under Salan's leadership the French forces in Indochina suffered a number of reverses which ultimately led to the Viet Minh victory. A few years later, Salan was to become infamous as the leader of the OAS, a terrorist organization of French Army officers and Algerian colonists dedicated to the violent overthrow of Charles de Gaulle.

Below German Legionnaires man a machine-gun post on a hill position overlooking Xieng Khouang. Between the end of World War II and the early Sixties, former *Wehrmacht* soldiers formed the backbone of the French Foreign Legion and made it one of the world's elite fighting units.

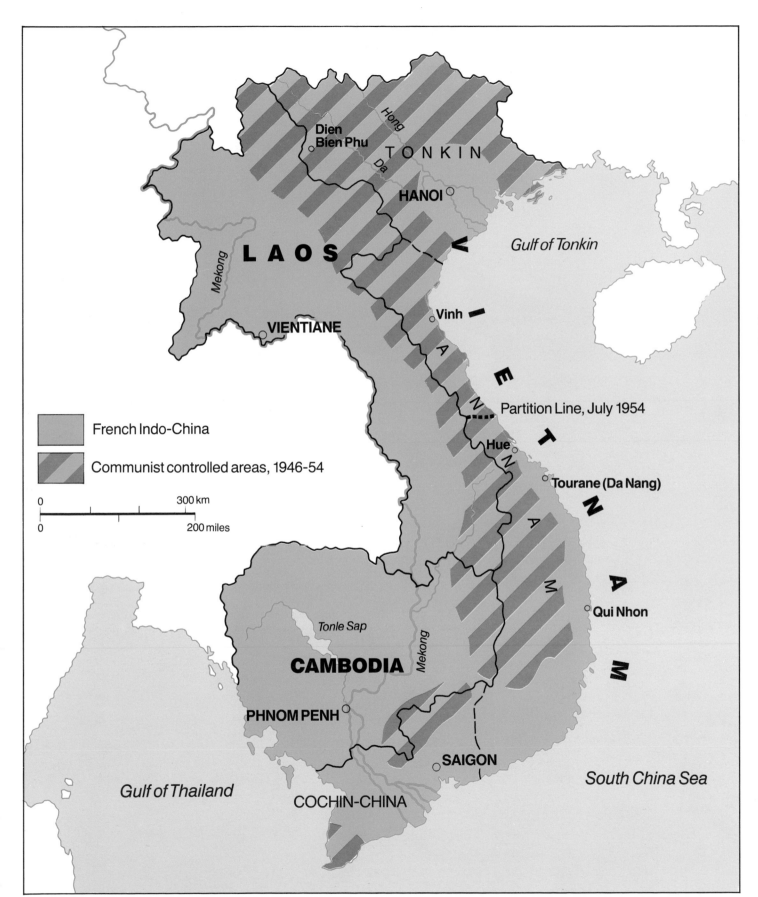

Dien
Bien Phu

Hong

T O N K I N

HANOI

Gulf of Tonkin

L A O S

Mekong

VIENTIANE

Vinh

French Indo-China

Communist controlled areas, 1946-54

Partition Line, July 1954

Hue

0   300 km

0   200 miles

Tourane (Da Nang)

Qui Nhon

Tonle Sap

CAMBODIA

Mekong

PHNOM PENH

SAIGON

Gulf of Thailand

COCHIN-CHINA

South China Sea

Left French Indochina, 1946-54, later to
become the independent nations of
Cambodia (Kampuchea), Laos, and
Vietnam.

Right French paratroopers drop near the Viet Minh-held town of Lang in July 1953. After two days of operation in the area, the French had driven the Viet Minh out and captured over 5000 tons of supplies.

Following pages An American river patrol operating in the Mekong Delta.

Giap and the Road to Dien Bien Phu

In June 1949, the French had some 150,000 troops stationed in Indochina but the military situation was pretty much at a stalemate. Then China fell to Mao's communist troops and the Viet Minh found themselves with a friendly ally to the north and, for the first time, with an ample supply of modern arms. Up to this point the Viet Minh had been fighting with a hodge podge of British, American, and French small arms; muskets, homemade grenades, swords, machetes, and even spears. But now all this would change. In September 1950, the Viet Minh's military commander Vo Nguyen Giap, his army advised, trained, and supplied by the Chinese, decided to abandon his usual guerrilla tactics and to take the military initiative. Giap sent his soldiers against a Foreign Legion camp at Dong Khe which they overran after heavy fighting. Giap then attacked a French garrison at Cao Bang and ambushed the relief column moving to the aid of their besieged comrades. Within weeks, most of the North Vietnamese countryside in the North and Northwest was in the effective control of the Viet Minh and the French Army had received massive – and unexpected – casualties.

Giap has become a legend and is often considered one of the greatest practitioners of the art of guerrilla warfare, even rivalling Mao himself. He was born in the village of An Xa in 1912, a year after Ho Chi Minh had left Indochina on his world travels. In 1922, Giap attended the Lycee National, a French school at Hue which boasted several prominent Vietnamese nationalists among its graduates including Ho Chi Minh. In 1927, Giap's nationalist activities caused his expulsion from the school; in 1930, he was sentenced to three years hard labor, also for political activity, but he was released after only a few months. Giap then entered the Lycee Albert Saurraut in Hanoi where he earned a law degree in 1937 and a doctorate in political economics in 1938.

During these years, Giap also joined the ICP. In 1940, his political activities forced him to flee to China where he met Ho Chi Minh for the first time. During his absence, Giap's wife and sister-in-law (who were both politically active), were arrested. His sister-in-law went to the guillotine and Giap's wife received fifteen years hard labor in Hanoi's Central Prison where she died in 1943. From 1940 onwards, Giap worked closely with Ho Chi Minh's guerrilla army. Like Ho, Giap was a committed communist but one who worked closely with the OSS during and just after the war. To the OSS, he was "Mr Van" and on several occasions Giap went to great lengths to stress his gratitude for US aid to the Viet Minh cause.

Over dinner with OSS agent Archimedes L.A. Patti, Giap spoke of the Viet Minh's communism as nationalistic rather than ideological. He explained how the Party had no desire to exchange "another foreign power in Vietnam for the French." Probably hinting at a possible bargain with the French, Ho Chi Minh, who was also present, talked of a "limited independence" for the Vietnamese. At a later meeting, Ho described his disillusionment with his earlier hopes that Western or Russian communists would understand or support the cause of Vietnamese liberation.

"In all the years that followed," Ho said, "not one of the so-called liberal elements have come to the aid of colonials. I place more reliance on the United States to support Vietnam's independence, before I could expect help from the USSR."

Whether or not Ho Chi Minh and Giap were nationalists first and communists second is a question that can never fully be answered, but much of their later behavior suggests that they were and that diplomats in Washington may well have missed a valuable opportunity.

In the last part of 1950, the Viet Minh's successes resulted in Paris sending General Jean de Lattre de Tassigny to command French forces in Indochina. A gifted soldier and leader, de Lattre achieved some quick, dramatic victories in 1951 but committed his troops to entrenched fortifications around major bases and around the cities of Hanoi and Haiphong. De Lattre also introduced airpower on a large scale into the fighting, using US supplied fighter-bombers to great effect. On December 22, 1950, Viet Minh troops operating near Tien Yen were hit with napalm and, just under a month later, a Viet Minh assault on French postitions at Hinh Yen was met with wave after wave of napalm carrying aircraft. Charred corpses littered the field and Giap was forced to call off the attack. Viet Minh losses were put at some 15,000 casualties and at least half of these were killed outright. It says something about the ferocity of the fighting that only a few hundred Viet Minh were taken prisoner. After further reversals at Mao Khe, fifteen miles north of Haiphong, Giap realized that he had overestimated his troops' capacity to wage open conventional warfare and the Viet Minh returned to its traditional guerrilla role of hit and run raids, ambushes, and other tactics of attrition designed to exhaust the French and wear down their morale.

Napalm was to become symbolic of the Vietnam war both then and later. Dropped from attacking aircraft, napalm explodes on impact to send a wall of flame across the ground incinerating everything in its path. Now banned as a weapon of war, it is truly effective only against dug in positions or concentrations of troops caught out in the open. As the US was to find later, napalm's great disadvantage as a weapon is that it is not selective. On several occasions, US aircraft used napalm on Vietcong units operating in or near villages, and American living rooms were filled with horrific pictures of burned civilians fleeing in panic or being treated in emergency aid centers. Ultimately, it was to be one of the many factors that influenced the American public's desire to get out of Vietnam as soon as possible.

The French had absolute control of the air. Later, American planes were to be faced with Soviet supplied surface-to-air missiles (SAM) and Mig fighters, but in 1950 the Viet Minh lacked even the portable, surface-to-air rocket launchers now common to modern warfare. But airpower is effective only against set targets or concentrations of enemy troops. It is rather wasted if the enemy is dispersed into small guerrilla bands operating off the countryside or, following Mao's dictum, hiding itself among the civilian population. When the Viet Minh temporarily abandoned its strategy of attacking entrenched French positions in concentrated numbers, the air weapon lost a great deal of its overall effectiveness.

France fought her Indochina war with career soldiers, colonial troops (including Vietnamese), and the Foreign Legion but, unlike the US, never used draftees to any extent. At the time, the Foreign Legion was one of the world's most effective fighting forces. Its ranks were swollen with volunteers escaping a war-ravaged Europe, most of whom had already seen years of

combat in one army or another. Many were German who brought to the Legion all the discipline and skill for which the German Army is famous. Veterans of the *Afrikakorps* and of the crack military units of the *SS* filled the non-commissioned ranks of the Legion while its officers – in a long standing tradition – were drawn from the elite of the French regular army and the best graduates of St Cyr, France's equivalent of West Point.

The harshness of Legion training and discipline is legendary but it was the only way an effective fighting force could be molded out of an international melting pot of mercenaries who had little or no loyalty to France. Today, the Legion is a shadow of its former self; it maintains a headquarters in Corsica and a few outposts scattered throughout the backwaters of the tiny remnants of France's colonial empire – Tahiti is the prize posting – but in the Fifties, the Legion was still one of the world's elite military units. The Legion's decline paralleled not just the loss of French colonies in Indochina and Algeria but also the German economic recovery. As West Germany began to recover from the devastations of World War II, more and more former *Wehrmacht* veterans opted to go home when their five year Legion enlistments were up.

De Lattre was dying of cancer and soon resigned to be succeeded in 1952 by General Raoul Salan who later became infamous as the leader of the OAS which waged a terrorist war against de Gaulle in the streets of Algiers and Paris. When Salan arrived, French troops had been engaging Viet Minh in a long series of running engagements for Hao Binh. Since he was unable to secure his communications with Hao Binh, Salan pulled back giving up several French positions on the Black River in the process. Salan's major strategic effort was Operation *Lorraine* in October 1952. Following the French retreat from the Black River, the Viet Minh had moved forward and Salan hoped both to secure large expanses of Vietnamese rebel territory and to defeat Giap's forces in a set battle. French territorial gains in Operation *Lorraine* were impressive but over-extended supply lines ultimately forced Salan to fall back before he had managed to bring the Viet Minh into a set battle. As usual, the Viet Minh had employed the time-honored guerrilla tactic of avoiding confrontation on anything other than the most favorable terms.

French morale was falling. Retreats from the Black River and the withdrawal after Operation *Lorraine* gave the Viet Minh ample opportunity to harass and ambush. Giap attacked French mobility by destroying roads and bridges wherever possible and he sent his soldiers to waylay the enemy as they hacked their way through dense jungle or waded across open rivers. The French controlled the major cities but in the countryside the Viet Minh was the only effective government. French troops continued to win small battles and temporarily to hold territory but, in the end, the Viet Minh remained a growing, undefeated force. In May 1953, Salan was replaced by General Henri Navarre who determined to lure the Viet Minh into a decisive battle which, if nothing else, would give the French an honorable settlement to the war.

The truth of it was that the war had been going badly for the French. The French populace at home was weary of the war and successive governments in Paris were seeking a face-saving way out. It was mainly the military who could not endure the idea of a defeat by what they saw as a rag-tag army of colonials.

In October 1952, hoping to lure the French out of the cities, Giap drove from the Red River to the Black River, mopping up French garrisons on his way, and then continued on across the Laotian border. The drive took six months and was done entirely on foot. By the end of April 1953, Giap's troops had reached the Laotian capital of Luang Prabang and set up the revolutionary Pathet Lao government. During their drive towards Laos, the Viet Minh overran a small French garrison and airfield at Dien Bien Phu in Northwestern Vietnam. It was here that the decisive battle of the first Vietnam war was to be fought.

In the summer of 1953, after yet another French offensive had proved ineffectual against his will of the wisp enemy, Navarre calculated that his only chance of winning was to lure the Viet Minh into a set battle. To do this he determined to build an impregnable fortress deep in rebel territory in a position to threaten Giap's lines of communication. If Giap was to carry on operations in Laos, he simply could not permit a French stronghold to lie in his rear. Not only that, but a seemingly isolated French outpost would seem an easy prize to the Viet Minh. Giap would *have* to attack and when he did, his troops would be annihilated by French airpower and massed artillery. That was what Navarre believed at least and the place he chose to build his impregnable fortress was Dien Bien Phu.

The fact that his own lines of communication would be dangerously extended did not worry Navarre. He was confident that the Viet Minh did not have the strength, logistical organization, or firepower to threaten Dien Bien Phu. With hindsight it is easy to see that the French made three fundamental miscalculations. First, they underestimated the military ability of General Giap (after all, the man was a school teacher – not a soldier); secondly, they thought the Viet Minh would be unable to get artillery up into the hills overlooking the fortress and that even if they did, it would be instantly destroyed by French counter battery fire; and thirdly (and most importantly), they thought the presence of an airstrip in the middle of the fortress meant they would be able to supply Dien Bien Phu by air. They turned out to be wrong on all three counts.

On November 20, 1953, Navarre sent three battalions of paratroopers to reoccupy Dien Bien Phu, which lies in a ten mile long valley about 180 miles from Hanoi. The paratroopers secured the airstrip and immediately began digging in. Over the months that followed, Navarre continued his build up with more equipment and more troops, throwing down an open challenge to Giap right in the heartland of his own territory.

Giap took the challenge. Over the next few months, the Viet Minh began its own build up in the area, assembling at least five divisions (50,000 men) in the hills surrounding Dien Bien Phu. More importantly they hand carried (or shipped via bicycles converted into wagons) tons of Soviet and Chinese donated equipment – radar, heavy mortars, multi-barreled rocket launchers, anti-aircraft guns, and up to one hundred 105mm howitzers. By late December, Dien Bien Phu was surrounded and the Viet Minh was operating more-or-less freely in Laos. A road running from Meng-Tzu in China to Dien Bien Phu had been secretly carved out of the jungle and the Chinese provided a number of Russian built trucks to move supplies, but the key to the battle was the Viet Minh's ability to keep its forces supplied by tireless muscle-power. Teams of peasants managed to hump the 105s up the trackless hills overlooking the fortress

Left German Legionnaires sight in a mortar during the fighting at Xieng Khouang.

Below Major Marcel Bigeard, commander of the 6th Colonial Parachute Battalion, during the battle for Dien Bien Phu. Major (later Colonel) Bigeard became one of the most legendary figures in the French Army, a veteran of World War II, Indochina, and the Algerian War.

Right The Lasserre Commandos training for tunnel operations against the Viet Minh. Like the Viet Cong after them, the Viet Minh specialized in digging tunnel complexes which could hide not only troops but vast stores of ammunition and supplies. The Lasserre Commandos were trained to locate these tunnels and to take prisoners for interrogation.

Below French troops battle Viet Minh in the area of the Cho Ben Pass in November 1951. More than 200 Viet Minh were killed after their flight into the mountains was intercepted and they were forced, for once, into a pitched battle.

by sheer will power alone. French patrols anxious to explore the hills were beaten back and, despite air surveillance, the French high command was largely ignorant of the extent of the massive Viet Minh build up.

Adding to the pressure on both sides was the up-coming Geneva Conference on Korea, which was to include a discussion on the future of Indochina. It was obvious to both sides that whoever won the battle for Dien Bien Phu was likely to win the battle of the conference table as well.

On March 13, 1954, Giap began his assault on Dien Bien Phu with a massive artillery barrage which took the French unaware. Dien Bien Phu had been converted into nine fortified strongpoints: *Gabrielle* in the north, *Anne-Marie* in the northwest; *Beatrice* in the northeast, and *Isabelle* in the south, with an inner ring of *Huguette, Claudine, Dominique, Elaine,* and *Francoise. Beatrice* was overrun on the first night after fierce hand-to-hand fighting. The battle raged for three days with appalling casualties and great heroism on both sides as waves of Viet Minh assault troops repeatedly charged into a wall of French machine-gun, mortar, and rifle fire. In the surrounding hills, Giap's artillery had been dug in and French air-power and counter-battery fire were unable to silence it. The unfortunate defenders were forced to endure a never ending rain of heavy shells. By March 15th, *Gabrielle* had fallen and, three days later,

Anne-Marie was finally abandoned after a bitter struggle.

Many believe that Giap could have completed his conquest of Dien Bien Phu in a week or so if he had carried on but – with some 3,000 dead and at least three times as many wounded – he paused and settled down for a longer siege. Valiant efforts were made to resupply the beleaguered garrison by air but the pilots faced concentrated Viet Minh anti-aircraft fire. On March 30th, a Viet Minh attack pushed to within a mile of Dien Bien Phu's main command bunker before being beaten back. At the same time, Viet Minh artillery shelled the airfield until it was useless. Supplies continued to be dropped by parachute but, as often as not, would drift into Viet Minh territory.

Regular army, Foreign Legion, and Vietnamese paratroopers who volunteered to relieve the Dien Bien Phu garrison became legendary in the French forces for their dangerous night drops into sniper and anti-aircraft fire. But despite the unquestioned courage of the defenders, the French position had become hopeless. By April 23rd, the Viet Minh had moved their lines to within six or seven hundred yards of Dien Bien Phu's center and had sealed off any chance of escape. Giap had replaced his losses and built up his forces for the final push. The French commander, General Christian de Castries, sent frantic appeals for new men and material but there was nothing

to be done. Giap's final drive began on May 1st and, after seven days of bloody yard-by-yard fighting, the Viet Minh overran the French command bunker. French losses totalled 2,300 killed and 5,100 wounded. Eleven thousand men, many of them the cream of the French Army, were taken prisoner by the victorious Viet Minh who themselves suffered roughly 23,000 casualties, including some 8,000 killed.

Negotiations in Geneva began on April 26th and dragged on into late July. The main outcome as far as Vietnam was concerned was that there would be an immediate cease fire by all parties; Vietnam would be divided along the 17th parallel into a communist North and a non-communist South; there would be a five mile demilitarized zone (DMZ) on either side of the border; French and Viet Minh forces would immediately withdraw north and south of the DMZ; there would be free movement of refugees across the DMZ for the next 300 days; and in two years' time elections would be held to decide the issue of reunification of the whole country. As a final point, the Geneva Accord recognized the independence of Laos and Cambodia.

Despite their military humiliation, few – least of all the French themselves – expected that the French would play no part in Vietnam's future. As it happened though, the United States was now taking an active role in Indochinese politics.

Below French forces exchange fire with Viet Minh guerrillas along the Nam Suong River near Pakseng in late 1953.

2 The Deepening Commitment

American support for a French War

Under President Roosevelt, US wartime policy had been opposed to French and British ambitions to re-establish control over their occupied colonies after the war. But in the turbulent years following World War II, particularly in view of the growing tensions of the Cold War, France's position as a pivotal European power was far more important to Washington than France's cynical manipulations to cling on to its Indochinese colonies. Between November 1945 and March 1946, Ho Chi Minh wrote numerous letters to US and UN officials seeking their support for Vietnamese independence, but these letters seem to have been largely ignored. As a clear signal to the West that his ambitions were fundamentally nationalistic rather than ideological, Ho dissolved the ICP on November 11, 1945, but the decision to ignore his letters seems to have been based as much on the West's refusal to take the Viet Minh seriously, as on a desire not to provoke the French. It wasn't until 1946, in fact, that Ho's politics became an issue and US officials began having hesitations about his communist affiliations.

In 1949, Nationalist China fell to the communists and in 1950, North Korea invaded the South. The Viet Minh's war

against the French came to be seen as nothing more than part of the Asian-wide communist expansion centered in China and emanating from Moscow. Support for the newly created, French-oriented, Bao Dai government of Vietnam became an essential part of US policy in Southeast Asia. Bao Dai was little more than a French puppet, and the US knew this, but also believed that his government might be a non-communist way to achieve Vietnam's independence. In February 1950, the US National Security Council (NSC) concluded that if Indochina went communist, then "Thailand and Burma could be expected to fall ... The balance of Southeast Asia would then be in grave hazard."

This, of course, is what later came to be known as the "Domino Theory;" the idea that if Vietnam went communist, its immediate and then nearby neighbors would rapidly follow like a row of falling dominoes. The Domino Theory was central to the thinking and policy of Presidents Kennedy and Johnson, but its origins can be traced back to the years immediately after the war. In any event, the NSC urged that "all practicable measures should be taken" to prevent a Viet Minh victory and – along with the Joint Chiefs of Staff (JCS) – called on the Pentagon to provide the French with military aid. Truman agreed and the French war effort received a grant of ten million dollars. This support grew rapidly and to the extent that when Giap's troops were moving on Dien Bien Phu four years later, the US was underwriting France's war costs to the tune of a billion dollars – nearly eighty percent of the total.

The decision to support France's war efforts was made shortly before the outbreak of the Korean War in June 1950. Korea merely confirmed Washington's concern about world-wide communist expansion and under the Truman Doctrine – evolved in 1947 to combat Soviet moves in Europe – containment became the overriding US policy in Asia. The use of American combat soldiers in Indochina was considered, but it was decided that this would be necessary only in the event of an invasion by Chinese ground troops. In 1952, a new president, Eisenhower, was elected but the Domino Theory did not lose its importance in US thinking about the Indochina problem.

The new adminstration feared that a Korean settlement would only encourage Chinese adventurism in Indochina. Based upon America's nuclear superiority over both the Soviet Union and China, the Eisenhower administration evolved a strategic policy of threatening "massive retaliation" for communist aggression. When the Korean Armistice was signed in July 1953, China – which quickly increased its aid to the Viet Minh – was warned in no uncertain terms that, if its forces moved into Indochina, the US response could well include nuclear strikes on the Chinese mainland. This was probably not an idle threat. After Korea, the American public would not have supported another long drawn out Asian land war easily, and the nuclear option might well have proved an irresistible alternative. Instead, US policy now hinged on supporting France

Above Operation *Condor* founders in the dense jungle near Dien Bien Phu. This French column was sent towards Dien Bien Phu to relieve pressure on the garrison there. After an exhausting march through the bush and numerous encounters with bands of guerrillas, the column found that the enemy had grown too strong for them to reach the beleaguered garrison. Their only choice was to turn around and march all the way back.

Left Foreign Legion mortar squad wait for the Viet Minh at Dien Bien Phu.

Far left Giap (right) and Ho Chi Minh (center) confer with a Communist Chinese advisor. During the last stages of the Viet Minh's war with the French, aid and assistance from Communist China reached massive proportions and assured the victory at Dien Bien Phu. Note that the portrait of Mao Tse Tung is given equal prominence with that of Ho Chi Minh.

and on keeping China out but, as yet, taking no direct role in the fighting.

Diplomatically, Washington's approach was to support the French while at the same time pressuring them into granting greater authority and autonomy to the Bao Dai regime. It was felt that this would win wider support from the Vietnamese themselves and would also ensure that France did not negotiate a peace which would give Indochina to the Viet Minh. The lure to obtain French support for both these aims was US aid – but aid is a two-edged sword. To get more American money and equipment, Paris gave Bao Dai's Vietnam more independence but, whenever they wanted more money, the French would broadly hint at their inability to carry on the war without it.

Despite clear warnings from the CIA to the contrary, US policy makers were still generally convinced that France could win the war as long as American aid kept flowing (and, of course, the Chinese stayed out). This was partly due to de Lattre's 1951 victories at Hinh Yeu and Mao Khe, when Giap made his premature move to finish the war, but after the Viet Minh returned to its earlier tactics of slow attrition, many US military observers seemed more impressed by the French Army's ability to win empty territory than by the guerrilla's ability to avoid unfavorable battles. The nature of the war that was being fought was all too often fundamentally misunderstood, a misunderstanding encouraged by French efforts to convince everyone that things were going well – even though they knew far better.

The fallout from Dien Bien Phu

In July 1953, General Navarre was given top secret instructions from Paris: his overriding orders were to defend Laos; to do whatever it was militarily possible to do to improve things *as a prelude to negotiations;* and – above everything else – to preserve "the safety of the French expeditionary force." Publicly he was supposed to be carrying out the so-called "Navarre Plan," a detailed scheme for France to regain the initiative on the ground and force a decisive victory over the next two years. Privately, however, Navarre's secret orders soon led him to the idea of the "unbeatable" fortification and an unmitigated disaster at Dien Bien Phu. Nevertheless, the "plan" he was supposed to be carrying out so impressed Washington that an extra $385-million was tacked on to the $400-million in aid scheduled for France's military efforts in Indochina for 1954.

Navarre's overt plan was, in part, his own doing. He believed it was necessary for France to regain the initiative; his campaigns against Giap's guerrillas prior to Dien Bien Phu did not succeed and annoyed Paris for their daring. His defence was that he was only trying to improve France's image on the battlefield and give the politicians a few more chips to bargain with. A few months after getting his sealed orders, Navarre sent Paris a secret report saying that a military victory was impossible and that the only realistic possibility was a stalemate with the Viet Minh. Numerous intelligence reports highlighted the declining influence of the Bao Dai government in areas controlled or penetrated by Giap's guerrillas. The Viet Minh were never universally popular, not even in the North, but they *were* Vietnamese, and as the war progressed they became the only immediate authority to the average, politically indifferent villager trying his best to carve out a meager living in a land split

Left 105mm howitzer manned by Legionnaires and Algerian troops during the March 1954 fighting at Dien Bien Phu. By March 18th, three of the nine French strongpoints had already fallen to the Viet Minh. For the rest of March, the two sides exchange massive artillery barrages.

Left A French soldier carries away a comrade killed in the Dien Bien Phu fighting.

Far left French troops take cover from Viet Minh artillery fire at Dien Bien Phu. The soldier on the right is carrying a US M1 Carbine; by the time of Dien Bien Phu, the US was underwriting eighty percent of the cost of the war.

amongst local warlords, bandits, and an ineffective national government propped up by a foreign army.

In February 1954, as Giap was preparing to accept Navarre's challenge at Dien Bien Phu, Washington announced that it was sending forty B-26 bombers to Indochina to make up for French losses and 200 civilian ground crew to maintain them. Fears that this was the first step in committing American troops to Vietnam were publicly discounted on the grounds that the French were winning the war. In the same month, an inspection tour led by the French Minister of Defence visited Indochina and found the situation to be militarily hopeless and politically unfavorable. The Eisenhower administration suspected France's dilemma – but didn't realise its extent – and in any case was divided on exactly what to do about it. The possibility of sending in US ground troops was considered again and again but shelved in the belief that the French could be pressured into improving things.

The first days of the Dien Bien Phu battle shattered Washington's hopes that France could hold onto Indochina. It was obvious that the French needed more support and preparations were made for Operation *Vulture* – a series of bombing raids on Viet Minh positions around Dien Bien Phu by USAF B-29s flying out of the Philippines with a fighter escort provided by carriers of the US Seventh Fleet. The use of a tactical nuclear weapon was also considered but rejected fairly quickly.

By the end of March, it became clear that if the French were to be saved at Dien Bien Phu the only really effective course would be to support the proposed bombing missions with American ground troops. This was politically undesirable without widespread support from other Allied powers and Operation *Vulture* was quietly dropped. During April, the US approached likely partners such as Thailand, France, the Philippines, and Great Britain in an attempt to create a unified approach to the Indochina problem. The Asian countries were willing to go along with American plans, but Britain was not and the French were interested only in a quick rescue mission and an honorable withdrawal for their battered army.

In view of the French debacle, US policy in Southeast Asia now had two aims. First, to build regional alliances aimed at containing communism and, second, to build a Western-oriented, stable government in what would soon become the Republic of South Vietnam. To achieve the first aim, the South East Asia Treaty Organization was created in September 1954, a military alliance modelled on NATO which promised joint action in face of communist aggression. Britain and France, however, were hostile to the SEATO pact which they saw as a clear signal of Washington's intent to replace the French in Indochina with an active American presence. To achieve the second aim, a stable South Vietnam, was a more difficult matter and, after considerable internal disagreement, the Eisenhower administration put its backing on the volatile character of Ngo Dinh Diem.

Diem's Rise to Power

A zealous Catholic, Diem was born in 1901 and considered the priesthood before opting to study for a career in the Vietnamese civil service. Appointed Minister of the Interior in 1933, Diem resigned two months later in protest about the low levels of

Right Vietnamese and French wounded seek shelter at Dien Bien Phu. Their wounds and the expressions on their faces say more than words can about the ferocity of the fighting.

Opposite Viet Minh artillery zeroes in on French troops defending the outer perimeters of Dien Bien Phu.

Below French trenches on the perimeters of Dien Bien Phu recall the lunar landscapes of World War I.

Vietnamese participation in France's colonial administration. Like Ho Chi Minh, Diem was an ardent nationalist but he was also vehemently anti-communist – an attitude which he formed very early. After his resignation, Diem retired from politics and refused a Japanese offer to become Prime Minister after their 1945 coup. In the same year, Ho Chi Minh offered Diem a cabinet post in his new Republic of Vietnam but, once again, Diem refused. He went to live near Saigon where he tried to persuade the French to grant Vietnam a significant degree of independence.

When the Bao Dai government was created, Diem tried unsuccessfully to persuade the Emperor (who, despite his playboy image, was a genuine nationalist with a fair skill for political intrigue) to hold out for better terms from the French before agreeing to head the new regime. In 1950, Diem went to live in the United States where his future career was given a great boost. He found support and sympathetic hearings from a large number of influential, anti-communist academics, politicians, and Catholic leaders including Francis Cardinal Spellman and a young Senator from Massachusetts, John Fitzgerald Kennedy.

Diem's American support and his genuine nationalism stood him in good stead. In June 1954, Bao Dai appointed him Premier whereupon Diem began working vigorously for an end to all French influence over Vietnam's future. A year later, Diem put aside the free, nationwide elections called for in the Geneva Accord and permanently divided the country along the 17th parallel truce line. The following October, Diem set up an election within South Vietnam to decide whether the new country should continue as a monarchy headed by Bao Dai or as a Republic led by himself. The referendum was organized by Diem's enigmatic – some say Machiavellian – brother, Ngo Dinh Nhu, and resulted in a not entirely convincing 99 percent vote in favor of the Republic.

The new President promptly began a "re-education" programme aimed at stamping out communist influences in his new Republic. Orders were issued for the arrest of persons considered a threat to national security and democratically-elected, local village councils were replaced by government appointed officials. Diem's political prisoners stood at some 20,000 in 1956 and included many non-communists hostile to his regime. Later it became fashionable to suppose that Diem filled his jails solely with Vietnam's communists, but he also jailed liberals and dissident politicians including supporters of General Nguyen Van Hinh, Diem's chief rival for power.

Despite many doubts about his commitment to democracy, Diem seemed to offer America the best chance for stabilising South Vietnam and turning it into the keystone in the SEATO bulwark against communist expansion in Southeast Asia. It was hoped that genuine democracy would follow not only to widen the base of Diem's support but also to broaden anti-communism throughout Indochina. To much of the American press, Diem was a sort of Vietnamese George Washington but the American administration knew better. Diem was far from perfect but he was the best of several bad choices.

Diem hitched his career to the US in no uncertain terms and in such a way as to antagonize the French. In December 1955, he cancelled economic treaties with Paris and withdrew from the French Union. The following March, the new Socialist

Left A street scene in Hanoi shortly after the fall of Dien Bien Phu. At the time the picture was taken, the victorious Viet Minh were moving into position for an attack on the heavily fortified French positions around Hanoi. But talks in Geneva settled the issue without a fight and the French withdrew peacefully.

Opposite Foreign Legion paratroopers reinforce the garrison at Dien Bien Phu. French and Vietnamese volunteers from all over Indochina volunteered to go to Dien Bien Phu as the fighting grew heavier. Many died or were captured but their courage made them legends in both the Legion and the French Army.

Below The last moments of Dien Bien Phu. On May 8th the Viet Minh finally overran the last few French positions at Dien Bien Phu, and marked the beginning of the end of French colonialism in Indochina.

government in France – in an atmosphere of anti-Americanism and co-existence with the Eastern block – told Diem it would withdraw its forces from Vietnam and, in April, it dissolved the high command in Saigon. A new and more divisive colonial war was brewing in Algeria while America, Britain, and France would soon clash in the July Suez crisis. The United States which had constantly tried for joint Allied action in Indochina now suddenly found itself with full responsibility for South Vietnam.

The CIA and the Start of the Covert War

Diem was fortunate in having a political base created for him largely by the CIA. The decision to abandon plans for unilateral American intervention in Indochina did not include covert warfare. The CIA was against overt intervention in Indochina partly because it was impractical, partly because it was politically inadvisable. But also because the Agency believed it could accomplish much the same thing by covert means. The idea was to undermine Ho Chi Minh's government through sabotage and rumor. In June 1954, Colonel Edward Lansdale took charge of a Saigon military mission with the second job of CIA Station Chief. His assignment was to "beat the Geneva timetable of communist takeover in the North."

The CIA had teams of agents throughout the North and these were quickly reinforced to make the Viet Minh's job as difficult as possible. Vital transport, communication, and food facilities were sabotaged to undermine the new government and breed discontent by increasing misery and dissatisfaction in the general population. Counterfeiting and other tricks were used to destabilize the currency. At the same time, "Black Psyche" rumors were started to frighten the general populace and send them fleeing South. The idea behind Black Psyche is to plant a rumor which is untraceable and turns the listener against

the subject; stories that the Viet Minh intended to nationalize all properties, for example, frightened countless Vietnamese farmers, merchants, and small businessmen. Reports that the Viet Minh were going to introduce new currency frightened anybody with savings and rumors of up-coming religious persecutions terrified the North's Catholics.

Combined with "White Psyche", traditional propaganda which stressed the virtues and opportunities in the South, Black Psyche fuelled an already uncertain situation and the droves of refugees fleeing south quickly turned into a flood. During the 300 days allowed for free movement between North and South Vietnam, something like 850,000 refugees – mostly Catholic – fled to the South where they became Diem's principal power base. Lansdale threw the CIA's support behind Diem, and supported him in his battles against ambitious General Nguyen Van Hinh, Bao Dai, and the Binh Xuyen, a criminal gang which controlled Saigon's underworld.

A few years later, Lansdale, now a General, was Kennedy's choice to head Operation *Mongoose,* the President's post Bay of Pigs plan to overthrow Castro. Lansdale brought all the enthusiasm from his days in Indochina and (before that) the Philippines but, by and large, very little came of the various schemes. Rumors were to be spread that Castro was out of favor with God and that the second coming was due at any time in an effort to alienate Cuba's Roman Catholic population from its government. Similar tricks had been used to frighten Vietnam's Catholics with the spectre of Ho Chi Minh and to convince all Vietnamese that the Viet Minh lacked the Mandate of Heaven – a fatalistic natural harmony which, to the Indochinese, conferred a semi-divine authority on leaders.

Lansdale's plans in Cuba called for "boom and bang": as well as economic disruption, industrial sabotage, counterfeiting

Above President Dwight David Eisenhower. It was during Eisenhower's Administration that the first steps toward a US commitment to the new Republic of South Vietnam were made and that the need to contain communism in the Far East and in Southeast Asia became a paramount part of American foreign policy.

Right French and Vietnamese prisoners of war are taken aboard landing craft at Viet Tri during an August 1954 POW exchange. These prisoners were some of the survivors of Dien Bien Phu. They had been force-marched into captivity and kept under conditions bordering on mass starvation. Thousands died. These were the lucky ones.

Left As Vietnam prepared for independence, there was a mass movement of the population. Catholics fled to the South; communists fled to the North. Here residents of Nam Dinh in the Delta prepare for evacuation.

Below South Vietnamese President Ngo Dinh Diem (foreground) visits a Strategic Hamlet near Pleiku. Diem was America's hope for a genuine democracy in South Vietnam but his government proved increasingly corrupt and unstable.

Right Refugees scramble for a place aboard a Dakota sent in to evacuate the Dong Hoi sector in September 1954.

Opposite Setting fire to a Vietnamese bamboo hut along the Bassac River. The entrances to Viet Cong bunkers were often concealed inside huts, and archery was one way to open the attack on them.

money, and contaminating vital sugar crops—exactly the sorts of thing which had been used in the chaos of Indochina following Dien Bien Phu. Contaminating crops can be an effective tactic. Not only does it cause economic disruption and personal hardship in primitive economies but—to an uneducated, superstitious peasant population—it fuels the idea that the government is out of favor with heaven. There is evidence that Lansdale's sabotage teams spread rice blast fungi (a few grams of which can infect several acres) over crops in North Vietnam.

Assassination was also a feature of Lansdale's bag of tricks. As head of Operation *Mongoose,* he was careless enough to suggest "liquidation" of Cuba's leaders in an official memo— but, despite lurid stories, the CIA has rarely involved itself directly in killing political opponents. In building Diem's regime, Lansdale's weapons were mainly bribery and skillful organization. The killing was left to the Vietnamese.

Vietnam was a country divided into regional loyalties and ruled by various political and religious sects. Typical of these, and a firm opponent of Diem, was the Hao Hao, a mystical Buddhist sect which ruled a large area to the southwest of Saigon. This region was broken up into numerous fiefdoms controlled by Hao Hao warlords who were often little more than bandits. Another such sect, also opposed to Diem, was the Cao Dai, a right-wing, quasi-political organization which drew from both Buddhism and Christianity and which ruled a vast area northwest of Saigon more or less as a separate principality. Richest and most powerful of the sects opposed to Diem were the Binh Xuyen, which controlled Saigon's vast network of organized crime. The three sects jockeyed for power but with internal divisions, mutual hatred, and (apart from Binh Xuyen) poor finance, they were easy targets for Diem and Lansdale. Against the first two, Lansdale used mainly bribery. The US paid something like twelve million dollars in subsidies to undermine the sects' power, and Diem's troops were able to take over Hao Hao and Cao Dai territories fairly easily.

The Binh Xuyen, however, was a far tougher and more sinister organization, which could only be overcome by armed force. A militantly anti-French sect formed from a variety of

bandit gangs in the 1940s, it was the Binh Xuyen which had captured some 150 European men, women, and children during the 1945 troubles in Saigon. Half of the prisoners had been killed outright and the remainder tortured. In return for a monopoly over organized crime in Saigon, the Binh Xuyen had supported Emperor Bao Dai's government both under the Japanese and under the French and, in return, they enjoyed his patronage.

To attack the Binh Xuyen was to take a big chance. Washington's support for Diem was not yet fixed and the State Department and sections of the Pentagon were arguing that he should be replaced by someone more suitable. The lack of an obvious candidate was the main reason that nothing had yet been done but, fully aware of these dangers, Lansdale and Diem bet everything on an all-or-nothing throw of the dice. Diem cancelled the Binh Xuyen's official sanctions as overlords of Saigon's vice and drug traffic and then ignored an order from Bao Dai to rescind his injunctions. In the last part of April 1954, Diem's troops attacked the Binh Xuyen in the middle of Saigon and, after days of street-by-street fighting which reduced a large part of the city to rubble, drove the sect into the outskirts where its leaders retreated into the jungle to carry out a futile resistance for several months.

The gamble paid off. Initially, Diem's attack on the Binh Xuyen had moved his critics in Washington to push for his quick removal. Orders for withdrawal of American support were, in fact, in the pipeline but were rapidly called back when—to the politicians' surprise—Diem won the day. Nothing succeeds like success and the CIA's protege now enjoyed, despite continuing reservations about his methods, full US backing as the only available, anti-communist Vietnamese strongman capable of asserting his authority over a bitterly divided country. Diem's conquest of the Bao Dai-backed Binh Xuyen also gave him the support necessary to usurp the figurehead Emperor and make himself President of his own Republic. American policy in Vietnam was now, for better or worse, linked firmly to Diem. The consequences of this decision were to prove far-reaching and when Diem finally fell in 1963, the US had been brought to the brink of the Indochina land war it had tried for so long to avoid.

3 The Hidden Quagmire

VC Preparations in the South

While the CIA and Diem were trying to beat Ho Chi Minh's takeover in the North, the Viet Minh were busily laying the groundwork for further revolution in the South. As countless Catholic refugees streamed South to give Diem his chief political base, some 100,000 Viet Minh moved North of the DMZ in line with the Geneva Accords. But they left behind them two or three times as many active guerillas, sympathizers, and one-time political allies, plus a small, hard-core revolutionary cadre who immediately set about building a new resistance movement dedicated to making sure that the elections scheduled for 1956 went in Hanoi's favor. Entire regions of what was shortly to become the Republic of South Vietnam were in fact controlled by the Viet Minh or sympathetic to it.

The majority of the Viet Minh were not communists, or were so in name only, but the hard-core cadre of the Viet Minh *was* communist and it was around these dedicated revolutionaries that the Viet Cong was built. Officially the Viet Minh called a halt to all revolutionary activity in 1954 in order to fight the up-coming election but no effort was spared to consolidate areas already under their control and to extend their influence into other regions. The Viet Minh's tactics included propaganda, intimidation, and, on occasion, violence. When Diem destroyed the sects, he eliminated his immediate competition and assured himself of the American backing he so desperately needed, but he also created power vacuums in large areas of territory around Saigon. His troops controlled the land but the population's loyalties were uncommitted and it was this battle that Diem was destined to lose.

The Viet Minh who went North were generally both dedicated guerrillas and Southern born. When they began to drift South again, they found safety among family and friends even in government controlled villages. In addition to the Viet Minh and its sympathizers, Diem's republic had a huge floating population who, if not exactly revolutionary in their outlook, could at least be easily molded into an anti-government force. Diem's crackdown on dissent and round-up of political opponents had only fueled the flames of discontent, and his half-hearted efforts at winning over the peasantry didn't work either. America had wanted a stable government with an increasingly broad base of popular support which was capable of holding the line against communism, but it soon found itself supporting a regime disliked by virtually all sections of the society and so concerned about fighting off opposition and subverting possible coups that a communist takeover seemed almost inevitable.

When Diem cancelled the scheduled 1956 elections, it destroyed the Viet Minh's plans for a more-or-less bloodless takeover. The political repression in the years following apparently did vast damage to the revolutionary organization that the communist cadres had been building and the dedicated party functionaries who escaped capture were forced into the

Far left Viet Cong raiding party, probably waiting in ambush. The weapon in the foreground is a B-40 anti-tank rocket. It was widely used by the VC, and very deadly.

Left South Vietnamese Marines subject a Viet Cong prisoner to on-the-spot interrogation. The prisoner's head is held under the water until he's about to drown. He's then brought up and questioned. If his interrogators don't like his answers, he's dunked again (and again) until he talks. These Marines no doubt enjoyed their work as their battalion had been badly mauled by the VC a few months previously.

mountains and jungles to begin again. The scale of the crackdown does not seem to have been Diem's idea. Local officials with old grudges against the Viet Minh simply rounded up or shot anyone they suspected regardless of whether they were currently politically active or not. In the short term, Diem's actions pushed back the Viet Minh's revolutionary time-table but, in the long term, he drove more and more people into joining the communists or allying themselves with them.

Gradually the communist cadres in the South began rebuilding their organizations in the old Viet Minh territories. They were supported in this by a steady stream of hard-core guerrillas and political commissars returning South across the DMZ or slipping in from Eastern Laos on a route that was to become known as the Ho Chi Minh Trail. After 1958, their organization was strong enough to begin small-scale hit-and-run raids on remote outposts of Diem's army – otherwise known to the Pentagon as the Army of the Republic of Vietnam (ARVN). The raids had two main purposes: to capture vital weaponry and equipment and to show the local peasantry that anti-government resistance was more than just talk. Viet Minh recruiting was stepped up and took in anti-government factions from all parts of the political spectrum although the organizational core remained firmly communist with direct links to the North.

The movement was then based chiefly in selected villages in the southern part of the Mekong Delta, the western sections of Quang Nam province in the North, and in the dense jungle to the west of Saigon. The organizational pattern was the cell; a small group which operated around its base-village and trained new recruits who then went to form new cells and pass on their newly acquired skills in guerrilla warfare and political ideology to others. In this fashion, the resistance movement spread quickly and created a large, highly trained guerrilla army with a central organizational core of disciplined Marxists. The pattern remained much the same in the years to come. Those skilled at guerrilla warfare gained greater responsibilities and command but the key to real advancement lay in party membership. Even later, many Viet Cong were more-or-less indifferent to politics, but, it was the communist element which took control of the movement's organizational structure, and because they controlled the structure (and hence promotion possibilities) they likewise controlled the movement's direction, overall policies, and ablest military commanders.

In December 1960, the revolutionaries created the National Liberation Front (NLF) or Viet Cong (VC). The old Viet Minh territories were under firm control and the VC had spread its influence into something like seventy-five per cent of Vietnam's villages. The VC's active guerrilla army stood at around 15,000 to 20,000 and was capable on occasion of fighting ARVN units to a standstill in open combat as well as carrying out hit-and-run raids more-or-less at will. In February 1962, the NLF formed a central committee made up of representatives of various factions opposing Diem but – despite the genuine liberal elements and the talk of future coalition governments – the communists were in firm control of the Front's overall policy and direction.

Until then, the South's hard-core communists had been members of the Lao Dong, the North Vietnamese People's Workers Party, but now they "split" to form a new southern-

Far left ARVN soldiers with a captured Viet Cong prisoner after a June 1962 sweep on a suspected insurgent village.

Left A burned-out Viet Cong village following a US/South Vietnamese air attack.

Below Pillars of smoke rise skywards from a US Air Force strike on heavily entrenched Viet Cong positions.

based People's Revolutionary Party (PRP). The new Party was little more than an extension of the Lao Dong. When the elections of 1956 failed to materialize, the Politburo in Hanoi decided to foster revolution in the South but — with the need to consolidate and rebuild the North — to avoid taking any direct role for the time being. In 1959, a conference of the Lao Dong's central committee confirmed the need for a military solution in the South but again put off any direct involvement. Revolution in the South was to be — at least on the surface — a Southern affair. Indeed, to a point, the interests of the Southern revolutionaries and Hanoi conflicted over priorities but, for the most part, the hard-core communist cadre below the DMZ was able to overcome regional differences and keep the movement in line with Hanoi's policies.

Non-VC villages were not overrun in the early days; instead they were slowly drawn into the revolutionary orbit. First came sporadic visits (usually at night) from VC cadre on recruitment missions or a sudden swoop by armed guerrillas to surround the village while the people were assembled for political lectures on the VC and its policies. As the revolutionary seeds took hold, these visits would become more frequent until local government authority was limited to the daytime or reduced to the times when ARVN troops were actually present. Government-appointed local and area chieftains or officials gradually backed away from trying to exercise any real authority or were assassinated in a pointed lesson to both the local populace and Diem's hard-pressed civil service. Quick fire-fights with government troops were frequently a useful tactic with marginal villages. Confronted by sniper fire, ARVN soldiers would often retaliate with little regard for finding the actual culprits and many innocent villagers were killed or wounded. Anti-government feeling usually grew accordingly.

Villages which had been converted were gradually reorganized with the emphasis switching from family to communal enterprise. Local leaders were appointed from the most promising villagers or from those who had been serving with the VC. Taxes were levied — frequently in rice or other food contributions — and lectures aimed at improving literacy and basic skills were a day-to-day routine. Inevitably one regular lecture was political "re-education" but, apart from rough treatment for obvious opponents and backsliders, such lectures were easy-going propaganda. Persistent lack of cooperation brought a more intensive education and, if that failed, exile or execution. Traitors or informers faced death as a matter of course but many escaped with re-education and menial duties. Even the politically indifferent usually cooperated more-or-less willingly. The government was no better than the VC and a lot further away. The average Vietnamese peasant knew little of things outside his small village and the VC had taken over its day-to-day running in such a way as to be the only real social authority that he had.

Under the VC's administration, one of a village's first projects was to dig a complex labyrinth of tunnels. Far below were storerooms holding the guerilla's tools of war, food, and so on. Other rooms could hide a VC unit for days as the ARVN or (later) the Americans patrolled the ground above. Passages led far into the jungle so, should the entrances be uncovered, the VC could slip away unnoticed as the hunters began to comb the myriad passages inch by inch. Entering a VC tunnel was a

This page The Viet Cong in training. In the early days, the US — like the French before them — seriously underestimated the VC, regarding them as little more than rag-tag irregulars. In fact, the VC were well-armed, well-led, and well trained. (*Above*) VC artillerymen in a jungle training camp. (*Below*) A VC guerrilla prepares to throw a grenade.

Far right Viet Cong guerrillas in Quang Ngai Province prepare panji stake booby-traps. Made with sharpened bamboo or nails, each spiked unit will be buried in shallow pits and disguised with leaves or grass. Any one stepping on them will be severely injured as the stakes are sharp enough to penetrate even the toughest leather. Panji stake traps were a VC favorite and surrounded many insurgent villages.

dangerous business. The passages were narrow, unlit, and usually boobytrapped as the guerillas retreated into the lower depths. Proceeding slowly downward, the lead hunter could never know if a VC rifleman lay a few feet in front or around a bend.

The usual tactic was to try to locate all the various hidden entrances, bottle them up, then use dogs or tear gas to flush the VC to the surface. But, without an informer, sealing off the entire complex often proved difficult and at least some of the VC would manage to slip away. If an informer wasn't handy, local villagers were usually rounded up and questioned until one broke down and led the hunters to the tunnel's entrance but even then it was still virtually impossible to be sure that all the exit points were covered. When the troops finished, the tunnels were blown up—often with little concern for any VC who might still be below—but the twisting pathways were so involved that it was unlikely that the whole complex had been destroyed. When the hunters left, VC and villagers would begin digging to make the complex operational again and to retrieve any overlooked stores.

VC Supply Lines

In the early days of the war, supplies from the North were relatively unimportant. It was much easier for the VC to improvise or to take what it needed from small government outposts. High explosives, for example, could be stolen or removed—with a very steady hand—from unexploded shells and bombs carefully gathered up from a battlefield. Panji stakes

Above A US CH-47 Chinook helicopter hits suspected VC positions with 55-gallon drums of CS gas. CS riot control gas causes intense burning to the eyes and lungs but is rarely fatal. It is used to flush the enemy out into the open. CS is a chemical weapon and its use in Vietnam caused some controversy. Communist accusations aside, however, the only chemical weapons known to have been used in Vietnam were CS gas and defoliants.

Right Burning a Viet Cong Village. In January 1966, the ARVN, the US Army, and soldiers from the South Korean forces sent to Vietnam launched Operation *Van Buren* which was aimed at denying the VC essential rice harvests. The operation attacked numerous suspect villages in important crop-producing areas.

(sharpened pieces of bamboo) placed in small holes and covered with leaves were capable of penetrating the toughest combat boot and crippling the wearer. This may not seem much to those who haven't experienced it but the tactic was very effective at slowing down and demoralizing wary attackers. In fact, during a quick fire-fight, wounding a man can be more advantageous than killing him. A corpse can be ignored but a casualty ties up others who have to carry him off or treat his wounds. On more than one occasion, the VC made crude but effective mortars from steel piping stolen from construction sites until the responsible engineers learned not to specify pipe dimensions that could be readily adapted to this purpose.

VC improvisation is legendary and deservedly so but there was also a steady source of the most up-to-date material available. For much of the time, the VC simply bought what they needed on the black-market. Corruption in Diem's Vietnam was a way of life and untold numbers of officials looked upon it as a simple perk that went with the job. It wasn't particularly Diem's fault; he made half-hearted efforts to stop it when he took office and, after his death, things were just as bad or worse. High civil servants and generals trafficked in opium and top ARVN officers took a cut of their soldiers' pay. Not all of them, of course, but so many that the few honest ones made little difference. As the flow of US equipment and aid grew, so did opportunities for turning a quick profit and American officials came to expect that the Vietnamese would demand a twenty-five to thirty per cent rake-off as a matter of course. Diem's brother lacked the President's sporadic outbursts of Catholic purism and actively encouraged corruption in order to gain the support of the civil service and to keep ambitious generals contented.

No on has bothered to try to calculate how much American material was diverted through the blackmarkets of South Vietnam (it's been suggested that the US sent enough cement over the course of war to pave the entire country to a depth of two or three feet) and there is no way of estimating how much of this material eventually found its way to the VC. What is certain, is that a great deal of this material *did* reach the VC. From the beginning weapons and ammunition were a familiar item on the Saigon black market and, as the war came to an end, Saigon was one of the world's major sources of illicit arms. VC purchasing agents were familiar figures in Saigon's underworld and there was no shortage of money-hungry intermediaries willing to deal with them. If cash wasn't readily available, cannabis or raw opium was a suitable alternative currency and the VC had ample sources for both in the fields of western and eastern Laos. As the war drew to a close, the VC itself became one of the chief suppliers of captured and "diverted" US material and weaponry to Saigon's bustling black-market but, by then, almost no one cared.

It wasn't just weaponry that the VC bought in the back streets of Saigon and in countless smaller black-markets scattered around the country. They also bought food, medical supplies, communications equipment, and other vital supplies. US aid designed to better the life-style of the average villager and dampen any revolutionary sympathies he might have often went directly into VC coffers. There was nothing more

Left VC positions burn following US Air Force strikes.

47

demoralizing to US troops than, having finally up-rooted a VC supply depot at great hardship and personal risk, to find "Made in the USA" stamped over most of the goods uncovered. Some of the more cynical decided to get in on the act and began dealing in the black-markets as well where, ironically enough, they could on occasion find themselves doing business with thinly disguised VC agents or their intermediaries.

As America's involvement grew, Soviet supplies from North Vietnam became more and more essential to the VC war effort but Soviet aid usually consisted mainly of weapons, ammunition, and sophisticated military equipment. Foodstuffs, medical supplies, and other such essentials had to be acquired by VC raiding parties or by their purchasing agents in the South and – despite many serious shortfalls as the war intensified – they could usually be acquired in sufficient quantities to keep things going. At the height of America's commitment, a few anti-war protestors began raising money to buy and ship medical supplies to North Vietnam and the VC. Few of them dreamed that the VC already enjoyed an excellent source of supply in the hidden market places of South Vietnam as well as

ample booty from over-run ARVN outposts and the litter of abandoned battlefields. The atmosphere of corruption ran through South Vietnamese society and gradually sapped the enthusiasm of even those who cared enough to try and remedy it.

Terrorism was one of the VC's chief weapons from the very beginning but, for the most part, it was practised very selectively. In the whole course of the war, thousands of important and minor government officials were assassinated, disappeared, or were intimidated into cooperation but the VC went to great lengths to avoid alienating the general populace upon which they were trying to build their movement. In Diem's day, American advisors were usually left alone unless they were taking an active battlefield role and American civilian personnel were off-limits save for active agents. Saigon nightspots were a sort of no-man's-land and there were several which boasted US advisors, ARVN troops, and VC agents as regular customers. Both sides were aware of each other but generally minded their own business.

In the mid-1960s, several bombings of Saigon bars were

alleged to be VC attacks on American personnel but, in many cases, the Americans were simply in the wrong place at the wrong time or the outrage was carried out by some of Vietnam's many other warring factions and blamed on the VC. NLF policy was to break the US-Saigon link – not to give Washington an excuse for further involvement. As America's commitment grew, however, this policy shifted. GIs became legitimate targets wherever they were but, for many years, the VC's war of terror was against the Saigon Government, not America. Those anti-American outrages which were actually the work of the NLF may well have been carried out by over-keen local units acting on their own, rather than as a result of orders from the top.

Treatment of prisoners by the VC was a different matter and ranged from mindless cruelty to relative decency depending on the temperament of the particular jailer rather than on any official line. Ordinary ARVN soldiers might be shot out-of-hand, or be assigned to political re-education classes, or be imprisoned in "tiger-cages" – bamboo boxes so small that the victim cannot stand properly. If left long enough, the unfortunate occupants of tiger cages can be permanently

Above left A Viet Cong booby-trap. Suspended over a jungle pathway and triggered by a tripwire, the clump of sharpened bamboo spikes will – when released by an unwary soldier – swing into the advancing patrol. Traps like these made patrols a nightmarish business.

Left Keeping a wary eye on the entrance to a VC tunnel complex.

Far left US Airborne troops move up-hill after being landed by helicopter. The rugged terrain made an ideal hiding place for their will-of-the-wisp guerrilla enemy.

49

crippled. Torture was a fairly common feature of Diem's political prisons but rarer for captured ARVN who, in any case, were not unknown to change sides. ARVN who engaged in rape and pillage faced quick execution if caught. As many Americans were to discover later, prisoners of the VC had to survive on the same rice and fish diet as their captors and wounded prisoners could die of simple neglect. Available medical supplies seldom ran to a surplus and VC wounded and the populace of controlled villages had first claims on such supplies as there were. Hardship, neglect, and persistent, skillful, political interrogations produced numerous phoney confessions.

VC assassinations were normally the responsibility of a special action-section which was responsible to the political wing of the NLF rather than to the military, and such decisions were usually taken at the higher levels. The weapons of assassination were chiefly machine guns, pistols, and the odd grenade. The victims were carefully selected for the damage the killing would do to Diem's regime or for some other obvious political gain. The killing of hostile or wealthier villagers might be done summarily on the spot as an object lesson or to elicit quick answers about enemy movements or other vital intelligence. Both sides did this sort of thing and, caught in the middle, most

neutral villagers learned to cooperate with whichever side happened to be asking the questions at the time.

By the time the US entered the war in force, the VC controlled most of South Vietnam's countryside and ravaged large parts of an increasingly apathetic ARVN army. The Government's only strong points were the cities and traffic between them was more than a little risky unless one took a plane. The VC had its own political officials, tax collectors, administrators, and assorted other general bureaucrats. In the countryside the VC was not only an alternative government but, in many places, the only government the villagers knew. As the American Army geared itself up to take over the burden of the war against the VC's guerrilla army, the CIA had evolved a different scheme. It would go to war on the VC as a functioning political unit by attacking or rounding-up the party cadre and various officials. Code named Operation *Phoenix,* the plan was to destroy the Viet Cong's organizational infrastructure (VCI) and hence its ability to wage effective war. In effect the CIA was preparing to do to the NLF what the NLF had been doing to the Saigon Government for the previous ten years. Operation *Phoenix* was highly secret and, when details finally emerged, very controversial – but it nearly worked.

Left US troops prepare to move in on VC positions. Note the gas masks in preparation for an attack with CS and smoke grenades.

Below Troops of the 173rd Engineer Company prepare to destroy a Viet Cong tunnel complex by mining it with explosives.

4 The Awakening

American dissatisfaction with the ARVN

In early 1963, a 2000-man regiment backed up by armored units, air power, artillery, and fifty US advisors moved in on the VC-held village of Ap Boc. Intelligence had reported that there was a major VC communications base in the village but that it was only lightly defended. America had by then been training South Vietnam's military for nearly a decade and, since Kennedy had become President in 1960, the amount of aid and number of military advisors sent to Southeast Asia had increased even more. The ARVN was slowly assimilating the new US-taught tactics and had achieved some successes in fire-fights with the VC. The result of an "Open Arms" program aimed at encouraging VC desertions to the Saigon Government looked encouraging and Ap Boc was intended to be a show-piece battle which would demonstrate to the world that the tide of communist insurgency was at last being stemmed. The outcome was a farce.

American helicopters dropped Diem's assault troops in front of the VC positions while other ground-based ARVN troops attempted to encircle the village and cut off the VC's line of retreat. But, instead of light-defences, the radio headquarters was held by some 400 hardened VC regulars who shattered the initial assault and brought down five helicopters in the process. A follow-up ARVN airborne attack missed its drop-zones and an emergency air strike succeeded only in bombing and strafing friendly positions. Back-up artillery was next to useless and despite a five to one superiority in man-power none of the ARVN commanders was willing to press the attack home. In the night, the VC simply sneaked off leaving some 165 ARVN and nine American casualties, and hopeless confusion behind them.

As well as being an embarrassment to both Diem and Kennedy, the significance of Ap Boc (and similar but smaller incidents) was that the US advisors and their commanders in Washington became steadily disillusioned with the ARVN's military capabilities. It wasn't so much a question of courage — given the opportunity, ARVN troops were capable of great bravery — but rather leadership. South Vietnam's generals seemed unable or unwilling to fight the war with the commitment necessary to check the VC. There was a growing feeling that, if the Viet Cong were to be defeated, it was the American Army itself which would have to do the job. More and more, the American military was calling for permission to take over responsibility for the war and for enough men to win it. What had been done up to now simply wasn't enough. The only alternative was to get out of Vietnam altogether.

Kennedy was in a dilemma. On the one hand he had no desire to hand South Vietnam over to the communists — an act which he believed would open the flood-gates to the rest of Southeast Asia. Equally he had to consider what would be the effect of abandoning Vietnam on America's other allies throughout the world. America was committed to various regional alliances against communist aggression in Europe,

Left Suicide by fire. In protest against the Diem regime's excesses, 73-year-old Buddhist monk Quang Duc set fire to himself in the streets of Saigon on June 11, 1963. Note the discarded empty gasoline can on the left. Duc's grim suicide found numerous imitators during South Vietnam's continuing domestic turmoil and even in Washington where an American anti-war protestor found self-immolation an effective way of making his views known.

Asia, and Latin America. If America left Vietnam in the lurch, it would make America's word worthless. Communist aggressors would be encouraged elsewhere and undecided countries would be driven into quick accommodations with Moscow or Peking. This worry was to continue as an unspoken undercurrent of American policy throughout the war and delay American withdrawal until Nixon was able to get an agreement which he felt – or least said – preserved US integrity.

On the other hand, Kennedy had no wish to involve the United States in a foreign war. The idea was both personally distasteful to him and politically risky. Memories of Korea were still prominent in the national consciousness and the American public was not likely to rally to the flag without a clear-cut reason. Kennedy already had suffered one embarrassing set-back in military adventurism abroad at the Bay of Pigs in 1961 and while he had regained much of his lost prestige by his handling of the 1962 Cuban Missile Crisis, there was still an election to fight in 1964. Kennedy had been elected by the slimmest of margins and a less than popular land war in Indochina was not likely to win him an election. There is some evidence to suggest that Kennedy was preparing to wind down US involvement in Indochina and write-off South Vietnam as a bad investment but, whatever he was planning, his death by assassination on November 22, 1963, put things into the hands of his successor,

Lyndon B. Johnson.

Despite Kennedy's misgivings, it was his Presidency which pushed America's commitment in Vietnam near to the point of no return. Kennedy believed that counter-insurgency and clandestine warfare were viable alternatives to conventional military force.

After the Bay of Pigs, he ordered the CIA's covert war on Castro (Operation Mongoose) and – soon after taking office in 1960 – he gave the go-ahead for a number of special warfare schemes to defeat the Viet Cong. He hoped that it would not be necessary to draw on America's regular forces for anything other than large teams of advisors whose task would be to make the ARVN self-sufficient as soon as possible. There was only one fatal flaw in his thinking; the ARVN forces were incapable of doing the task assigned them. As more and more American advisors flooded in to fill the gaps, they began to take an increasingly active role in the fighting. The distinction between an 'American-supported war' and an 'American war' grew less and less clear but Kennedy always avoided making that final commitment.

In 1961, Kennedy sent General Maxwell Taylor on a fact-finding visit to Vietnam. Taylor's report confirmed what Washington already knew; morale and discipline in the ARVN forces was deteriorating rapidly and unless something was

Far left VC prisoners captured by ARVN forces during June 1962 anti-guerrilla operations. Blindfolds were standard practice to prevent prisoners from gaining useful intelligence.

Left US advisor and ARVN soldiers gathering palm branches during the construction of a strategic hamlet in early 1963. The Strategic Hamlet program was designed to separate the rural population from the VC by enclosing them in fortified villages. The idea worked for the British in Malaya but was not especially successful in Vietnam where the insurgents and the peasants came from the same ethnic and cultural background.

Right Madame Ngo Dinh Nhu, the "Dragon Lady". Madame Nhu was the flamboyant and outspoken sister-in-law of South Vietnam's President Diem. Her remarks about "Buddhist barbecues" intensified American uncertainty about her brother-in-law's desirability as president. After the coup in which Diem and her husband were killed, Madame Nhu and her daughter went into a luxurious exile in the South of France.

done, and done quickly, the VC were poised for victory. Taylor recommended that Washington send some 8,000 US troops to Vietnam to demonstrate the seriousness of America's commitment and to coordinate the war effort. The mission would officially be for flood relief and other engineering duties but the reality would, of course, have been something quite different. Secretary of Defense Robert McNamara saw the plan as inconclusive and argued for a far greater number of troops which would be capable of winning the war. Kennedy refused to commit himself but he did increase the number of advisors and boosted Saigon's already substantial package of military aid.

When Kennedy took office, the number of American advisors in South Vietnam stood at just under 900 (not counting a large number of CIA and other intelligence personnel). A year later the figure stood at just over 3,000 and, by the end of 1962, there were over 11,000 advisors in Vietnam. The excesses of the Diem regime were widely reported in the Western press and were becoming a political embarrassment. Diem was handed a list of necessary reforms which, it was hoped, would improve his image in the eyes of the American public and bring the various quarrelling factions of South Vietnam together sufficiently to carry the war to a successful conclusion. The old Military Aid and Assistance Group (MAAG) in Saigon which had been responsible for the training of South Vietnam's Army since 1955 was transformed into the Military Assistance Command Vietnam (MACV) with the specific mission of reorganizing the ARVN forces and centralizing war-planning. Nonetheless, Kennedy continued to pin his hopes for a successful conclusion to the war on the techniques of counter-insurgency.

America's Counter-insurgency Campaigns
Central to America's counter-insurgency campaign was the "Strategic Hamlet", a network of fortified villages designed to separate the NLF from the general population of the countryside. Villages were surrounded by barbed wire and rows of panji stakes. Watch towers were erected and (usually) a few ARVN troops maintained a small garrison. The idea was to keep the VC out and, by improving their life-styles with US financial aid, motivate the villagers to defend themselves. In theory, there was to be no forced relocation but, in some areas, this was unavoidable – in particular, the sprawling rice paddies of the Mekong Delta where the villages tended to be spread over a wide area. For the most part, the Strategic Hamlet scheme destroyed the traditional economic and social patterns of Vietnamese villages and, with little US aid actually reaching the peasant population, caused increasing resentment towards the Saigon Government and its US backers.

The low popularity of the scheme was hardly improved by the "Free-Fire" strategy that went with it. Vast areas of the countryside not within the strategic hamlet or safe zones were designated Free-Fire areas. Anybody within these areas was liable to attack by helicopter, artillery, or fighter-bomber. Known or suspected VC pathways and assembly areas were shelled randomly to break-up the enemy's pattern of movement and even the vaguest report of human activity in the proscribed areas could bring an immediate artillery barrage or air strike. The idea was to make the enemy keep his head down and to stop non-NLF from wandering out of the safe areas. The fact that ammunition was being used on what was more often than not

empty space didn't matter – harassing the VC was enough.

The Strategic Hamlet plan was the contribution of Sir Robert Thompson, a noted British counter-insurgency expert whose opinions were highly valued in Washington. During their successful campaign against communist guerrillas in Malaya, the British had used the Strategic Hamlet tactic with great effect and pushed the idea to the Americans and Diem (who saw the added advantage of being able to keep a closer eye on the population). But what works well in one part of the world, does not necessarily work well in another. In Malaya the insurgents were usually of a different ethnic origin from the population that the British were trying to protect in their Strategic Hamlets. This was not the case, however, in Vietnam. Not only were the NLF Vietnamese themselves but, in many cases, they came from the very same villages that were being sealed off.

The plan was reasonably successful in the short-term but, in the long run it was a failure. Many Strategic Hamlets were simply attacked whenever the VC wanted to re-supply themselves. Some were "liberated" by a gradual subversion. VC agents would make brief visits to explain NLF policies and generally propagandize anybody willing to listen. Gradually VC sympathy would spread and the Government's local agents would find themselves in increasingly unfriendly territory. The original plan had been to fortify some two-thirds of South Vietnam's villages in just over a year and, in 1962, the Diem Government claimed some 3000 completions. After Diem's death, however, investigations suggested that the actual number was much less.

A more fruitful counter-insurgency scheme was America's efforts to enlist the support of the various Montagnard tribes living in Vietnam's central highlands. These simple tribesmen had long been at war with the Vietnamese who considered them little more than sub-human savages. The Montagnard were a generous and honorable people and many of the tribes were highly warlike. Due to their hatred of the Saigon Government, some Montagnard tribes were cooperating with the NLF but, given their general dislike of anything Vietnamese, it was fairly easy to turn their energies into fighting the Viet Cong. This project was chiefly the responsibility of the CIA working in cooperation with the US Army's Special Forces, better known as the "Green Berets", one of the world's elite military units.

The Special Forces were designed to act as an elite commando unit and as specialists in counter-insurgency warfare. The basic unit was a small team – like the British Special Air Service (SAS) – of specialists each of whom was capable of taking over the role of any other member of the team. Training was intensive and stressed intelligence and initiative as well as fighting skill. A would-be green beret would pass from basic training to jump school and, from there to the Army's Special Warfare School at Fort Benning, Georgia, where a series of specialized courses trained them in all aspects of modern warfare and counter-insurgency. Many recruits were bi-lingual and others underwent intensive language courses designed to make them so.

The Special Forces' unique training and their elite status made them highly disliked in the regular Army but they captured Kennedy's imagination. To Kennedy, the Special Forces could defeat insurgent movements by using the guerrillas' own tactics

Above Secretary of Defence Robert McNamara (left) and General Maxwell Taylor (center) on a tour of US bases abroad.

Above left General Duong Van "Big" Minh. General Minh headed the South Vietnamese military Junta for a few weeks after the Army's anti-Diem coup before being ousted himself. As the North Vietnamese tanks converged on Saigon in April 1975, General Minh was again called to power in the hope that he could find a last-minute compromise with the communists. This time, his rule lasted for only a few days.

or by training the armed forces of friendly governments. In Vietnam, Special Forces advisors worked closely with elite ARVN units (many of whom had also received CIA-sponsored training in America's counter-insurgency schools) and regular forces. Special Forces advisors were trained in the language, customs, and traditions of the people with whom they were to work and many had a genuine appreciation of the indigenous culture. The result was often a close working relationship of mutual trust which produced better soldiers than those simply instructed by regular Army advisors – many of whom were simply doing a job in a country they didn't understand and didn't like.

Most Green Beret advisors achieved an instant rapport in the villages of the Montagnard tribes. They lived among the tribesmen enlisting their support and helping in the daily tasks but, whatever the provocation, avoiding interference in tribal custom. One advisor, for example, just shrugged his shoulders and watched as the tribal chief executed his adulterous daughter with an ancient French rifle. Supplies and goods for the tribes were delivered regularly by helicopter and soon Montagnard units were being trained in modern weaponry and fighting alongside US forces with courage and distinction.

In theory the programme converted the Montagnard's ancient hostility towards anything Vietnamese into a war on the Viet Cong. On occasion, the practice was a bit different. Persuading the more warlike Montagnard tribes to kill Vietnamese was an easy matter. Raiding parties of tribesmen armed with a variety of weaponry (including the small cross-bows the Montagnard were famous for) were sent on "hunter-killer" missions to seek-out VC units or hit known Viet Cong villages. Sometimes the advisor went along with the war-party and sometimes not but – either way – it was a bit of an effort to restrain tribal enthusiasm for killing *any* Vietnamese the raiders happened to run across. The fighting skill of these hunter-killer war-parties cleared many a tribal area of major VC activity – on the other hand, it didn't do much towards increasing good will among the general Vietnamese population.

Growing American Disenchantment with Diem's Government

By early 1963, it had become clear that one of the chief obstacles to America's efforts in Vietnam was Diem's Government. There had been an attempted coup in 1960, and since then Diem seemed to be more concerned about subverting his generals' plots than with fighting the war. Diem's commanders were ordered to avoid casualties and losses of equipment by any over-zealous pursuit of VC guerrillas. Generals who showed signs of ability were handicapped rather than encouraged lest they became the focus of popular sentiment. Corruption, political repression, and simple bungling by Diem's government were causing waves of unfavorable publicity in the American press. As in 1954, Washington was divided on exactly what to do about Diem and the CIA had toyed with the idea of killing him since 1957. He was clearly a serious drawback to everything Kennedy wanted to accomplish but no one could come up with an obvious alternative. What finally brought down Diem's regime were his excesses against Vietnam's Buddhists.

Diem's chief support came from his fellow Catholics and aid programmes always managed to favor Catholic villages. In

Left US military advisor instructs ARVN troops in map reading before going on a search-and-destroy exercise in March 1963.

59

May 1963, Vietnam's Archbishop Ngo Dinh Thuc—who happened to be Diem's older brother—issued an order forbidding people from carrying flags on Buddha's birthday. The ancient capital of Hue was the center of Vietnamese Buddhism and, on May 8th, a crowd gathering at the local radio station to protest this order was met with fire hoses and tear gas. When the crowd still refused to disperse, a (Catholic) provincial official gave the order to fire. Nine died as the crowd panicked and ran. The Government tried to blame the killings on a Viet Cong terrorist bomb but nobody believed it and the Buddhists found themselves at the center of a growing public opposition to everything Diem stood for. It wasn't simply a religious quarrel but rather a protest which focused the discontent of all aspects of Vietnamese society.

In June, Buddhist monk Thich Quang Duc sat down in the middle of Saigon, soaked himself in gasoline, and turned himself into a living funeral pyre. Duc's macabre self-martyrdom pushed his fellow monks into organized anti-Diem protest throughout South Vietnam's cities and made virtually every American aware of what was going on through constant re-plays of the grisly suicide on TV. Diem's sister-in-law, Madame Nhu, a handsome, cruel-looking woman nicknamed the "Dragon Lady" after an old American comic strip character, only made matters worse with her light-hearted remarks about "Buddhist barbecues." The crisis dragged on for weeks and the Government looked totally incapable of dealing with it.

On August 21st, Nhu—Diem's increasingly unstable brother—ordered his elite, CIA trained Special Forces to attack Buddhist pagodas in Hue, Saigon, and other major cities. In Saigon alone, some thirty monks were shot out of hand. Nhu rounded-up and imprisoned thousands of student demonstrators who had taken to the streets to protest his attack on the Buddhists and then he publicly accused the CIA of plotting against the regime. A month earlier Nhu had informed Vietnam's chief military commanders that he was planning to stage-manage a phoney coup. It was a total bluff but the generals—who had been making plans for a real coup of their own—were caught unprepared, didn't know whom to trust, and backed-off from their various schemes for a short while longer.

In Washington, opinion was pretty much divided between a faction of the State Department led by Averell Harriman which argued for Diem's removal, and the top echelons of the CIA, under its Director John McCone, which favored keeping him—despite his faults—because there was no obvious candidate to put in his place. The President's brother, Attorney General Robert Kennedy, argued that if Diem was overthrown, and the US was unable to come up with a satisfactory replacement, Washington should begin winding down its commitments in South Vietnam. Kennedy, however, was undecided and nothing definite came out of endless top-level discussions. Following Nhu's move on the Buddhists, however, Diem's opponents in the State Department took matters into their own hands and triggered a coup in Saigon.

Through local agents, the CIA was in contact with some of the Vietnamese generals plotting against Diem. Harriman's group sent a message to America's new ambassador to Saigon, Henry Cabot Lodge, authorizing him to give US support to the dissident generals and an anti-Diem coup. They cleared the message with Kennedy by telephone and—having caught the

Above Lyndon Baines Johnson, who became President after Kennedy's assassination. Not wanting to commit the United States to a full-scale war, Johnson escalated America's involvement in South Vietnam step by step. In the end, his small steps added up to the major war he had wished to avoid.

Right A GI carries two small Vietnamese children to safety during a fire-fight with the Viet Cong.

President in a "do-something" mood—got his go-ahead. Lodge was ordered to proceed before Diem's backers in the CIA were even aware that a coup had been authorized. When McCone heard the news, he repeatedly tried to get Kennedy to change his mind but the President had now committed himself and when the plotting Vietnamese generals informed Washington in late October that they were ready to move, they were assured of American support. On November 1st, Diem found his Presidential palace surrounded by tanks and armed troops who just sat and waited for events to unfold.

For the rest of the day, Diem and Nhu used the radio and telephone to negotiate with the leaders of the coup, any of his former supporters who would answer, and Ambassador Lodge. Lodge told Diem that he really wasn't sure what was going on or of Washington's position but that it was his understanding that both Diem and Nhu would be given a safe passage abroad in exchange for their resignations. The brothers decided to take matters into their own hands. They slipped into a secret underground tunnel and escaped into the streets of Saigon. They managed to elude capture until the next morning but, when discovered, they were arrested, thrown into a transit van, and promptly shot by a junior officer. When Kennedy heard of the killings, according to Maxwell Taylor, he "leaped to his feet and rushed from the room with a look of shock and dismay on his face which I had never seen before."

Three weeks later, Kennedy himself lay dead in Dallas' Parkland Hospital and Lyndon Johnson became President. One of the first thoughts to cross Johnson's mind was that Kennedy's assassination had been a revenge killing for Diem's murder but, at the end of the day, there was no evidence to back up this idea and there have been a succession of theories ever since. What *is* clear is that Kennedy's death left the United States on the brink of

direct involvement in the Vietnam war. Johnson was to take the final steps and the war has been thought of as largely his doing ever since but all he did was to continue initiatives already set in motion by Kennedy and Eisenhower. Johnson took over Kennedy's administration almost intact; he made no major changes in the cabinet, CIA, or other advisory agencies for some time. With few exceptions, the Kennedy administration was in favor of letting America's armed forces do the job the Vietnamese Army seemed incapable of doing. Johnson took over his domestic duties very quickly and with considerable political skill but he had very little appreciation of the subtleties of foreign policy. Within a few years he found himself hopelessly immersed in a seemingly endless war which he couldn't lose but which he couldn't win either. Only then was it obvious that he had listened to the wrong advice.

Inset left Random US 50 caliber machine-gun fire at the entrance to the An Lao Valley designed to discourage any enemy who might be trying to use the cover of darkness to move in or out of the area. In so-called "free-fire-zones", suspected VC pathways and assembly points were shelled, bombed, or fired upon in a more-or-less random pattern to inhibit the enemy's movement.

Main picture UH-1B "Huey" helicopters move in for a landing near Tuy Hoa. The mission was Operation *Bolling*, a 1967 search-and-destroy sweep in Phu Yen Province. The helicopter added great mobility to US forces and had its first major military role in Vietnam.

Above President John Fitzgerald Kennedy. Kennedy's death in November 1963 left Vice President Johnson in command of an uncertain US commitment to Vietnam. There is some evidence that Kennedy was flirting with the idea of withdrawing US support for the Saigon Government and removing American advisors but the truth will never now be known.

Top right A US advisor looks on as an ARVN soldier distributes psychological warfare material to a Vietnamese peasant in an effort to win the "hearts and minds" of the rural populace.

Bottom right South Vietnamese soldiers patrol the mangrove swamps of the Ca Mau Peninsula as part of a 1962 ARVN operation against VC in the Mekong Delta.

Far right A US inshore patrol craft of the so called "Brown Water Navy", cruises through the outskirts of the city of Ca Mau.

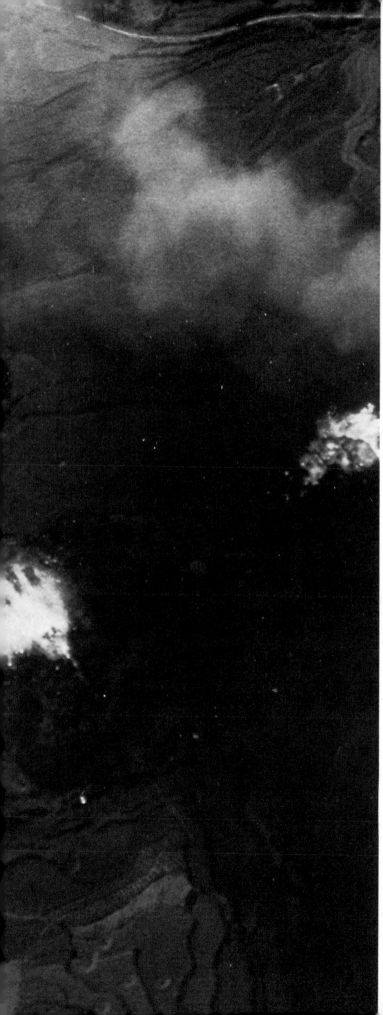

5 The Slide into War

The Maddox Incident

In late July 1964, the American destroyer *USS Maddox* entered the Gulf of Tonkin and soon slipped across the fifteen mile limit and into the coastal waters of North Vietnam. The *Maddox* was operating as a "ferret," a standard type of electronic intelligence mission which provokes the target country with deliberate border incursions in order to test its defences. Radar frequencies, radio transmissions, and response times are monitored and analyzed to seek blind spots in the defence network. The *Maddox* continued her mission in North Vietnamese waters and on August 2nd, she suddenly found herself under attack by three patrol boats. The attackers were easily beaten off but, two days later, the *Maddox* and a second destroyer, the *USS Turner Joy*, were attacked by another wave of North Vietnamese patrol boats. Neither ship was hit and, after four hours, they sent their attackers fleeing home after sinking two and damaging two others. The next day, President Johnson announced that he was ordering retaliatory air strikes on North Vietnamese naval bases and oil storage installations. Flying off the carriers *Ticonderoga* and *Constellation*, American fighter-bombers flew some sixty sorties. Up to thirty North Vietnamese naval craft were sunk or damaged beyond repair and extensive damage was done to fuel depots and maintenance facilities.

Johnson went before Congress asking for the authority to do what ever had to be done to defend American forces in Southeast Asia. The incidents in the Gulf of Tonkin and reports that the North Vietnamese were moving troops into position near the DMZ in preparation for a possible invasion of the South, provided an air of urgency and Congress quickly responded with everything Johnson wanted. Known informally as the Gulf of Tonkin Resolution, the Bill was little more than an open ticket for Johnson to use US armed forces in Indochina when and how he wanted without having either to seek Congressional approval beforehand, or to make a formal declaration of war.

The maneuvering which lay behind the Gulf of Tonkin Resolution is still something of a mystery. The draft of the Resolution was written some two months earlier and it is obvious that the Johnson adminstration was looking for some pretext to get a Congressional stamp of approval before escalating US involvement further. Johnson was by then fighting the 1964 election campaign against the conservative Republican Senator Barry Goldwater. Goldwater was a hard-liner on communist aggression and Johnson wished to appear less hawkish than Goldwater but nevertheless firm in his determination to defend South Vietnam. His speeches at the time of the Gulf of Tonkin incidents invoked images of Pearl Harbor-like treachery by Hanoi but it was clear that the American public was not going to respond with anything like the sort of fervor and national outrage which sent the US into World War II.

Although few, if any, doubted America's ability to win a war in Southeast Asia, the mood of the US public was uncertain. There were those anxious to stop the communist menace there and then but, on the whole, these were a small if vocal part of a

Left A swathe of destruction left after a US Super Sabre has carried out a napalm strike on suspected VC positions.

67

largely disinterested population. They were, in any case, pretty much balanced by an equally vocal – although somewhat smaller – minority opposed to everything that the United States was trying to do in Indochina. On the whole, the American public saw Vietnam as a far-off place populated by a strange and alien people. It was certainly less important than the numerous domestic issues that were then dividing US society, such as Civil Rights and racial conflict.

The man on the street probably thought in a vague sort of way that stopping communism in Southeast Asia was a good idea but it was not a cause for flag waving and certainly not one worth dying for. Even at the height of the war, Johnson's supporters argued chiefly on the basis of the need to support the country's leaders and the need to finish a job already begun. The humanitarian and geopolitical principles supposedly involved in the conflict rarely excited anyone and even the Marine Corps was forced to meet its manpower needs with draftees for a time – an unheard of humiliation for a service which has always prided itself on being a volunteer outfit. Committing America to a full-scale war before the 1964 election would have been politically risky and, while the Johnson administration was now set on winning in Vietnam, it would have to wait awhile to do it.

Washington now saw North Vietnam as the main enemy rather than the VC itself. It was clear that Hanoi was firmly committed to overthrowing the Saigon Government and furthering a VC takeover by force. Soviet weapons and supplies were flooding down the myriad jungle pathways nicknamed the "Ho Chi Minh Trail" but, as yet, no regular troops of the North Vietnamese Army (NVA) were operating in the South – at least not in any numbers worth mentioning. A few irregular NVA units and some North Vietnamese advisors were fighting alongside the VC but it was still the NLF's war. Nevertheless, Washington was convinced that the key to victory lay not simply in defeating the insurgents but, more importantly, in breaking Hanoi's willingness to support and supply them. The Johnson administration was determined to provoke Hanoi into a fight while at the same time making it appear that the US was the victim of naked aggression.

America was already conducting clandestine warfare in the North. Since Colonel Lansdale's campaign of the mid-1950s, the CIA had specially trained squads of demolition, sabotage, and psychological warfare experts engaging in sporadic hit-and-run raids along the coastlines of Southern China and North Vietnam. Some were commando raids pure and simple while others left behind small teams for longer term sabotage and intelligence-gathering. The idea was to disrupt and harass communications and conduct economic sabotage. The teams were chiefly made up of former refugees from North Vietnam or Nationalist Chinese volunteers from Taiwan. A long-term hope was also to build active resistance movements in both North Vietnam and Southern China but, in the event, this proved futile.

Covert operations against North Vietnam were stepped up as US involvement in the war increased and, by late 1964, these operations were part of a highly secret scheme known as OPLAN-34A. In addition to increasing the covert campaign against Hanoi, the plan involved bombing targets in the North with a fleet of some thirty old bombers repainted with Laotian markings and flown by CIA-recruited Laotian, Thai, Vietnamese,

Far left A US Marine squad leader calls for his men to move up on VC positions. Note his Armalite AR-15 (M-16) rifle, now the standard American forces issue. The M-16 fires a 0.223 calibre, high velocity bullet whose shock effect more than makes up for its small mass.

Left North Vietnamese soldiers train for the war in the South. When Johnson committed US troops to Vietnam on a large-scale, North Vietnam quickly began sending large numbers of its own forces to the South. Before this, Hanoi had been content to encourage the Viet Cong insurgency with equipment and a small commitment of manpower.

Below The destroyer *USS Maddox*. Operating on a top-secret, intelligence-gathering mission in the Gulf of Tonkin, the *USS Maddox* was attacked by three North Vietnamese patrol boats on August 2, 1964. The attack was easily beaten off but the incident led to the passing of the Gulf of Tonkin Resolution by the US Congress – a Bill which virtually gave Johnson a blank check in his powers to use American forces abroad.

and Nationalist Chinese pilots from a secret base in Laos. Under the code-name DeSoto, the *USS Maddox* was sent into the Gulf of Tonkin to ferret out intelligence on North Vietnam's coastal defence network for future OPLAN-34A operations and other vital military data for an escalating, undeclared war with Hanoi. What is still unclear is whether or not the *Maddox* was also directly involved in another OPLAN-34A mission going on at the same time.

During the *Maddox*'s sojurn in North Vietnamese waters, an OPLAN-34A vessel put a commando unit ashore in the vicinity of the coastal city of Vinh. Some believe that the attack on the *Maddox* was a retaliation for this covert raiding party or that the North Vietnamese mistook the *Maddox* for the clandestine, OPLAN-34A vessel. Another suggestion is that the *Maddox* was acting as an escort for the commando ship or engaging in other actions designed to provoke the North Vietnamese into attacking her. Perhaps the full truth will never be known but whether by accident or by design, the Gulf of Tonkin Resolution gave Johnson what he had wanted all along – approval "to take all necessary measures to repel any armed attack against the forces of the United States and to prevent

further aggression."

By now American casualties in the South were mounting and each was played up by the Administration as an attack on the United States. Including the debacle at Ap Boc, in which three US advisors had been killed, some thirty Americans had died in Vietnam's wars since 1945. Long since considered legitimate targets by the NLF, American personnel were to suffer greatly at the hands of terrorist attacks during 1964. In early May, an attack on the transport ship *USS Card* in Saigon's harbor sank the vessel and, as an American inspection team was having a look at the wreckage, terrorists threw bombs into the crowd. On Christmas Eve, a bomb attack on the US Bachelor Officers Quarters in Saigon killed two Americans and wounded over fifty others.

The first American killed in Vietnam, OSS Major Peter Dewey, had been caught in a Viet Minh ambush near Hanoi in September 1945. His jeep apparently lacked the proper US identification and the shooting was accepted as accidental by the OSS. Ironically his last report recommended that America "clear out of South East Asia". It wasn't until mid-1959 that another American serviceman on active duty in Vietnam was killed, when two advisors were killed in an insurgent attack on ARVN positions at Bien Hoa. But in 1959, the number of US advisors officially in Vietnam was only a few hundred. By the time of the Ap Boc battle, the figure stood at just over 11,000 and, by the end of 1963, 16,500. By mid-1964, the number was 21,000.

The first weeks of 1965 were to irreversibly transform Vietnam into an American war. In January, VC troops attacked and occupied the village of Binh Gia near Saigon. Before they withdrew, after four days of intense fighting, the VC had killed six Americans and over 175 ARVN regulars. In the early morning hours of February 7th, a VC mortar barrage caught US personnel at Camp Holloway and the neighboring Pleiku Airbase by surprise before a wave of guerrillas cut their way through the wire. The result was eight dead and well over 100 wounded in addition to some twenty aircraft destroyed or seriously damaged. Johnson immediately announced the launching of Operation *Rolling Thunder*, a long-planned campaign of air strikes against North Vietnam which the administration had continually postponed until it was fairly certain that the American public would accept a major escalation in the fighting.

At the end of March 1965, a VC attack on the US Embassy in Saigon left twenty dead and 175 injured but by then Johnson had already committed the United States to a land war in Indochina. General William Westmoreland, who had assumed command of MACV on June 20, 1964, argued that the ARVN forces were not sufficient to protect US airbases, particularly the major American field at Danang. The incident at Pleiku highlighted the vulnerability of airfields to guerrilla attack but, after Johnson signed an order on February 26th for American forces to defend American airfields in South Vietnam, it was the US Marines – and not Air Force security troops – who landed at Danang on March 8th. Two battalions of Marines waded ashore from landing craft in front of the bemused crowd of on-lookers but the show was just the beginning. With the arrival of the Marines in Danang, America's troop strength in Vietnam reached some 27,000. The floodgates had been opened once and for all and, by October 23rd, the number stood at 148,000.

Below A USAF F-100 Super Sabre turns to make a strafing pass against a VC position in the Mekong Delta.

Miscalculations on both sides

In many ways, America's involvement in Vietnam was the result of serious political miscalculations in both Washington and Hanoi. In Hanoi, the planners appear to have concluded (quite rightly) that Saigon could not hold out against a Viet Cong armed with a steady supply of advanced Soviet military equipment shipped from the North and supported by regular NVA troops, but (wrongly) that Washington would not enter into a major land war in Southeast Asia. In Hanoi's opinion, America would continue to support Saigon with plentiful supplies, advisors, CIA special-operations, and airstrikes south of the DMZ, and against the Cambodian and Laotian portions of the Ho Chi Minh Trail, but any US ground-operations, they calculated, would be carried out chiefly in support of ARVN forces. Eventually, any war of attrition like this would weary the American public who would become increasingly angered by US casualties as the Saigon Government grew closer and closer to collapse. This strategy had worked on the French and, sooner or later, Washington would abandon Saigon to its fate.

Here, too, Hanoi got things pretty much right but they misjudged the level of commitment that Washington was in the first instance willing to make. By August 1967, Johnson had 525,000 American troops in South Vietnam and, before Nixon began the US wind-down in June 1969, the figure peaked at 541,000. Neither did Hanoi take into account the boost in morale given to ARVN forces by the introduction of American troops on a large-scale. Fighting alongside American forces and largely under American direction, ARVN performances improved

Above ARVN Special Forces are put ashore by a US Navy river patrol boat to set up an ambush for VC guerrillas operating in the Mekong Delta.

Right US Navy inshore patrol craft (PCE) cruising near Viet Cong positions on the Duong Keo River.

considerably. Washington also put diplomatic pressure on its allies and under terms of the SEATO Treaty, contingents of Australian troops began arriving in Vietnam early in June 1965 to be followed in turn by forces from New Zealand and South Korea. Efforts at persuading Britain to send even a token force from its legendary Gurkha regiments, however, came to nothing and Johnson was to become increasingly bitter over European disinterest.

Hanoi, then, underestimated the scale and intensity of the coming war, but they made a far more serious mistake in believing that the United States would not bomb north of the DMZ for fear of a wider war with China or the Soviet Union. China's probable response was certainly America's main worry and every step of the coming campaign against North Vietnam was riddled with endless debates about whether or not Peking would intervene. What would China do if America bombed in the Hanoi region or near the Chinese border? Or mined Haiphong harbor? Or made limited invasions of Cambodia, Laos, and across the DMZ? In the event, America did all these things but as the war grew in intensity so did America's belief that China would not intervene unless there was a clear attempt to overthrow the Hanoi Government. There was no clear evidence either way, but China was distracted by its own internal turmoil and was engaged in a deep ideological struggle with the Soviet Union. When the Johnson administration had finished its discussions, there was always the feeling that Peking would keep out of the war at each rung up the ladder of escalation. Hanoi's main error was in misjudging America's willingness to

bomb North of the border and the country was to suffer greatly in the coming years. Shortly after assuming the Presidency, Johnson approved the preparation of plans for a possible bombing campaign against the North. The plans were completed by mid-April 1964—a list of ninety-four primary targets in North Vietnam which, it was hoped, would cripple Hanoi's war effort and dampen its enthusiasm for fomenting revolution in the South.

America's main error in all this was its faith in the awesome destructive power of the US Air Force and its doubts about the capability of the North Vietnamese to endure the methodical devastation of modern aerial bombardment. Critics who argued that the scale of bombing was not enough to make Hanoi backtrack were over-ruled. Johnson went to war in small steps. From the tragic day in Dallas which made him President, Johnson was constantly told that if something wasn't done quickly, South Vietnam would fall. Johnson listened, deliberated, and sooner or later approved the smallest level of escalation which he thought would do any good. Many of his advisors were pushing for a far larger American involvement far sooner, but Johnson was understandably afraid of committing the United States to a major war and of the political effect it would have on his Presidency. At the end of the day, Johnson's war was probably just as intense and extensive as it would have been if he had done what his more hawkish advisors had been suggesting all along, but he didn't do things that way. A step at a time. That was Johnson's way. It was as if he felt that the American public would accept a war that they became

Below A PCE moving at full speed during search-and-destroy operations in the Mekong Delta.

Above A Super Sabre hits a VC position with a general-purpose bomb during operations in late 1965.

accustomed to gradually; but doubtless he also hoped that each level of escalation might just do the trick.

The Chaos after Diem

Whatever hopes Johnson may have had that the United States could defeat the NLF without a deeper commitment rapidly vanished as the government of South Vietnam floundered in a political vacuum that hovered on anarchy. Diem's regime had been overthrown but the military junta which took over looked even less efficient. The junta's first leader, General Duong Van "Big" Minh, was a large, jovial man educated in the French tradition but he quickly proved incapable of controlling his fellow officers or of re-organizing his government to take account of the countless political factions that had emerged with the fall of Diem's police state.

In the turmoil of Diem's fall, the NLF stepped up its campaign and began attacking government villages and military outposts across the country. Casualties were heavy and the ARVN forces soon found themselves driven back to the safety of Saigon and the provincial capitals. The junta's generals were professional soldiers but they were not the sort of militant anti-communist crusaders that Diem had been. Washington

was forced to increase its aid and promises of support in order to stave off the possibility that the junta would try to seek an accommodation with the VC, or accept a French proposal for the neutralization of all Indochina. The Minh-led coup had not been the only plot against Diem and, on January 29th, 1964, General Nguyen Khanh's troops seized control of the three-month-old junta. Bloated by American aid and equipment, the South Vietnamese Army was now a major political force and was more-or-less to rule the country until its fall in 1975. Ironically, when North Vietnamese and NLF troops finally entered Saigon, South Vietnam's last leader was General "Big" Minh.

To the Americans, Khanh and his clique seemed a god-send. Unlike their predecessors, they appeared young, efficient commanders gifted with the personal courage, skills, dedication, and life-styles of professional soldiers. Their origins were largely lower middle-class and their careers were made solely in the military. They were genuinely nationalistic and anti-communist but also, it must be said, opportunistic. Khanh, for example, spent a year and a half with the Viet Minh as a young man before leaving (some say he was thrown out) to begin a military career under a French programme aimed at increasing the number of Vietnamese officers in the colonial

Above 1965. The Marines storm ashore at Danang in full battle-gear. As they landed in pure Iwo Jima style, the Marines were greeted by beach-partying US advisors and holiday-making South Vietnamese enjoying the local color.

Left A 1st Cavalry UH-1B helicopter equipped for rocket attacks on entrenched Viet Cong takes off as part of Operation *Pershing* in July 1967.

army. Within a short time, General Khanh had alienated most of the myriad political factions (and their countless splinter groups) that he was trying to unite into a workable government and, by July, various generals were plotting a new coup.

With the fall of Diem, South Vietnam's Catholics – one of the country's more powerful minorities – saw much of their influence in the government begin to erode. Within a few months, vocal Catholic factions had become one of Khanh's busier political opponents and – partly in reaction to this – various anti-Catholic groups with Buddhists at their head began their own agitation. The result was growing social unrest, sectarian murders, and a demand by both sides for civilian government. Khanh's response was a "constitution" which increased his own authority. Violent political protest erupted almost immediately from all sides. The streets of Saigon were filled with demonstrators, counter-demonstrators, and bands of rioting youngsters often bent solely on looting and murder. Unknown terrorists planted bombs. Although Saigon suffered most, the rioting quickly spread to Hue and Danang as well.

In September, the streets of Saigon were filled with various ARVN forces in three separate attempted coups, but Khanh managed to hang on – largely because none of the plotters could find enough support to make himself leader of a new junta. As the turmoil increased, the Americans under their new Ambassador, Maxwell Taylor, let it be known that they too favored a civilian government. Khanh was forced to accept this and he rapidly created a civilian National Council led by 90-year-old Phan Khac Suu and with an aging teacher, Tran Van Huong, as Prime Minister. The National Council proceeded to offend the Buddhists, the Catholics, the junta (officially, the Military Council) and virtually everybody else of any importance. The generals promptly tried to overthrow the National Council and Khanh rapidly allied himself with his former enemies, the Buddhists, to put himself back in power.

Needless to say, the Khanh-Buddhist alliance was not universally popular and, in late February 1965, a Catholic faction of the army tried its own coup. Things hung in the balance for three days but, in the end, the majority of generals went against the plotters. Although this latest coup against him had failed, Khanh was not to return to power. His fellow junta members simply voted him out of office and sent him into a pleasant exile. For the next three months, South Vietnamese politics teetered on chaos as Catholics, Buddhists, generals, and various politicians sought to out-maneuver each other in a shifting pattern of alliances. On June 12th, three generals – Nguyen Huu Co, Nguyen Van Thieu, and Nguyen Cao Ky – managed to establish a National Leadership Council and take over with Ky as the effective leader.

Ky was a flamboyant figure and a skillful pilot with westernized tastes in colorful flying suits and a fast life-style. He had personally thwarted at least two previous attempted coups by switching sides at the last minute and threatening to lead his fighter-bombers against the plotter's forces. To most US observers, including Ambassador Taylor, the idea of "Air Vice-Marshal" Ky heading the Saigon junta was disturbing if not a disaster. Taylor tried his best to keep Ky out of power but, when months passed without further coups and it looked as if Ky's government had the united support of the military, the American authorities began to see him as the leader they had

Above left The North Vietnamese Navy holds gunnery practice in the Gulf of Tonkin. Their Navy was mainly geared for coastal defence.

Left A Marine helicopter lands supplies for ARVN troops on a mission against the VC. The ARVN and an American advisor clear the helicopter on the double so it can take off before enemy gunners zero in.

Far left The interrogation of an NVA prisoner. In a brutal, dirty war like Vietnam, there were excesses on both sides.

been waiting for all along. It was at that moment that Ky precipitated a major confrontation with the Buddhists and almost single-handedly returned the Saigon Government to the brink of anarchy.

Frightened that Ky was trying to increase his personal power, the Buddhists began demonstrating in March 1965, for a civil government and the junta's resignation. Anti-American demonstrations and rioting multiplied throughout South Vietnam's cities and, in Hue and Danang, large numbers of soldiers and local officials went over to the protestors. On April 5th, Ky and 1500 Vietnamese elite troops landed at Danang airbase to re-take the city but had to fly back to Saigon when hostile crowds surrounded the gates of the base and the US commander closed the field. Rioting and demonstrations spread, and within the week, Ky's junta, now divided, called for a national congress of all political groupings and promised free elections within half-a-year to vote in an assembly.

Things gradually quieted down but, on May 14th, Ky sent 1000 of his best troops with back-up air support from his own air force unit to seize Danang in a lightning coup. The country exploded in protest and large elements of the army looked on the verge of revolt. The Buddhists of Danang fortified their pagodas and Ky's local commander refused to force them out. Putting his most firm supporter and ruthless commander, Colonel Nguyen Ngoc Loan, in charge, Ky ordered his forces

Right General William Westmoreland, in combat fatigues, watches Vietnamese troops train at the Military Police School.

Right A Huey hovers to off-load members of the 101st Airborne (World War II's famous "Screaming Eagles") in a search-and-destroy mission near the DMZ.

into the pagodas which eventually fell after considerable blood-letting. Ky's forces then besieged Hue. Saigon was rife with rioting, self-immolating buddhists, swirling clouds of tear gas, and club-wielding police. On the last day of May, an angry mob burned down the US Consulate in Hue.

Ky played a waiting game at Hue and, as the effects of his siege took hold, rebel commanders and officials began trying to mend their fences with the junta in Saigon. On June 8th, Ky's forces moved into Hue but, realizing that fighting was now futile, the Buddhist leaders ordered only passive resistance. Influential rebels were treated more-or-less lightly but others were rounded up and imprisoned ruthlessly. America tried to stand neutral during what became known as the "Buddhist revolt" but the US always treated the junta as the lawful government of Vietnam. When it was all over, Ky's junta was firmly in place. Washington at last had something remotely like the Saigon Government it had been seeking when Kennedy gave the go-ahead to overthrow Diem nearly three years before.

Vietnam becomes an American War

Vietnam became an American war during a National Security Council (NSC) meeting on April 1st, 1965 when Johnson agreed to increase the bombing campaign against the North and to let General Westmoreland use US troops to seek out and engage the enemy's forces. Khanh's government had fallen a month

Above ARVN airborne troops shoot their way through the streets of Danang during the Buddhist insurrection of 1963.

Left A CH-47 Chinook bringing in much needed supplies and ammunition to an American artillery position engaged in a fire-fight with the Viet Cong.

Following pages A US A-1 Skyraider passes over VC-held jungle while escorting a rescue helicopter moving in to pick up a downed pilot.

Right A VC commando squad in action near Hue. The VC proved to be a formidable enemy.

Below A US casualty is loaded aboard a truck for transport to a hospital and – perhaps – eventually home.

before and there looked no hope of finding some formula which might bring even a semblance of stability to Saigon. Ky's clique of discontented officers had originally sought Washington's support for Khanh's removal but their advances were rejected in no uncertain terms. Ambassador Taylor even went so far as to threaten the withdrawal of US aid if the plotters didn't stop their bickering and scheming. Continued American pressure forced Khanh to continue his half-hearted efforts at creating a civilian government but, when that collapsed and Khanh himself fell shortly afterwards, Johnson had little choice but to take final steps in making the war an American responsibility. It was either that or abandon Saigon altogether.

When Johnson took the final step, the decision remained unpublicized as if he hoped the American people would fight a war without quite realizing what was happening until it was all over. Nor did Johnson's administration take the last step with any coherent idea of what had to be done to win. Taylor and others had long argued for bombing the North in retaliation for guerrilla activities in the South but Johnson's advisors had no real idea of what it would take to make Hanoi back-away from supporting the NLF. The JCS had approved an Air Force plan for

a twelve-week intensive bombing campaign aimed at eliminating all ninety-four priority targets in North Vietnam but this was rejected in favor of a more gradual effort. Later in the war, the bombing would reach an intensity far beyond the original plan but its aim then would be to stop the NVA in its tracks and to bring Hanoi to the Paris peace table.

On the ground, Westmoreland's forces were to score some notable successes during the first few months of the war and they halted the NLF's drive just at the point of victory. But the NLF casualties and desertions were quickly replaced by new recruits, and "pacified" areas were reinfiltrated once the US/ARVN troops left. NVA regulars too were brought to battle and defeated but just as quickly replaced by new troops moving south. There was always something more to do – attack NVA/VC sanctuaries in Laos and Cambodia, for example – and requests for more troops were made virtually every month. There began to be talk of an American "presence" in South Vietnam for anything up to the next fifteen years. In the end, the decision to unleash America's armed forces in Vietnam turned out to be just another small step in an endless series of small steps that led inexorably to a deeper conflict than anyone had foreseen.

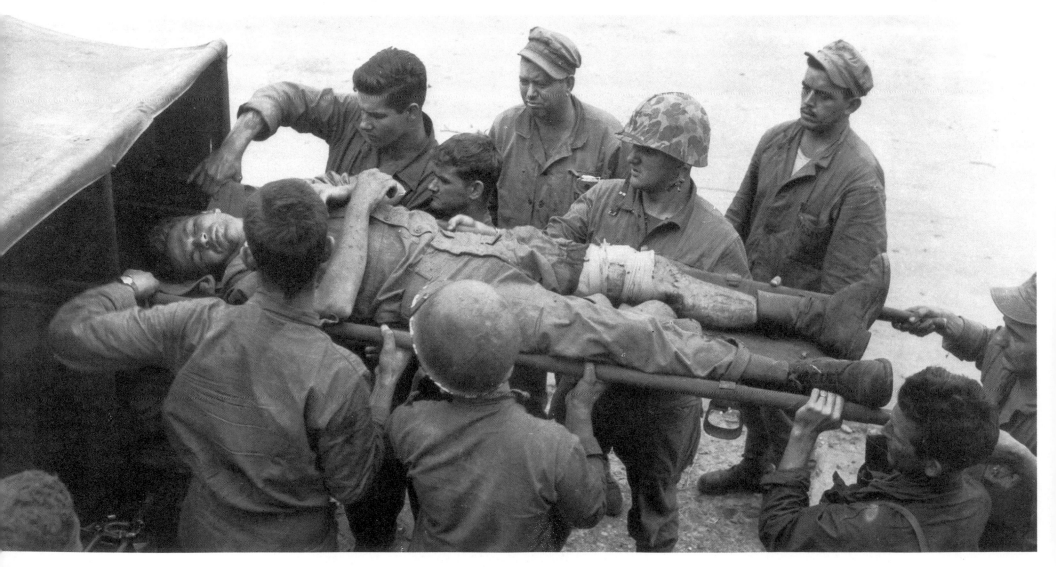

Left US hovercraft used for rapid assaults and pursuits over river and swampy areas. Delta regions of Vietnam occasioned the first military use of these unwieldy looking vehicles.

Right Battling for the Bien Hoa Bridge area against heavy VC opposition, a US Army Sergeant fires his M-60 machine gun from the shoulder.

Below ARVN airborne troops, backed up by tanks, shoot their way through the streets of Danang during the Buddhist insurrection. The soldier in the foreground is carrying an M-79 grenade launcher.

Left A quick evacuation of a casualty. The rapid evacuation of casualties by helicopter and other motorized transport saved many lives in Vietnam.

Below South Vietnamese tanks move against the Buddhists of Danang. This uprising led to the overthrow of President Diem.

Left An M-60 machine-gunner in position for a long fire-fight with the enemy. Belts of 7.62mm ammunition festoon his position.

Below The 1st Air Cavalry Division arriving at An Khe in July 1965. Specially trained for using helicopters, the 1st Air Cavalry were one of the most effective American units in Vietnam.

Right A US monitor of the 91 and 92 River Assault Squadrons on patrol in the Mekong Delta.

Far left Troopers of the 101st Airborne fight from old VC positions as the VC attack US artillery during Operation *Hawthorne,* near Kontum, in June 1966.

Left Catholic Nuns escort Vietnamese children to the airstrip at Vinh Long in Operation *Little Lift* during November 1968. Some two million people were made homeless by the war.

Below Artillery support for the 1st Cavalry from a 105mm howitzer during Operation *White Wing.* Light, mobile, and fast-firing, the 105s were the artillery work horse of the war.

Right Troops rush in for homeward bound helicopter transport after a search-and-destroy patrol against the VC.

Below Marines carry a wounded comrade to a waiting helicopter. Helicopter missions to evacuate wounded were known as "dust offs".

6 The Shadow War

The CIA at War

Nguyen Van Tai spent over four years shut up in a cold, totally white, 30 x 30 foot room fitted with the barest minimum of furniture. For four years Tai never stepped out of that room, and, apart from a succession of interrogators, he never saw another human being until a few hours before the fall of Saigon in April 1975. Tai had been captured during a routine ARVN sweep near Saigon at the end of 1970. His captors had struck lucky for, purely by chance, their prisoner turned out to be one of Hanoi's most important agents in the South since 1962 – a leader of VC terrorist teams in the Saigon area, the main architect of the VC's attack on the US Embassy during the 1968 Tet offensive, and a former deputy minister of the North Vietnamese secret police. Tai was tortured by the Vietnamese then taken over by the CIA who tried more subtle methods of breaking him down.

According to former CIA agent Frank Snepp, Tai claimed to be nothing more than an NLF-active peasant but his captors noted that this "peasant" devoured French and Vietnamese literature when it was offered to him and that he did regular exercises in his cell to keep himself fit. He was constantly monitored by secret cameras and tape recorders and considerable effort and guile were expended in breaking him psychologically: his room was kept cold (because of a common Vietnamese fear of the effects of chilly air); he was confronted with more cooperative prisoners who had once worked with him; he was interrogated continually but – to disorient him – irregularly; to play on any lingering guilt feelings, he was constantly reminded of the father he had once betrayed to the North Vietnamese security police; and was taunted with reminders of the wife and children he had left in the North and feared he would never see again.

During the long weeks and months of interrogation Tai let slip many details of his own career but – unlike many of his fellow prisoners – he was never broken sufficiently to reveal crucial details of NLF and North Vietnamese activities to his captors. When the 1973 cease-fire was signed, the CIA left Tai in the custody of the South Vietnamese who thought him far too important and dangerous to include in the general exchange of prisoners. When the North Vietnamese Army stood on the outskirts of Saigon two years later, Tai, the long-silent, long-suffering prisoner, was a few hours away from becoming a conqueror with less than kindly memories of his long captivity. At the suggestion of a high-ranking official, Tai's South Vietnamese captors unceremoniously bundled him aboard a plane, flew him out over the ocean, and threw him overboard without a parachute to make sure he never took his revenge.

Indochina was a CIA battlefield and had been one since Colonel Lansdale's action teams had tried to undermine the Viet Minh in the mid-1950s and Tai's story is not untypical of the brutal and uncompromising shadow-war that paralleled the conventional Vietnam war. The Agency fought its hidden war by proxy. It armed and trained the Montagnard tribes of the

Left Operation *Hawthorne*, June 1966. Troopers of the 101st Airborne fight from positions formerly occupied by the enemy.

Right A VC prisoner is questioned by the South Vietnamese Marines' 4th Battalion following a March 1965 raid in the Delta. The VC's interrogation methods were no less brutal.

Vietnamese highlands and the Meo tribesmen of Laos. It sent teams of saboteurs and agents into North Vietnam and used any South Vietnamese official it could recruit to spy on the Saigon Government. It planned and waged a war of terror on the Viet Cong. In partnership with the South Vietnamese Special forces and police (whom it trained and equipped) often in direct opposition to the efforts of the State Department and Pentagon, the agency boosted the careers of Saigon politicians it favored and hindered those it opposed. As America's involvement in Vietnam grew, so did the CIA's until in the end the CIA station in Saigon was the largest in the world with 1,000 or so full-time personnel, not counting agents and contracted employees in the rest of Indochina.

For all this commitment, however, the CIA did not play an important role in Johnson's war cabinet. Its generally pessimistic views on how the war was going and what could be done, were not what Johnson wanted to hear. He didn't like reading long, detailed intelligence analyses and prefered simple solutions. Moreover, Secretary of Defence McNamara's policy of "Graduated Response" had largely replaced the "Massive Retaliation" of the Eisenhower years. McNamara proposed to escalate military force in small steps to match an enemy's actions. This fitted in with Johnson's cautious approach to the war in Vietnam and the hesitant President usually accepted McNamara's ideas.

At the April, 1965 NSC meeting that finally turned Vietnam into an American conflict, the CIA's McCone was the odd-man-out. Ever since he and McNamara had visited Vietnam a year before, McCone had argued that Washington's step by step escalations were too little and probably too late. The day after the NSC's decision, McCone circulated a memo stating this in no uncertain terms. He wrote of an "ever-increasing commitment of US personnel … mired down in combat in the jungle in a military effort that we cannot win and from which we will have extreme difficulty in extracting ourselves." Giving US ground forces a more active role in Vietnam, McCone said, would work "only if our air-strikes against the North are sufficiently heavy and damaging really to hurt the North Vietnamese." McCone also correctly foresaw the political effects of the increasing anti-war movement. "With the passage of each day," McCone said "and each week, we can expect increasing pressure to stop the bombing. This will come from various elements of the American public, from the press, the United Nations and world opinion. Therefore time will run against us in this operation and I think the North Vietnamese are counting on this. Therefore I think what we are doing is starting on a track which involves ground force operations which, in all probability, will have limited effectiveness against guerrillas." McCone's all or nothing analysis was the opposite of McNamara's policy of graduated response favored by Johnson, and CIA access to the President's ear suffered accordingly.

As the war went on, the CIA under McCone and his successors, Raborn and Helms, remained sceptical of the benefits of bombing the North and, to a certain extent, they were joined in this by an increasingly disillusioned McNamara. It soon became obvious that the North Vietnamese were not being intimidated by the bombing and that copious war materials and men were still reaching the South. In its reports and policy papers to the NSC and McNamara, the Agency increasingly

Left The ugliest side of an ugly war. ARVN forces question a VC suspect near An Ninh, April 1966.

Below Chinese Nung mercenaries working with the US Special Forces interrogate a suspected VC sniper. After fifteen minutes, he confessed to being the rifleman who had fired on refugees earlier in the day.

THÀ CHẾT KHÔNG ĐỂ VŨ KHÍ RƠI VÀO TAY ĐỊCH

TRAP MEWAL   BUÔN JOK   EA MBIT   XÃ EA-HDING   EA KMUR

stressed the determination of the North Vietnamese to simply outlast the United States, however much damage the bombing managed to do. Hanoi's determination to topple the Saigon Government also remained unchanged. One 1967 report concluded: twenty-seven months of bombing have "had remarkably little effect on Hanoi's overall strategy in prosecuting the war, on its confident view of long-term communist prospects, and on its political tactics regarding negotiations."

A full-scale invasion of the North had long been ruled out because of the demands on American manpower, the effect on world opinion, and, most importantly, the very high risk that it would cause a wider war with China. A few hawks were constantly calling for such an invasion and for a methodical bombing campaign aimed at reducing North Vietnam to a pile of rubble. The Strategic Air Command's former commander General Curtis Lemay, for example, spoke of "bombing North Vietnam back into the stone-age." Lemay (who led the US contingent in the Anglo-American fire-bombing of Dresden) and others who shared his opinions didn't understand the type of war that Johnson was trying to fight. Unlike World War II, US goals in Vietnam were extremely limited. Washington's aim was to defeat VC insurgency in the South. Hanoi was being "punished" in order to make it cooperate but the overriding objective was to contain the conflict within Indochina – *not* to escalate things into a wider war with China or the USSR.

The CIA is only one of several US intelligence agencies. Two others are the Defence Intelligence Agency (DIA), which comes under the Pentagon, and the National Security Agency (NSA), which is based at Fort Meade, Maryland. The NSA is responsible for code breaking and signal intelligence (SIGINT) – the interception and breaking of all forms of electronic communication. Both the NSA and DIA have larger annual budgets and more manpower than the CIA and the three agencies are constantly squabbling about their respective domains, sources, and responsibilities. In addition, the Joint Chiefs of Staff (JCS) draw upon Army, Navy, and Air Force intelligence departments which may occasionally disagree with everyone else including the Pentagon's own DIA.

Although the CIA's views on the effectiveness of the bombing campaign and on Hanoi's overall "wear-down" strategy were to be proved more-or-less correct, it wasn't a case of Johnson and the NSC ignoring intelligence so much as a question of which intelligence they chose to listen to in a frighteningly complex world of bureaucratic in-fighting and conflicting opinion. When McNamara asked the CIA to submit an analysis of the bombing campaign and its effectiveness, for example, both the JCS and the DIA fought the decision tooth and nail. When McNamara grew sceptical of the benefits of increased bombing, he found himself in a long-running disagreement with Westmoreland and the JCS but largely in agreement with the CIA which, in turn, was arguing with the State Department about whether or not China would come into the war if the US undertook a limited invasion north of the DMZ or mined the ports of North Vietnam.

Far left top Viet Cong prisoners are taken aboard US 1st Cavalry helicopters for questioning back at Brigade Headquarters during Operation *Thayer II* in February 1967.

Far left below Montagnard tribesmen line up behind banners of their local villages to pledge loyalty to the Saigon Government in January 1965. The banners name the villages which the tribesmen are honor-bound to defend. The Montagnard tribes had an ancient hatred of Vietnamese and made excellent allies for the Green Berets' war against the VC. The tribesmen's pledge of loyalty to the Saigon regime was half-hearted but, once their word was given, they would generally keep it to the very end.

Left American Special Forces out of Cai Cai on a patrol near the Cambodian border.

Battles in the Secret War

Like any spy agency, the CIA's chief function is to gather intelligence but – despite the tons of paper that crossed the Agency's desks – it seems to have missed out on forecasting most of Hanoi's major moves. There were many successes – for example, the CIA correctly interpreted Hanoi's outfittng of a new NVA construction unit in 1959 as evidence of North Vietnam's intention to re-build the Ho Chi Minh Trail and take a more active role in the South – but the Agency seems to have missed the big ones. The agency was also generally correct in its interpretation of Hanoi's wait-it-out strategy and of its determination to continue the war in the face of US bombing. It also seems to have understood China's likely reactions to American escalations. The trouble was that the Agency seems to have only pushed these points when it was too late. The CIA's most spectacular failure was not warning Washington about the 1968 Tet Offensive despite clear indications that the NVA/VC were planning something big. On the other hand, no other intelligence agency saw it coming either.

The Agency – and its competitors in the intelligence business – also failed to warn Washington of a major NVA drive across the DMZ at the end of March 1972, Hanoi's biggest push since 1968. The ARVN high command had read the signs and predicted the attack exactly but, at the time, American

intelligence was forecasting that there would be no major NVA action across the DMZ – only less ambitious activities elsewhere. Intelligence analysts in the CIA and other agencies who did read the signs more-or-less correctly were largely ignored by their superiors who seemed to be more concerned with providing Nixon's National Security Advisor, Henry Kissinger, with reports that fit in with his long-running diplomatic efforts to secure a ceasefire. During Hanoi's 1975 offensives, the strength of the NVA thrusts were continually ignored or misinterpreted as South Vietnam collapsed like a house of cards. Even the North Vietnamese were surprised at the speed of their victory and the rapid disintegration of the ARVN forces.

Counter-intelligence activity in Vietnam was something of a disaster. Later estimates suggested that the NVA/VC had up to 30,000 or even 40,000 active agents throughout the ARVN and the Saigon Government. Many of these were obviously major officials and some were certainly double agents or simple information peddlers, but there were nevertheless a large number of highly-placed spies who sent the VC or Hanoi every bit of information passing through their hands. Throughout the war, US military operations were continually compromised at considerable cost in lives and effort. In the end the US military simply neglected to inform their ARVN counterparts about forthcoming operations or did so only at the last possible minute

to try and avoid leaks. Such tactics helped but couldn't even begin to solve the problem.

One of many examples of this was a high-level December 1974 meeting of the ARVN command in Saigon. The purpose of the meeting was to try and predict forthcoming NVA activity. It was decided that Hanoi was incapable of capturing and holding South Vietnam's provincial capitals and major cities but that the NVA would almost certainly strike at Tay Ninh province to the north-west of Saigon. ARVN forces were then concentrated in or near this area and the western highlands – where no attack was expected – were not reinforced. This was actually a CIA analysis passed on to the Saigon Government who quickly took it over as their own but, no sooner had it become agreed policy, than a still unidentified senior South Vietnamese official passed it on to Hanoi.

Needless to say, Hanoi was delighted to know where Saigon expected them to attack and where the ARVN forces were deployed. The NVA promptly prepared a campaign aimed at the lightly defended western highlands which achieved both total surprise and a spectacular success. The victory helped persuade the generally cautious Politburo in Hanoi that a final triumph could be achieved a lot more quickly than they had thought and the NVA campaign was stepped-up. Saigon fell some four months later. Hanoi's benefactor was never caught

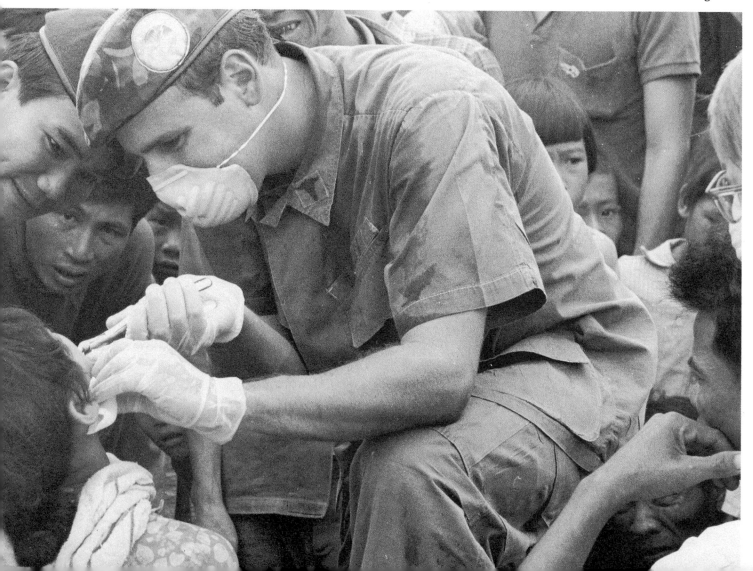

Far left Sick call in the South Vietnamese village of Ta Ly under the direction of a US Navy medical corpsman. American medical help was part of the effort to win over the hearts and minds of the people.

Left Dr. Arthur J. Goldberg, USNR, treats the teeth of a South Vietnamese woman as fascinated villagers look on. American pacification programmes in South Vietnam made tremendous strides in eliminating disease and making up for long years of medical neglect. Sadly, most of these advances were reversed when the South fell to the North in April 1975.

but the CIA had a long-standing list of at least four high-ranking suspects in the Saigon Government. Each of the suspects apparently owed his early career to CIA sponsorship and support. According to Frank Snepp, fear of having to expose one of its proteges as a NVA spy lead the CIA to shelve the whole business.

The CIA had its own extensive network of agents throughout the NLF who yielded valuable intelligence. But periodic memos from Washington and the Saigon station ordering intensive spy recruitment led to the Agency enlisting large numbers of VC-plants or enterprising Vietnamese con men who simply passed on cleverly made-up stories which did little except drain the operating fund of large sums of money. On one occasion, a well-placed CIA mole in the NVA was able to pass on the details of the latest proposals at the Paris peace talks but this gave the Agency one up only on the highly secretive Kissinger who had been keeping his diplomatic maneuverings pretty much to himself. Hanoi was a closed and security-conscious society and the Agency always had great trouble in recruiting agents there. There were some successes but the details remain secret even today as do the activities of the long-term spies sent in on covert missions such as OPLAN-34A. The Agency's reluctance to talk about the scheme is understandable. In 1968, when Johnson ordered a wind-down of the war north of the DMZ in an effort to bring Hanoi to the peace table, OPLAN teams operating in North Vietnam were simply abandoned. Over the next few years, the active teams were gradually rounded-up or fled to avoid capture when they realized that they were on their own.

Some good intelligence did come but it came far too late and often revealed earlier intelligence blunders. For years, Washington targeted the Ho Chi Minh trail with endless bombing raids aimed at interrupting the continual flow of Soviet supplies to the South. Like virtually everybody else, the CIA was convinced that the Ho Chi Minh Trail was the VC's life-line and the Agency waged its own covert war against the Trail with Montagnard and Meo tribesmen. When the military began to suspect that large amounts of supplies were also coming in through the Cambodian port of Sihanoukville, and then overland to NVA/VC strongpoints in Laos, Cambodia, and South Vietnam, the CIA disputed this with a blizzard of facts and figures and continued to direct the bulk of their operations against the Ho Chi Minh Trail.

When Nixon ordered the invasion of Cambodia in 1970 to clear out long-standing NVA/VC sanctuaries, however, documents and prisoners captured during the invasion gave a different picture of the "Sihanoukville Trail". The CIA had put the total military supplies shipped through Sihanoukville between 1966 and 1970 at some 6000 tons. The military had strongly disagreed throughout and put the figure at something around

Top right Special Forces on operations near Ba Xoai.

Bottom right Fifty caliber machine-gunners mount guard at the Bo Dup Special Forces camp.

Below VC suspects captured during operations on the Plaines des Joncs, 1965.

18,000 tons. The actual figure turned out to be around 26,000 tons, perhaps as much as eighty per cent of the total supplies that reached the South. Not only that, but, as it happened, the Agency had had the right information all along. A spy working through the China desk had access to much of the paperwork for shipping into Sihanoukville and was sending in regular reports which, after processing and editing, were forwarded to the CIA section assessing the problem of the Sihanoukville Trail. Sadly this additional information did not impress the responsible official and was simply set aside in favor of the prevailing idea that Sihanoukville was relatively unimportant.

Something of the complicated geopolitical flavor of the Vietnam war can be seen in a CIA proposal to assist the Soviet Union in getting its war supplies to the NLF. In less complicated times, this would have sounded like treason but, with the US trying to balance a limited war in Indochina against a wider peace with China and Russia, the proposal, however improbable, had an element of Catch-22 practicality about it. The Sixties and Seventies were highlighted by the ideological split between the Communist Giants and for a time, China would not even allow the USSR to ship its war material over Chinese territory to Hanoi. This gave the world a picture of two major communist powers squabbling over petty details while their "imperialist" enemy waged a war with another Marxist country. As the USSR was left with the long sea route to Haiphong

harbor, the CIA suggested that the US help establish an alternate Soviet supply line through Thailand and Laos. Had this proposal gone ahead, the CIA's price would have been to ask Moscow to put pressure on Hanoi to moderate its demands in the South.

The Agency's most successful work by far was in penetrating the Saigon Government and – to a slightly lesser extent – the ARVN. Bugs were planted in the Presidential Palace in Saigon almost from the beginning and in the offices and homes of almost anyone thought capable of influencing South Vietnam's ever-changing leadership. Officials who supported a strong South Vietnamese Government which would be averse to any sort of agreement with the VC, were bought or had their careers boosted. The Agency tried to persuade Saigon's self-seeking generals to broaden the base of their governments to include the country's dissident factions but, in the end, invariably opted to accept the most pro-American, anti-communist leadership available irrespective of its popular base.

Snepp tells the story of Tran Ngoc Chau, a nationalistic but dedicated opponent of the Saigon Government in 1970. When the South Vietnamese authorities decided to frame him as a communist sympathiser by falsifying his dossier and then throwing him into jail, the CIA went along with the plot quite

willingly and, along with other US personnel, cooperated in confirming the story after Chau's arrest. Chau spent some four years in prison and, when local agents wanted to evacuate him during the fall of Saigon, the idea was turned down and he was forced to stay behind. Efforts to put ARVN personnel directly onto the Agency payroll ran into conflict with US military intelligence who kept careful guard over their own preserves. The CIA got around this by recruiting former American advisors who had worked closely with the South Vietnamese so they could keep friendly with their old contacts.

The Agency came close to pulling off the greatest intelligence coup of the war by some clever desk-work in Washington but the coup was bungled by bureaucratic in-fighting. In 1966, CIA analyst Samuel Adams became curious about a long-standing estimate of 270,000 for the number of active VC. He began digging through countless old piles of intelligence reports and, after several months of diligent analysis, he decided that the true figure should be something like 500,000. His report triggered a bitter quarrel between the CIA and the military who steadfastly maintained that there were no more than 300,000 VC insurgents at the very most. In September 1967, the CIA director Richard Helms ordered

Adams to agree on a figure with the military and with the DIA (who wouldn't agree with the CIA's figure either). After all it looked fairly silly if different branches of the US Government couldn't even agree on how many enemy they were fighting.

Adams soon found that the military and the DIA had no intention of putting the figure at more than 300,000 and says that he was told off-the-record that the officers were specifically ordered not to go above this number. If Adams introduced evidence it was either dismissed out-of-hand or the breakdowns of VC battle units were adjusted so that the total still came out less than 300,000. The official Washington line was that the VC was a "spent force"; two years of US firepower and bombing had turned the tide. The VC was relatively quiet and had been suffering as many as 150,000 casualties a year plus a large number of desertions. Frightened about having yet another divisive argument in official circles (and one which contradicted Johnson's optimistic line that America had turned the tide) Helms ordered Adams and his fellow negotiators to concede the point and the CIA reluctantly agreed to an estimate of 300,000. Shortly afterwards, the military revised the figure again to less than 250,000.

Within three months of this one-sided compromise,

Far left South Vietnamese Rangers interrogate a VC prisoner with the aid of a water-filled jar. The prisoner was one of four taken in an attack on Cau Me in the Mekong Delta. It is not certain how many of these prisoners reached the comparative safety of the POW compounds.

Center Vietnam was a war which respected neither age nor sex. Anyone could be the enemy. This woman was held as a suspected VC or VC sympathizer during operations in the Tam Ky area.

Below An Airborne patrol moves through the idyllic woodlands of the Vietnamese Highlands.

however, NVA/VC attacks hit every major city in Sout Vietnam in the now famous Tet Offensive. While US forces were in no danger of an overall defeat, they were plunged into pitched battles across the country. Casualties were running high and it was clear to everyone that the VC was far from being a "spent force". It was obvious that the NLF's manpower resources were a lot larger than the official estimate. McNamara, already involved in a number of tactical disagreements with the JCS, began asking probing questions and Johnson came to realize that he faced a far bigger — and longer — war than he had ever thought. He was informed that there were at least twice as many VC as previous estimates had suggested. Angered that Helm's decision to concede the issue may well have been in part responsible for thousands of US dead and wounded during the Tet Offensive, Adams spent some time actively trying to get the CIA's director fired but nothing came of it in the end.

One of the CIA's most controversial operations during the Vietnam conflict was to enlist the support of the Montagnard tribes of central Vietnam and the Meo tribesmen of Laos. The Montagnard project was comparatively small-scale but, for the most part, highly effective. It was taken over by the military in 1963 after the Agency personnel and the Special Forces advisors who were dealing directly with the Montagnard aided the tribes in pushing Saigon for national autonomy on their ancestral lands. Three years later, an agreement between the South Vietnamese Government and the Montagnard was reached but Saigon promptly broke it. By the early 1970s, General Ky's westernized wife was trying to claim a large area of Montagnard land and disillusioned tribesmen then serving in ARVN units began to desert.

Like the Montagnard, the Meo tribes of Laos were initially recruited by specially-trained CIA operatives and Special Forces personnel operating covertly. The official neutrality of Laos, after all, had been guaranteed by a May 1961 super-power agreement in Geneva. In the beginning, the Meo — who lived in the highlands near the Plaine des Jarres — were recruited to harass the communist Pathet Lao guerrillas just as the Montagnard had been organized into units specifically to harass the VC. But the Meo homelands lay adjacent to the strategic Ho Chi Minh Trail and the tribesmen were soon carrying out hit-and-run guerrilla raids on North Vietnamese troops and supply units moving South. To protect its vital supply line, the NVA soon began its own search-and-destroy operations along the Trail and into the Meo's homelands. To enable the Meo to hold their own, the Agency sent them more advisors and increased the flow of military supplies. The result was a mini-war in an obscure corner of Laos which the world never saw.

Within a few years, this mini-war had grown into something a lot bigger. The Meo were fielding a 25,000 to 35,000 man, well-equipped army, which, at times, was engaging a NVA force two or three times larger. The battles were not just over the Ho Chi Minh Trail but, later, over the Meo Homelands and over certain strategic Laotian mountain peaks where the US had placed navigational beacons to guide B-52 bombers flying out of Thailand to attack targets in North Vietnam and Laos. The CIA's Meo army had been given the task of guarding the beacons as well as harassing North Vietnamese operations in Laos and along the Ho Chi Minh Trail. Fed up with harassment

from the Agency's Laotian army, Hanoi ordered the NVA to clear the area once and for all and the CIA's secret-war became an open conflict in which the very survival of the Meo people was at stake.

When it was exposed to the press and general public, the Agency's secret war caused a great deal of controversy but it was not – as many believed – a case of the CIA going off on its own to stir up trouble in foreign parts. The operation was approved by the White House and by select members of Congress who were privately briefed. Few, if any, suffered guilt feelings about using the Meo except for some on-the-spot CIA operatives and Special Forces who worked with them directly and saw what the war was doing to the customs and traditional life-styles of a people they had come to respect and like. When the project was exposed, it simply became part of the anti-CIA crusade in the press and Congress during the early 1970s, but many of the politicians and newspapers who publicly expressed their outrage had known about it all along.

When the Vietnam war finally ended with the fall of Saigon in 1975, the Meo had for all practical purposes ceased to exist. A few thousand Meo refugees trickled across the Thai border but, when they were first recruited in the early Sixties, their population had been some 250,000 or more. Their leader, General Vang Pao, had escaped to live in Montana but behind him he left a people who were either dead, living in miserable Thai refugee camps, or scattered throughout the Laotian highlands. Journalist Thomas Powers once interviewed a former CIA field agent who had worked with the Meo from 1962 to 1966. The ex-operative spoke of his immense admiration for both Vang Pao and his people. He tried to warn Pao that US backing was probably going to prove a short-term thing and that the Americans were only likely to be around for something like three years but, the conflict had its own logic and Pao got so involved with the war that he was overtaken by events. Like many of those who worked with the Meo, the agent was saddened by an outcome no one had foreseen.

Both the Meo and the Montagnard were a warlike people and getting them to fight VC, Pathet Lao, or NVA regulars didn't take much persuasion. Occasionally, battles fought by these irregulars had distinct elements of the macabre. Both the Meo and the Montagnard frequently collected ears to keep a running tally of Vietnamese or Pathet Lao killed in action. Despite later denials, US advisors either ignored the practice or actively encouraged it in order to motivate their tribesmen. A few Montagnard preferred taking heads to ears and both peoples often went at their work with an enthusiasm that made them a danger to any Vietnamese or Laotian in the vicinity. On the not infrequent occasions (especially in the early Sixties) that bounties were paid for dead insurgents or NVA there were problems making sure that the severed ears, heads, or hands actually belonged to the enemy. Neither the Meo nor the Montagnard regularly specialized in torture but it was not unknown when they wanted to extract information quickly or when they captured Vietnamese or Laotians who had perpetrated atrocities against local tribesmen. These people made natural allies but they were put to work in a wider war that was not of their doing.

Top left A swift boat gunner mans his fifty caliber.

Bottom left Pausing for an urgent reload before attacking VC positions.

This page A US patrol awaits helicopter evacuation after a fire-fight with the VC. The ease with which troops could be lifted from the terror of combat to the comparative safety of well guarded rear areas, was one of the factors in the high incidence of post-service trauma suffered by Vietnam veterans.

Operation Phoenix

The most notorious CIA project during the Indochina war was Operation *Phoenix* which turned into a terror campaign against the NLF. *Phoenix* began as part of the "pacification" program aimed at boosting support for the Saigon Government in the rural population on the one hand, while neutralizing the VC's political organization on the other. Originally the pacification program was a loose knit group of projects ranging from various village-aid programs undertaken by civilian organizations and the military, to intelligence gathering activities undertaken by the Vietnamese in cooperation with the CIA. Largely through the influence of McNamara, who believed in the long-term gains of pacification, the programme was centralized under military control in May 1967 with General Westmoreland having overall authority. The project was known as Civilian Operations and Rural Development Support (CORDS) but within it, was the CIA's programme for gathering intelligence on the NLF's political apparatus. Tagged the Intelligence Coordination and Exploitation Program (ICEX), it was soon to be renamed the "*Phoenix* Project".

The idea was to identify the Viet Cong Infrastructure (VCI) – the political cadres and various bureaucrats which enabled it to function as an alternative government throughout much of the Vietnamese countryside. Sources of information were prisoners, informants, agents, and general gossip. Information was collected, categorized, and computerized to build up a list of VC personnel by village, district, and region. Having identified an important VC, special Vietnamese police, ARVN, or para-military units would then attempt to capture him – or her – for interrogation. The hope was that each new capture would reveal more information on other VCI in a chain which would eventually destroy the NLF as a functioning political body. A similar operation was run by the US Green Berets in close cooperation with *Phoenix* and the CIA. Known as the Luc Luong Dac Biet (LLDB), the Special Forces and their ARVN counterparts (trained by the Green Berets and the CIA) carried out an intelligence-gathering campaign against the VCI and the NLF's military command.

Interrogation of the VCI was far from gentle as the case of Tai shows, but at least this important North Vietnamese agent

Below US Marine search-and-destroy patrol wades through waist deep water near the DMZ. The troops are garlanded with belts of ammunition for their M-60 machine-gun.

had the comparative luxury of the CIA's attempt to break him psychologically. In a South Vietnamese cell, questioning was little more than direct physical torture. The CIA established over fifty interrogation centers throughout South Vietnam and these were backed by specialist departments in the police cells of the Saigon Government, but even in these official interrogation centers, extracting information was often more brutal than in Tai's case. In the field, LLDB interrogations were often quick and to the point. The usual method was to question a group of suspects together and, if there were no answers, kill one to show the others that the interrogators meant business. Another tactic was to take two or three suspected VC for a helicopter ride. The one the interrogators wanted to break was questioned and, if he stayed silent, one of the others was tossed overboard. Veterans of the LLDB say the method usually worked but, if not, the second prisoner was thrown out. If that didn't work, the VC suspect was flown into base and turned over to the professional interrogators but he usually talked when he saw his friends heading into open space. On more than one occasion, the talkative suspect was tossed out anyway after he had told his captives everything they wanted to know or thought they could find out.

Stories like these shocked the American public when splashed across newspaper headlines but the men who did the killing point out that they were fighting a ruthless and determined enemy who committed similar atrocities every day. Vietnamese villagers suspected of cooperating with the government were killed by the VC as a matter of course as an example to others. On many occasions, the VC rounded-up unsympathetic local villagers – innocent men, women, and children – and drove them at gun-point against the barbed wire of isolated Special Forces, US Army, or ARVN outposts while a wave of armed guerrillas came on behind. The defenders had the grisly choice of either shooting down the innocent to hit the VC or of allowing the attackers to breach their outer defences. Sometimes the VC wired their victims with explosives, turning them into human bombs before herding them onto the American defenders. Frequently, officers fresh from the States would hesitate before shooting into these waves of innocents – a fact that the VC was well aware of – but the new officers soon

Below Montagnard tribesmen are issued weapons at a Special Forces camp near Ban Me Thuot. The Montagnard showed a surprising agility in adapting to modern weapons and tactics.

learned. VC interrogations were as brutal as anything the LLDB indulged in. Again uncooperative villagers would be gathered together to watch the execution of one or two government officials or their innocent relatives. The Montagnard were handled even more brutally. As feared and despised enemies of the VC they were often treated to little more than rape, pillage, and genocide. Many returning veterans became increasingly embittered by the failure of the American public to understand that the brutality and cruelty of the war was two-sided.

To return to the *Phoenix* Project, things went wrong almost from the beginning. The sources were all-too-often unreliable or corrupt. In a study of South Vietnam's villages, Harvard's Dr. Samuel Popkin found several incidents of the information being based on simple malice. One woman reported her brother-in-law as a VC tax collector. After his arrest and torture by the South Vietnamese, he was found to have been the victim of a cruel prank. In another incident a South Vietnamese *Phoenix* official was found extorting money from innocent villagers for keeping them off his lists of VC suspects. The system was widely abused to settle old grudges or for simple profit. VCI quotas were handed down from above but local officials frequently went to no more effort than borrowing recent body-counts from the military and including them in their reports of VC bureaucrats neutralized. Para-military and commando raids on NLF villages often simply shot everyone in sight and then listed the dead as VCI killed.

The Saigon Government adopted the *Phoenix* Project under pressure from the CIA but adopted it with enthusiasm. For 1969, the *Phoenix* administrators set a target of 20,000 VCI to be neutralized. At the end of the year, the South Vietnamese reported 19,534 successes but US estimates of VC agents still at large remained virtually the same. The South Vietnamese apparently spent their time largely running prisoners in and out of police stations to boost the arrest figures and borrowing corpses from military body-counts. Actual *Phoenix* raids by South Vietnamese "provincial reconnaissance units," police, and ARVN forces rounded-up or killed hundreds of possible VCI but many of them seem to have been nothing more than innocent bystanders, VC sympathizers, or minor NLF bureaucrats. In some cases, corrupt (or secret NLF) *Phoenix* officials put the VC's enemies on the government hit-list.

Phoenix wound up being more an assassination program than a pacification project. It's been estimated that something like thirty or forty per cent of those "neutralized" by *Phoenix* and LLDB were killed out of hand. Special *Phoenix* hit-squads went after targeted individuals with pistols, knives, or the garrotting cord. The small hit-teams worked chiefly in the cities and in nearby villages which were more-or-less under government control. Para-military raiding parties operated mainly in the more remote villages or those largely under NLF control. Unlike the raiding parties, the hit-squads normally got the person they were sent for without excess bloodshed but the victims were often killed for personal reasons or for financial gain without regard to their political activities. The tactics were common to terrorist killings everywhere: answering a knock on the door was followed by a bullet; ambushes from dark city alleys or from jungle roadsides; the sniper's rifle.

Para-military raiders hitting a village would head for the victim's hut to take out the target with machine guns and

Far left top A tank fords the Beh Hai River on the DMZ. Because of the terrain – sometimes mountainous, sometimes marshy – the use of tanks was somewhat restricted in Vietnam.

Far left bottom The standard issue Chemical-Biological-Radiological gas mask of the US forces. Apart from defoliants and riot control agents, such as CS gas, chemical weapons were not used in Vietnam. The round objects on the lower cheeks of the mask are the air filters.

Left A US soldier makes friends with Vietnamese villagers. Part of the US pacification programme included stationing Marines and GIs in local villages where it was felt that mutual exposure would make for friendship and understanding on both sides.

grenades. If the target was to be brought back for interrogation, he would simply be bundled off while the team shot their way out. Before 1968, hit-and-run teams (such as those operating under OPLAN-34A) would occasionally try kidnapping North Vietnamese officials for interrogation but Johnson stopped these raids as part of his post-Tet peace feeler. In the cities, suspected VCI or NVA agents were usually rounded-up in police raids but more than one suspected person was the victim of a quiet, commando-style kidnapping. For *Phoenix,* the Saigon Government revived some of Diem's old security laws and it was easy for regional committees to send suspects to jail for up to two years without trial.

The CIA later admitted that over 20,000 VCI had been assassinated under the auspices of the *Phoenix* Program; the South Vietnamese figures – no doubt grossly inflated to keep US funds flowing in – were practically double that. Something like one-third of *Phoenix's* VCI "neutralizations" were actually fatalities. But the project came close to working. Despite, the appalling mismanagement, corruption, and random violence, there is evidence that the terror campaign did genuine damage to the VCI. In the midst of all the chaos, true VCI *were* identified, targeted, and successfully brought in for interrogation or killed. The hard-core political cadre (always well hidden) were driven deeper underground and the ranks of the lesser bureaucrats were decimated in areas where the *Phoenix* teams actually applied themselves to the job at hand.

William Colby, the CIA operative in charge of *Phoenix* and later the Agency's director, believed he could fight the VC on its home ground, on its own terms. The CIA would wage a "people's war". The difficulty was that Vietnam was no longer a people's war. The chief enemy was now the NVA divisions in the South and their hard-core VC guerrilla allies. *Phoenix's* main targets had been the sort of rice-farmer-by-day, guerrilla-by-night part-timers; once they had been the basis of the movement but now they no longer carried the major burden of the war. In the end, whatever chance *Phoenix* had of real success was lost in the project's misuse and the corruption which alienated as many or more of the Vietnamese "silent-majority" than VCI it eliminated. At the same time, the other aspect of the pacification program (aid packages and projects designed to win the "hearts and minds" of the general rural populace) were an overall failure leaving largely indiscriminate terror as the only obvious result.

Colby later claimed to have won the people's war but this is a clear exaggeration. What *Phoenix* did do was to cripple parts of the VCI but – through mismanagement – leave other parts of it with little or no injury whatsoever. Had *Phoenix* been more discriminatory in weeding out its own corrupt local Vietnamese agents and selecting exactly who it targeted, things might have been different. Colby remained a controversial figure. In this later career in the Agency's upper echelons, his management of CIA policies and apparently eager cooperation with Senate investigating committees produced bitter in-fighting and split America's best known intelligence service into warring splinter groups. Some of his more embittered enemies within the Agency went so far as to suggest that Colby had been working for the KGB all along.

7 Johnson's War

The men who Fought

The months following the Gulf of Tonkin incidents caught the Politburo in Hanoi somewhat by surprise. Johnson had launched sporadic retaliatory bombing raids across the DMZ and a series of air-strikes (Operation *Barrel Roll)* against the Laotian parts of the Ho Chi Minh Trail. But the early months of 1965 saw the beginnings of Operation *Rolling Thunder,* a methodical series of air-strikes on military targets in North Vietnam and the landing of US Marines at Danang. It was clear that Washington wasn't going to let South Vietnam go under but Hanoi still wasn't sure exactly how far Johnson was prepared to go. Operation *Barrel Roll* had been only a minor irritation; the bombing was in Laos and had little overall effect on the flow of supplies and men to the South. But *Rolling Thunder* was a far greater worry even though bombing was restricted to barracks, bridges, ammunition dumps, and other military targets below the 20th parallel. Hanoi, Haiphong, and other targets in the northern part of the country were still off-limits to America's fighter-bombers.

Like the Johnson administration, the government of North Vietnam throughout the war was divided between the bold and the cautious. On the one hand, no one in Hanoi was prepared to abandon the fight for the South but there was considerable debate as to the best way to go about meeting the American threat. Unless there was a full-scale US/ARVN invasion in the North, Hanoi had little doubt about its ability to wear down US determination in the same way the Viet Minh had outlasted the will of the French people to support a seemingly endless and expensive war thousands of miles from home. The more immediate problem was to find the most appropriate tactics for meeting the American threat. Supplies of Soviet weapons to the VC, even with increased NVA back-up, wouldn't be enough to prevent the NLF from being pushed back from the brink of victory to the point where it became an ever decreasing threat in the South.

An NLF on the retreat would rapidly lose its appeal to South Vietnam's vast, largely apolitical, rural population and the Saigon Government would gain accordingly. Hanoi believed it held the advantage; North Vietnam – it thought – was almost safe from invasion or unrestricted aerial bombardment and could therefore fight in the South without fear of incurring the full weight of American fire-power. In effect, Washington would be fighting with one hand behind its back. Hanoi could send its forces south without worrying about defending its homeland and more-or-less call the tune in what promised to be years of conflict with America's armed forces. Hanoi could increase or decrease the fighting at will while Washington could only respond. America would be slowly bled until it was forced to seek a peace on North Vietnamese terms.

Giap had no doubts about his ability to win in the South but – to a large extent – he was reliving his past glories. The Army America sent to Vietnam in 1965 was not the same type of

Right A soldier of the 1st Air Cavalry blasts a VC bunker during Operation *White Wing.*

Following pages A phosphorus bomb bursts, hurled from a US Air Force Skyraider at a VC position.

Far right Jungle patrol. Troops of the 5th Cavalry cross a stream during a sweep operation near Bong Son in February 1966.

Right Three members of the USAF's Combat Control Team watch ARVN paratroopers drop into a VC-held area near Saigon. The Air Force squad had jumped in first to stake out a landing zone for the Vietnamese.

Below Heavily laden with equipment, men of the 1st Infantry Division leave a helicopter drop and charge toward VC positions in the woods near Phuoc Vinh. The courage, discipline, and professionalism with which a largely conscript Army fought, amazed the enemy.

Army the French had fought the Viet Minh with a decade before. Its strengths and weaknesses were quite different but it took Giap a long time to learn the differences. From the beginning, Giap seems to have believed that the key to final victory lay in inflicting a decisive Dien Bien Phu-like defeat on the American Army and he spent much of his time and countless North Vietnamese lives trying to engineer one. He reasoned that a catastrophic defeat would rapidly sicken the American public's taste for an Indochina war and make Washington eager to negotiate but – while he never came near another Dien Bien Phu – the United States grew tired of the whole business far more quickly than he thought.

The army that America sent to Vietnam was the best equipped in the world and fought with courage, the discipline of good training, and in the best traditions of the US military. But it was essentially a conscript army serving a brief tour of duty in a country that few Americans cared the slightest about. Officially the Air Force, Navy, and Marine Corps were made up of volunteers but only the latter could lay a genuine claim to fielding an almost totally professional force. The Air Force and Navy were composed of volunteers but a large proportion joined simply to avoid being drafted into the Army and for what was commonly thought to be better training opportunities in such fields as electronics, data processing, equipment

maintenance and so on. Pilots and officers in the Navy and Air Force tended to be career men but the ranks had large numbers of short-termers who largely saw themselves as civilians in uniform.

The advisors that Washington sent to South Vietnam over the years were largely professional soldiers but, as the American build-up began in the mid-sixties, draftees became the mainstay of all the services. Soldiers – professional or conscript – were sent to Vietnam on a year's rotation. Many professionals signed for second or even third tours but, by and large, the prevailing attitude was follow orders, don't volunteer, stay alive for a year, and get back home. With the exception of certain elite units such as the Special Forces, and some detachments of Marines or Airborne, soldiers sent to Vietnam were shipped over individually to join forces already in the field. This is in almost direct contrast to World War II where units trained and served together for the course of the war and formed a deep sense of camaraderie and unit pride. Again, unlike World War II where the average age of the combat soldier was twenty-six, in Vietnam it was nineteen.

The draft (Selective Service) system caused increasing bitterness as the war went on and those who found themselves in Vietnam became more-and-more indifferent to anything but staying alive and going home when their tour was finished.

College and university students could get deferments for their periods of study and, when those ran out, there was always graduate school and further extensions of their deferments. This had an unintended weeding-out effect so that the burden of the war fell on those who couldn't or wouldn't qualify for further education – poor whites, Hispanics, and Blacks. Universities such as Berkeley became the centre of the student anti-war movement but the protestors had the benefit of deferments and those who didn't frequently fled to Canada before the draft caught up with them. Many protestors went to jail out of conscience but they were a small minority of the anti-war movement as a whole.

Students who did go into the Army when their number was called often found themselves curiously pitied by their comrades in arms and by their more fortunate fellows left behind to enjoy the traditional campus life-styles or the newer wine, cheese, and pot parties of the protest movement in university communities. Veterans coming home were generally greeted with disinterest by the public at large or treated as some sort of war criminals by youthful radicals. Certainly large numbers of Americans supported the war's aims but there was an increasing disillusionment with the way it was being carried out and the serving soldier or veteran felt a growing alienation even from those who were loudly backing him. At the end of the

A helicopter gun-ship supports the US Navy's river patrol boats in the Mekong Delta by strafing VC positions. Shown are twin .30 caliber machine-guns fitted aboard a Navy UH-1B helicopter.

day, even the so-called "silent majority" couldn't really understand what the war was all about or why their sons were being asked to die in it.

Draftees and their parents were told that America was fighting to preserve freedom and to stop the advance of communism but, when he got to Vietnam, the soldier found mainly indifferent allies and cynical comrades. Junior officers fresh from the States tended to be a lot keener than the combat veterans they found themselves commanding. For the Pentagon, one of the war's side benefits was the opportunity it gave for young officers to gain combat experience but many of the Junior officers faced hostility from their own troops if they were too eager. Enlisted men – and not a few junior officers – due for rotation home adopted a why-get-killed-now? attitude and risked as little as possible with the tacit understanding of everyone else. This general malaise affected career soldiers as well as draftees. One career Sergeant due to fly state-side at the end of the week was ordered to lead a hunter-killer patrol into VC territory in the Mekong Delta by a green Second-Lieutenant fresh out of university and Officer's Candidate School. The Sergeant refused in very direct language and he was taken before the company commander on charges. The commander had been in Vietnam for a lot longer than the Second-Lieutenant; he let the whole thing quietly slide and the Sergeant – who had already distinguished himself in combat – flew home on schedule.

Earlier in his Vietnam tour, the same Sergeant was on a night patrol led by another green Lieutenant. His unit had captured two VC and interrogated them. The Sergeant then ordered the prisoners taken into the bush and shot. The Lieutenant objected on the grounds of basic human decency and he refused to listen to the Sergeant's arguments that bringing the VC prisoners back alive through hostile territory was very likely to get the patrol spotted and killed. The Sergeant then shot the two VC himself and, on returning to base, was brought up on charges. Again the charges were dropped quietly and – a few weeks later – the Lieutenant was killed on another patrol while trying to bring in some VC prisoners alive.

Blacks made up a large proportion of the enlisted regulars of America's armed forces and – because of the inequities in the draft system – a high percentage of its conscripts as well. During the Sixties, America was torn apart by civil rights struggles as the Blacks campaigned for the equality that had been denied them since being set free from slavery during the Civil War a hundred years before. Black ghettos in Los Angeles, Detroit, and, over a ten year period, almost every other US city saw heavy rioting, protest marches, and rallies aimed at ending the injustices of centuries there and then. Johnson, who as part of his call for the "Great Society," actually passed more civil rights legislation than Kennedy had even attempted, inspired very few with his speeches on the need to fight in Vietnam. Black troops found themselves risking their lives for Vietnamese freedom while back home their families and friends were having to fight to win their own most basic civil rights. To make matters worse, the blacks made up the majority of the combat troops and seemed to be doing most of the dying. To many blacks, even long-serving career soldiers, Vietnam became a white-man's war from which they felt increasingly alienated and one they saw no reason to fight in.

Far left A machine-gunner of the 1st Cavalry Division passes a flaming Vietnamese house during Operation *White Wing* in January 1966. *White Wing* was originally code-named *Masher* but President Johnson found the term objectionable(!).

Left Marines rake NVA positions on Hill Nui Cray Tre near the DMZ with machine-gun fire.

Below Marine Hueys touch down at Fire-base *Cunningham*. The mobility of helicopters prevented forward fire-bases from being cut off in the manner of Dien Bien Phu.

Giap knew all the weaknesses of America's conscript army and was confident of his ability to break its will in the rice paddies and jungles of Vietnam. After all, the French had fielded a fully professional army against him and he had repeatedly crippled it before the final humiliation at Dien Bien Phu. The French army could have continued the fight even after Dien Bien Phu; it was the French people who lost taste for war and Giap fully expected the United States to go the same way. When it came to open combat with the NVA, however, America's conscript soldiers held their ground, fought Giap's troops to a stand-still, and broke his divisions one by one. In the end Giap won all right but his victory was won in the hearts and minds of the American people who were sickened by the war. He was never able to repeat his past glories and defeat the American Army in the field.

The build-up of American forces in Vietnam continued during most of 1965. After the Marines landed at Danang in March, the 1st Infantry and 101st Airborne ("Screaming Eagles")

Divisions arrived in July. In September they were joined by the 1st Air Cavalry Division. The North Vietnamese build-up continued too. The 32nd NVA Regiment had been in South Vietnam since the beginning of the year and the 33rd NVA Regiment arrived in the late summer, while the 66th was winding its way down the Ho Chi Minh Trail. Their commander, General Chu Huy Man, positioned his forces near Pleiku and prepared to repeat a tactic that had worked well against the French. He would attack an isolated American position and then ambush the relief column. What the NVA hadn't considered in these plans was the Pentagon's newest piece of military technology – the helicopter.

During the night of October 19th, the 33rd NVA Regiment attacked the American Special Forces outpost at Plei Mei but, thanks to the spirited resistance of the defenders, failed to over-run it. The US command prepared a relief force of ARVN troops but in the expectation that it would probably be

Right Marines of G Company, 4th Marine Regiment, clamber up a steep hillside to attack NVA positions near the DMZ during Operation *Hastings* in July 1966.

Left South Korean and US Marines manning an observation post take a musical break.

Below A helicopter lands Marines on a former VC-held hill during Operation *Double Eagle* in the coastal province of Quang Ngai in February 1966. Over 5,000 Marines took part in the operation which was aimed at encircling and trapping the thousands of Viet Cong believed to have been operating in the area.

ambushed. In due course, the relief column *was* ambushed but, forewarned, they were able to fight their way out of it with the aid of the Cavalry helicopters who airlifted in artillery pieces to pound the NVA positions. The Green Beret camp was relieved and the NVA pulled back to re-group. US and ARVN forces were airlifted onto their likely escape routes and, after some futile searching and some lucky intelligence, the American 1st Cavalry managed to cut off the retreat of the 33rd NVA. The 33rd suffered massive casualties in a series of futile efforts to break through. In the end, the 33rd – or what was left of it – finally trickled off in round-about escape routes and joined up with the as yet unbloodied 66th NVA in a renewed assault on the camp at Plei Mei.

US helicopter assault troops landed in the Ia Drang Valley and met the NVA head on. One assault company was cut-off and, by the next day, the entire 1st Battalion of the 7th Air Cavalry was engaged in bitter fighting with a determined NVA. US artillery, fighter-bombers, and massed B-52s, pounded the North Vietnamese positions and within forty-eight hours, the 66th NVA was decimated and retreating. ARVN paratroopers were deployed by helicopter to block the remnants of the retreating NVA as they tried to escape across the Cambodian border. Giap had apparently hoped to cut South Vietnam into two parts on a line running roughly from Pleiku to Qui Nhon on the coast but, whatever he had in mind, the plan was in ruins and three of the NVA's elite regiments had been battered into a rag-tag band of stragglers. The only criticism of the operation was the reluctance of the US commanders to engage in hot-pursuit of the fleeing NVA. Had they done so, North Vietnamese casualties would have been higher but, even so, American dead totaled close to 300 men.

The key to the battle was the helicopter and this was a personal justification for Secretary of Defence McNamara who had pioneered this new form of mobile warfare a few years before. The helicopter's military career began in the early 1950s and achieved great success in Korea where it was used for the rapid evacuation of wounded troops, aerial reconnaissance, and for opening a quick supply-line with the front. By the Sixties, larger helicopters capable of airlifting large numbers of troops and heavy artillery were under development and, in January 1963, what was to become the 1st Air Cavalry Division was formed at Fort Benning, Georgia. Two helicopters were the mainstay of the Air Cavalry: the Bell UH-1 "Huey" Iroquois and the Boeing CH-47 Chinook. During the battle of Ia Drang, US helicopters moved 105mm artillery pieces nearly seventy times and kept the batteries constantly supplied with shells. Moved to different strategic locations during the course of the battle, the guns were able to pound away steadily at a hapless NVA which was never out of range.

The Chinook was the workhorse carrying artillery and heavy supplies to troops already landed by a fleet of Hueys. Landing Zones (LZ) were selected by aerial reconnaissance or by foot patrols of specially-trained "pathfinders". Traveling at well over 100 miles per hour at tree-top level, Hueys armed with heavy machine guns and rockets would fly around the area of the LZ laying down a hail of fire into the surrounding bush. These were the "gun-ships" made famous by the Vietnam war. Troop-carrying Hueys would then land to disgorge human cargoes while the gun-ships kept a careful eye overhead or

Far left South Korean troops clear out VC pinned down in a Vietnamese Catholic Church.

Left Burning down a hut in a VC village during Operation *Thayer II*.

Below Troops of the Royal Australian Regiment return from a patrol near Bien Hoa. The Australians sent men and equipment to honor their SEATO commitments.

Far right top A flight of US Ranch Hand C-123's spray Viet Cong areas with chemical defoliants to kill off the covering jungle. The four aircraft spray a 1000-foot-wide area with each pass. Because certain of the defoliants used – particularly Agent Orange – contained highly toxic, long-lived chemicals which may cause physical and genetic damage to human beings, the use of anti-plant agents was to become highly controversial.

Far right below An improvised helicopter gun-ship.

Right Mortar team of the 1st Cavalry fires on the enemy during a search and destroy mission in the Song Re Valley. The 81mm M-29 mortar was a standard infantry weapon throughout the war.

Above A US Navy Seal (Sea, Air, Land) team goes ashore on a secret operation in the Rung Sat special zone of South Vietnam. The Seals are the Navy's equivalent of the Special Forces. Each man receives intensive training in underwater demolition, commando operations, weaponry, hand-to-hand combat, and paramilitary warfare, and is a qualified parachutist.

harassed any enemy left in the vicinity. If the mission was a hit-and-run raid, the helicopters would return to base and wait for orders to go back and take their troops out again.

But decisive battles like this were not the order of the day in Vietnam. The vast part of a soldier's combat tour was spent either doing nothing but waiting or carrying out "search-and-destroy" patrols. They ranged from small patrols of a few men – "hunter-killer" missions aimed at intelligence gathering or capturing one or two prisoners for interrogation – to operations involving a company or more. These would move through an area trying to locate VC units and bring them to battle. The VC normally either avoided contact or laid an ambush. Prior to the battle of the Ia Drang Valley, US Marines first saw action in search-and-destroy missions outside Danang while the US 173rd Airborne Brigade carried out similar missions north-east of Saigon in the so-called "Iron-Triangle" in cooperation with the Australians.

VC ambushes were not always full-scale actions. Often the search-and-destroy patrol was simply fired at by snipers who then ran off to find another spot to shoot from later on. Booby traps became legendary. Grenades were set on various trip-wires to catch the unwary moving through the bush. Leaf-covered pits filled with Panji stakes or landmines lay underfoot. Thorny branches were bent back and fastened to trip-wires. When triggered, they would sweep forward to catch a platoon walking in single-file. The frustration of combat like this was unimaginable. The enemy's traps were everywhere killing or maiming but the VC seemed always to slip away before he could be caught. If the patrol found VC, it was usually on the enemy's terms when he lay in wait for a quick ambush before disappearing again. Nothing typified the frustration and alienation of the American soldier more than these dangerous, often fruitless patrols against a hidden enemy who preferred to harass rather than to confront. The war soon seemed endless and more and more farcical as the months wore on.

"Reconnaissance-in-force" was the other principal US tactic against the VC. These were full-scale drives into known VC territory aimed at clearing and pacifying the area. When the United States began to take a direct part in the war, it was intended to use American forces chiefly in reconnaissance-in-force operations against the NVA, with the ARVN taking over the responsibilities for day-to-day search-and-destroy missions and pacifying newly cleared areas. It rarely worked out this way in practice. Frequently the operations did little more than devastate large parts of the countryside creating vast numbers of refugees who streamed into the cities. Hundreds of VC were killed but, after the US forces withdrew, the enemy would reinfiltrate. Air mobility meant that forces could be put-in and withdrawn at will so closing with VC units was a lot easier but – like the French before them – the Americans often found they were grabbing at empty space while the guerrillas melted away. A large number of the missions became simple searches for hidden VC storerooms and weapons dumps in order to deprive the enemy of the means of making war.

Between late January and early March 1966, Operation *Masher* (it was formally retitled *White Wing* after Johnson objected to the name) cleared the northern parts of Binh Dinh province. Over 1000 NVA/VC were killed and some 1700 captured but the vast majority of the prisoners were only

Far right top Troops of the 1st Cavalry move down a hillside after a helicopter drop during a search-and-destroy mission in the Cay Giep mountains.

Far right below 1st Cavalry mortar team in the Bong Son District during Operation *White Wing.*

Center ARVN troopers standing guard over a VC suspect while the convoy pauses during its journey.

Right An M-60 machine-gunner of the Royal Australian Regiment.

suspected insurgents. At roughly the same time, Operation *Double Eagle* sent the US Marines into the border areas of Binh Dinh and Quang Ngai provinces to engage the 325th NVA Division but the North Vietnamese apparently had advance warning and managed to slip away. Later in the year, Operations *Thayer* and *Irving* used massive air bombardment and nearly 300,000 pounds of napalm. *Irving,* reported about 1000 enemy dead (plus 500 or so "possible" kills) and just over 1000 prisoners. To make up for their losses, the VC stepped-up their recruiting program and Hanoi sent more men down the Ho Chi Minh Trail to replace their battered divisions in the northern provinces of South Vietnam. Estimates vary but, overall, it seems that despite such losses enemy strength in the South actually increased in 1966 and 1967.

Entering a VC village was a hazardous business but, if the enemy had vanished, there were only the unsmiling, uncooperative faces of the villagers. It was then a matter of interrogation – sometimes simply asking questions but sometimes less gentle – and frequently a long tedious search for the enemy's underground labyrinth of tunnels. At the height of the war, most villages built tunnel complexes to shelter from bombing raids and artillery but VC tunnels ran deeper and far longer. When an entrance or air-vent (usually a hollow bamboo pole poking out slightly in the underbrush) was found, smoke grenades were thrown in hopefully to reveal other entry points. Frequently, tear gas was thrown in to harass any VC below and to drive them further underground. Then a "tunnel-rat" decked in flak jacket and gas mask would descend inwards to begin combing out any enemy and searching for the valuable supply rooms far below.

When they were finished, the troops would do their best to destroy the tunnel complex or at least make it uninhabitable. Sometimes it would be mined with explosives or pumped full of acetylene gas then ignited. Occasionally little was done apart from filling the tunnels with powdered tear gas (usually CS) to contaminate the passageways while blowing up or bull-dozing over the entrances. Other times, each of these methods was used to some degree in an effort to insure that the VC wouldn't be able to use the complex again. But the tunnels often ran for miles and it was usually impossible to make sure that large sections were not salvageable with a little effort. Tunnel warfare in Vietnam was one of the most unpopular tasks the American soldier faced.

Like the French before them, the Americans opted for a fortification strategy – but with a difference. Major fortified bases of divisional strength were established along the coast in places such as Danang, Phu Bai, and Cam Ranh. Around these were a number of smaller "fire-bases" sited where they could offer each other artillery support and easily back up operations in the field. They were designed both to act as a first-line of defence for the main divisional bases, and as a base for mounting attacks against the NVA/VC. The fire-bases were strategically placed near enemy areas or lines of communication as an inducement to bring him to battle and where regular search-and-destroy patrols could be mounted. Fire bases varied from platoon to company size and – depending how permanent they were intended to be – were often crude constructions of barbed wire surrounding dug-in troops, a command bunker, and positioned artillery.

It was in these fire-bases that the war sapped the will and morale of the American soldier. They spent their days staring at the surrounding bush looking for an enemy who might or might not be there, or waiting to go on yet another search-and-destroy patrol that promised little but danger or death. In the back of his mind there was the sure knowledge that the VC were watching, waiting for a night when the guards had been lulled into carelessness by the unbelievable boredom. Then a few VC commandos would cut through or crawl under the wire to throw grenades and leave behind a wall of gunfire. Even worse was the possibility of a major VC attack often during the rainy season when the defenders were deep in mud and soaked to the skin and when air-support was hindered by the weather. Here waves of VC would pour in during the slow time of the night and the defenders would find themselves cut off and engaged in bitter hand-to-hand fighting.

Pushing the VC back frequently took the whole night and occasionally the defenders had no choice but to flee into the jungle and wait for morning and helicopter support from the main base. On more than one occasion, besieged fire-bases had to call for artillery fire on their own positions. Most of the time, though, was spent just waiting and thinking – thinking about the next patrol, thinking about when a VC hit-and-run attack might come, thinking about why the United States was fighting this seemingly endless war in the first place. The enemy was fully aware of the demoralizing effects of manning a lonely outpost against a guerrilla army which just bided its time. Cannabis – and occasionally harder drugs – became a regular diversion and the traffic was encouraged by the NLF. The other most popular

Facing page A CH-47 Chinook helicopter unloads a construction team. Armed with explosives and chain-saws, the team cleared a landing zone for in-coming supply helicopters during Operation *Cedar Falls*.

Below Helicopter assault on the Plaine des Joncs.

diversion was simply counting the days until it would be time to go home.

The Light at the End of the Tunnel

In 1967, General Westmoreland decided to go after major VC areas once and for all. The major operations were *Cedar Falls, Junction City* and *Fairfax. Fairfax* was a long-term series of aggressive patrols by US infantry, Green Berets, and ARVN Rangers in the countryside around Saigon. The goal was chiefly to harass and ambush enemy units operating during the night. In the Spring, some 25,000 US and ARVN troops moved into Tay Ninh province to clear the area and hopefully to capture the headquarters of the communist party of South Vietnam. If the VC's political headquarters was in fact there, the top cadre managed to escape across the Cambodian border but roughly 3000 other NVA/VC were killed. The American Army, however, suffered some 1,900 casualties in the operation and this fueled the doubts of a US public about Washington's role in Vietnam and of an increasingly critical US Congress.

Operation *Cedar Falls* was aimed at clearing the Iron-Triangle northeast of Saigon once and for all. The 1965 sorties of the 17th Airborne Brigade, ARVN, and Australian forces into the Iron-Triangle had hurt the VC but far from finished it. When the allies withdrew, the guerrillas had gradually drifted back. The area was covered with dense foliage (which American planes had tried to destroy by spraying with a combination of highly inflammable oil and gasoline) and had been an insurgent sanctuary since the days of the Viet Minh. This time the Iron-Triangle was going to receive the full weight of US

Far right top 1st Cavalry advances on VC positions during Operation *White Wing.*

Far right below Chinook lands troops on a secured mountain ridge during Operation *White Wing.*

Right Troops of the 1st Cavalry move some local civilians to safety while the village is being cleared of VC during Operation *White Wing.*

firepower. *Cedar Falls* began on January 4th with massive artillery barrages and saturation bombing from flights of B-52s. Four days later, helicopter assault troops and infantry backed by armor seized positions on the edge of the Iron-Triangle to block VC escape routes.

An armored cavalry thrust to the Saigon River, divided the area, and then the positioned forces began to move in to close the vise. Miles of VC tunnels were uprooted and bulldozed over and the dense foliage was sprayed with herbicides to kill the guerrilla's leafy shelter. The operation captured large amounts of VC supplies and weaponry but enemy casualties were in the hundreds rather than the thousands hoped for. Again the hard-core VC and NVA in the area had gotten wind of the operation (given the scale of preparation, it wouldn't have been too difficult) and slipped off well in advance. Something like 7,000 civilians were made homeless and flocked into the shanty-towns on the outskirts of Saigon or into the growing number of refugee camps. According to a later report by General Westmoreland, major VC activity in the Iron-Triangle was hindered for some six months.

The use of chemical herbicides became one of the war's most controversial aspects. The herbicides were used either to clear dense foliage which screened VC activity or to attack VC rice crops and deprive the NLF of its vital food supplies. The VC had ways of replacing lost food supplies which the villagers did not and the refugee problem was only heightened. Various anti-plant agents were used but the most controversial was Agent Orange. Agent Orange is a 50/50 mixture of two chemical defoliants developed during World War II, 2,4,5,-D and its cousin 2,4,5,-T. Unfortunately, the latter contains the highly lethal compound Dioxin as a by-product and, without stringent manufacturing conditions, 2,4,5,-T can have far higher concentrations of Dioxin than would normally be expected. Dioxin has been responsible for several pollution disasters in recent years. Very small amounts of it are lethal and it has now been shown to cause genetic damage as well. Ill-health and malformed babies in both post-war Vietnam and among US veterans has caused widespread protest and a number of former soldiers have sued the US Government for damages.

Elsewhere the US Army and Navy carried out a combined operation designed to clear the VC out of the Mekong Delta. Engineers built a Delta base for Navy assault patrol-boats by dredging the river to make a new island home for the river fleet. The patrol boats, armed with machine guns and mortars, patrolled the delta in sorties ranging between twenty and forty miles from their base. They were backed up by helicopter assault troops and air-strikes against inland targets. Armed hovercraft joined the fleet to operate in areas impassable to the patrol-boat strike-force. This was one of the first uses of this unique form of transportation in a military role but it has now become a more-or-less standard feature of the world's coastal defence forces. Despite constant harassment, however, the VC remained fairly well entrenched in the Delta.

In the North, the US established what became known as the "McNamara Line", a 160 long chain of electronic surveillance equipment designed to monitor NVA traffic slipping across the

DMZ. The gadgetry included infra-red sensors to detect body heat, highly sensitive sound detectors, and radar. Specially equipped aircraft made regular patrols over the area listening for NVA radio traffic. Not only would they record the transmissions for intelligence purposes but, in addition, would triangulate the source and direct artillery fire or aircraft strikes onto the NVA below. Behind the McNamara Line lay a series of US fire-bases to block NVA infiltration routes but the tactic was a two edged sword. The NVA moved long-range artillery to the DMZ and were able to shell the forward American bases. For all that, the McNamara Line was not much of a success.

It was fairly easy for the NVA to go around it and, in any case, the DMZ was not a major infiltration route compared to the Ho Chi Minh Trail. Also the North Vietnamese developed some fairly simple spoofing techniques which sometimes had US bombers and artillery pounding away at empty jungles. Finally, General Westmoreland had lost an argument with McNamara for increased bombing north of the DMZ and never gave the idea his whole-hearted support.

In March, the NVA began a long artillery assault on US Marine positions at Con Thien, near the DMZ. Memories of Dien Bien Phu sprang to mind but in the months that followed, electronic intelligence, artillery, and massed air-power (both long-range B-52 strikes and sorties by tactical fighter-bombers) were used in a highly coordinated campaign to break-up concentrations of NVA troops assembling in positions where

they could move on Con Thien. By the end of the summer, the NVA threat had begun to melt away.

In April, the Marines began another series of bloody engagements to take the NVA-held hills around the US base at Khe Sanh. Backed by artillery and concentrated air-strikes, the Marines took the hills and fortified them. In other major fighting, the NVA attacked American and ARVN positions at Loc Ninh, Song Be, and Dak To. In each case, the defenders decimated the ranks of the attacking NVA. There were nearly 1,000 dead North Vietnamese at Loc Ninh and some 1,500 killed at Dak To.

In many ways, 1967 seemed to be the turning point of the war. The NVA had been broken in every set battle it had attempted and VC activity was considerably down on the year before. Generals and politicians began talking about the "light at the end of the tunnel" and the approaching day when the US could begin withdrawing its troops and turn the war over to the South Vietnamese. But the VC were not yet – as many thought – a "spent force" and the battered NVA troops in the South were only the beginnings of the commitment that Hanoi was prepared to send down the Ho Chi Minh Trail or across the DMZ. In South Vietnam, the 1966 elections had created a constitutional assembly and, in September 1967, a half-way honest ballot had voted General Nguyen Van Thieu in as President after he had earlier succeeded in largely deposing Ky in a bloodless takeover by the ruling military clique. Johnson used the South Vietnamese elections and the nearly three years

Below Helicopter assault moves out to engage the enemy.

Left Members of the 173rd Airborne Brigade set off smoke grenades for the spotter planes during Operation *MacArthur* in the highlands near Dak To in November 1967.

Below Search-and-destroy patrol moves through a village in the Bong Son District during Operation *White Wing*.

of comparative political stability to highlight progress in the fight for freedom in Indochina. As it turned out, though, Thieu's government was as corrupt as Diem's ever was and more open about it. The battle for the hearts and minds of South Vietnam's general population was not won and, as events would soon show, was actually being lost.

The anti-War Movement at Home

In the United States, the anti-war movement was at its height and powerful Congressmen and Senators such as William Fulbright were increasingly testing Johnson's authority to carry on the war. The Gulf of Tonkin Resolution had been passed in the heat of the moment and Congress was now becoming more-and-more restless over the lengths to which the Johnson administration had gone on the basis of the Resolution's rather vague language. In October 1967, nearly 40,000 demonstrators converged on the Pentagon to protest against the war. Anti-Vietnam rallies were regular occurrences in America's campus communities and often ended with bands of military-age youngsters burning their draft cards before eager TV reporters while chanting "Hell no! We won't go."

It's difficult to categorize the anti-war movement in the United States as it was made up from many diverse walks of life. A number of the protesters were genuine pacifists or at least believed that Vietnam was an immoral war which they wanted no part of; others were stand-by members of the anti-everything, quasi-student-radical movement that had been

going since the early Sixties; and some just found it a convenient way to avoid military service. Fighting for liberal or radical causes was something of a way of life in the Sixties but, whatever the individual motives, there was a real concern and disquiet about the war that spread far wider than the actual protest movement itself. Even every-day Americans were uncertain about the war and became increasingly more so as the death toll mounted. Johnson knew that his support was more passive than active – a status quo acceptance of things – and that that support was becoming more and more fragile.

Hard as it tried, the Government just couldn't "sell" the war to the American public. In his TV addresses to the nation, Johnson's folksy-accented "my fellow Americans" and down-home manner – which were probably well-suited to his years of campaigning in his home state of Texas – failed to inspire the country at large and became something of a popular joke. The Pentagon tried to confirm military progress in terms of "body-counts" of NVA/VC dead but the media kept accusing the generals of deliberately inflating these numbers and in any case the body-count that mattered most to the average American was the number of US casualties. Johnson was in a dilemma. On one hand he was trying to assure an increasingly disquieted US public that he wanted to secure a just peace and bring the boys home as quickly as possible but, on the other, he was bending over backwards to convince Hanoi of his determination to persevere in what promised to be a very long war. Neither Hanoi nor the American public were convinced.

Above The troopship of the Mobile Riverine Force. Note the floating pier for accommodating smaller craft and the helicopter landing pad.

Left VC prisoners combed out of local mountain caves are marched back to base camp during a search-and-destroy mission in the An Lao Valley, some 400 miles northwest of Saigon. The mission was part of Operation *Thayer* in February 1967.

Center left VC prisoners cleared out of a tunnel complex in the Thanh Dieu Forest of the "Iron Triangle" during Operation *Cedar Falls*.

Far left top A 1st Cavalry radioman moves through the cloud from a smoke grenade dropped by the commander of an over-flying helicopter to mark positions of suspected VC bunkers during Operation *Pershing* in July 1967.

Far left below Members of the 173rd Airborne Brigade prepare for the final assault on Hill 875 fifteen miles southwest of Dak To.

Far right top Men of the 1st Cavalry are dropped on a seek-and-destroy mission near Duc Pho during Operation *Oregon* in April 1967.

Far right bottom A unit of the 173rd Airborne Brigade in the dense jungle below Hill 875.

Right A US assault support patrol boat hit by NVA fire in the Mekong Delta. The crew are attempting to repair the damage while returning fire.

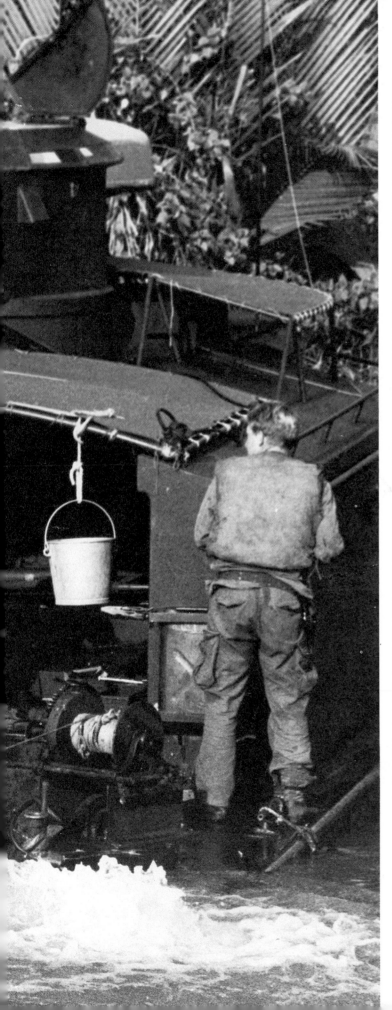

Above A Navy river patrol boat crewman mans an M-60 machine-gun during a fire-fight with the VC. The boat was engaged in a psychological warfare project (part of the Open Arms Programme) along the Bassac River when the VC began firing from the banks.

Right Members of the Royal Australian Regiment train for ambush tactics against bands of VC regulars.

Left A casualty is carried away during the November 1967 fighting for Hill 875, a bitterly contested communist strongpoint in the wooded Central Highlands near Dak To.

Far left top Members of the 173rd Airborne dig themselves in in former NVA bunkers after the first stage of the battle for Hill 875. The fight cost the lives of 280 US soldiers and close to 1,400 NVA regulars.

Top center A Navy Seal keeps a silent watch by a jungle stream.

Far left below Waiting to move up on Hill 875.

Left US helicopter patrol over the Mekong Delta.

8 Decline and Fall

The Tet Offensive

Giap was prepared to take a gamble. His divisions had been battered whenever they met the American forces in conventional combat and the VC – if not exactly on the retreat – was at least being pushed backwards. Hanoi was perfectly aware of the growing US peace movement and of the deep divisions the war was causing in American society. What Giap needed was a body-blow that would break Washington's will to carry on and at the same time would undermine the growing legitimacy of the Saigon Government once and for all. In one sense, time was not on Giap's side. While Hanoi was sure that the Americans would tire of the war as the French had before them, the longer it took, the stronger the Saigon Government might become. Another year or so of American involvement could seriously damage the NLF and leave the ARVN capable of dealing with its enemies on its own. Giap opted for a quick and decisive victory that would be well in time for the 1968 US Presidential campaign.

Giap prepared a bold thrust on two fronts. With memories of the victory at Dien Bien Phu still in his mind, he planned an attack on the US Marines' fire-base at Khe Sanh. At the same time, the NVA and the NLF planned coordinated attacks on virtually all South Vietnam's major cities and provincial capitals.

If the Americans opted to defend Khe Sanh, they would find themselves stretched to the limit when battles erupted elsewhere throughout the South. Forced to defend themselves everywhere at once, the US/ARVN forces would suffer a multitude of small to major defeats which would add up to an overall disaster. Khe Sanh would distract the attention of the US commanders while the NVA/VC was preparing for D-day in South Vietnam's cities but, when this full offensive was at its height, it was unlikely that the over-stretched American forces would be able to keep the base from being overrun and Giap would have repeated his triumph of fourteen years before.

It's highly doubtful that the NVA/VC expected to hold all or even some of the cities and towns they attacked, but the NLF apparently did expect large sections of the urban populace to rise-up in revolt. With a few exceptions, this didn't happen. South Vietnam's city dwellers were generally indifferent to both the NLF and the Saigon Government but the VC clearly expected more support than it actually got. The object of attacking the cities was not so much to win in a single blow as it was to inflict a series of humiliating defeats on the Americans and to destroy the authority of the Saigon Government. When

Right US Air Force helicopter crewman fires a mini-gun to cover a rescue operation over South Vietnam. The mini-gun is a modern version of the old Gatling. At its lower rate of fire, the mini-gun performs like a standard machine-gun, but at its higher rate of 6,000 rounds per minute the effect can be devastating. Newer versions installed aboard fighter aircraft can literally saw an enemy plane in half or – armed with special armor-piercing shells – destroy a tank with a brief burst.

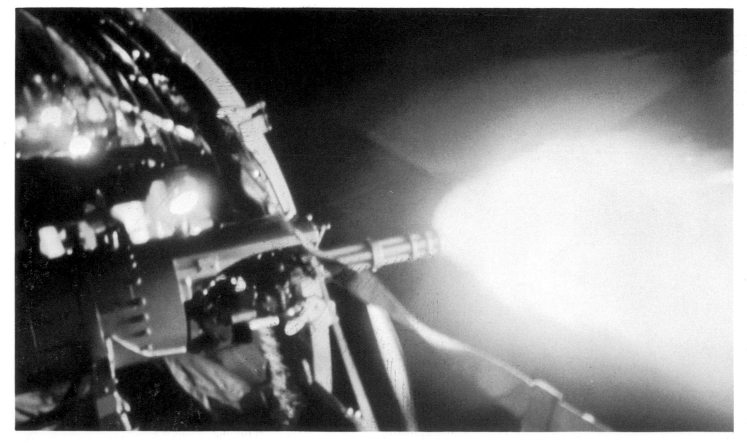

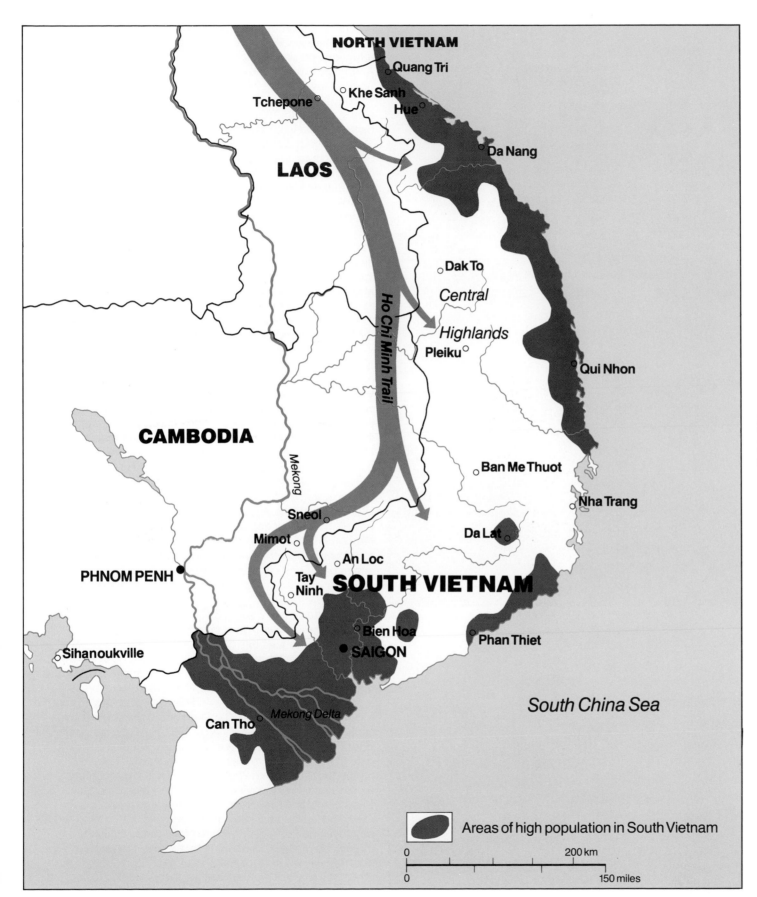

NORTH VIETNAM

Quang Tri

Tchepone

Khe Sanh

Hue

Da Nang

LAOS

Dak To

Central

Highlands

Pleiku

Qui Nhon

Ho Chi Minh Trail

CAMBODIA

Ban Me Thuot

Mekong

Nha Trang

Sneol

Da Lat

Mimot

An Loc

PHNOM PENH

Tay Ninh

SOUTH VIETNAM

Bien Hoa

Phan Thiet

SAIGON

Sihanoukville

South China Sea

Can Tho

Mekong Delta

Areas of high population in South Vietnam

0   200 km

0   150 miles

Left South Vietnam at the time of the 1968
Tet Offensive, when the VC/NVA
launched coordinated attacks in virtually
all the major cities and important towns.

the US/ARVN forces finally drove the NVA/VC back into the jungle, there would be left behind a wasteland of rubble, refugees, and simmering discontent. Stung by their defeats, the Americans would lose heart for the war and what was left of the Saigon Government would be forced to reach an agreement with the NLF and Hanoi which – after a time – would simply take over in the South. This offensive would begin in January 1968 at the time of the Vietnamese Tet (New Year) holidays.

The village of Khe Sanh lay in the northwest corner of South Vietnam just below the DMZ and close to the Laotian border. Khe Sanh had been garrisoned by the French during the first Indochina war and became an important US Special Forces base early on during the second. Its importance lay in its proximity to the Ho Chi Minh Trail. From Khe Sanh, US artillery could shell the trail and observers could keep an eye on NVA traffic moving southwards. If necessary they could call in air-strikes or alert CIA/Meo raiding parties across the border in Laos. Special Forces working with local Montagnard tribesmen also harried NVA traffic in the area and were a definite nuisance to Hanoi. In 1967, the Marines took over Khe Sanh and converted it into a large fire base. The Special Forces moved their base to the Montagnard village of Lang Vei.

Towards the end of 1967, it was obvious that Giap was planning something. Broadcasts from Hanoi were speaking of great victories and of taking the war into the cities of South Vietnam. Two NVA divisions – the 325th and the 304th were spotted moving into the Khe Sanh area and a third was positioning itself along Route-9 where it would be able to intercept reinforcements coming in from Quang Tri. The two NVA divisions near Khe Sanh had fought at Dien Bien Phu and the warning was clear. Westmoreland picked up the gauntlet and began to reinforce the base despite predictions of up-coming bad weather which could hinder air support and interfere with vital supply planes. Appearances to the contrary, Westmoreland had no intention of duplicating the French mistakes at Dien Bien Phu. American airpower was capable of delivering devastating attacks on concentrations of enemy troops and – apart from anti-aircraft guns – was unopposed. Helicopters and parachute drops by low-flying cargo planes reduced the dependence on re-supply by road.

By late January, some 6,000 Marines had been flown in to reinforce the Khe Sanh garrison and thousands of reinforcements had been moved north of Hue. The NVA build-up also continued; 20,000 North Vietnamese were ultimately moved in around Khe Sanh but other estimates put the number at twice that. Initially, Giap would position his artillery in the DMZ and then send his assault troops against the fortified hills surrounding Khe Sanh which the Marines had captured in the dogged fighting in 1967. Having captured the hill positions, Giap reasoned, the NVA artillery could be moved onto the heights above the beleaguered base. Then – as happened at Dien Bien Phu – waves of determined infantry would steadily grind away until the defenders were pushed into a corner and finally over-run. The White House and the US media became convinced that the decisive battle of the war had begun. TV news reports were so obsessed with Giap's threatened replay of Dien Bien Phu that day-to-day life at Khe Sanh became lead-story material even when it showed nothing other than anxious Marines waiting for something to happen.

Far left top Revolutionaries or refugees? This North Vietnamese photo purports to show villagers of a strategic hamlet in Binh Tri Thien Province rising up during the 1968 Tet Offensive but it looks more like a hasty – if not forced – evacuation. Note what appear to be VC or NVA observers standing among the trees.

Far left middle US Army 175mm gun at fire-support-base J.J. Carroll shelling NVA positions around Khe Sanh in aid of the beleaguered Marine garrison.

Far left below Marines load a 105mm howitzer during a January 1968 artillery exchange at Khe Sanh.

Left Marines charge an enemy machine-gun nest during the battle to re-take Hue.

Right The mini-gun in action: this weapon has six 7.62 caliber barrels turned by a 28-volt electric motor and a selector mechanism allowing choice between 400 or 6,000 rounds per minute.

Below MPs take a VC into custody following the attack on the US embassy in Saigon on January 31, 1968 – the opening day of the Tet Offensive.

The first attack began shortly before dawn on January 21st, when the NVA attempted to cross the river running past the base. It was beaten back but followed by an artillery barrage which damaged the runway, blew up the main ammunition stores, and damaged a few aircraft. Secondary attacks were launched against the Special Forces' defences at Lang Vei and against the Marines dug-in on the hills surrounding Khe Sanh but these attacks were aimed more at testing the defences than anything else. The next day, helicopters and light cargo aircraft flew in virtually every few minutes replacing lost ammunition but the weather began turning worse.

The NVA began a concentrated artillery barrage and moved their troops forward to begin building a network of entrenched positions in which they could prepare for further assaults on Khe Sanh's outer defences. Anti-aircraft guns and the worsening weather made in-coming supply flights difficult and supporting US forces moved-up to engage the NVA in running skirmishes designed to break-through on Route-9. Air strikes on NVA positions around Khe Sanh were intensified and – despite the weather – pounded the North Vietnamese hour after hour. Electronic sensors of the types running along the McNamara Line surrounded Khe Sanh. Seismic disturbance devices warned of even the smallest movements of the enemy

and highly sensitive listening devices enabled the Americans to monitor everything from normal conversations to radio communications. Overhead, high-flying signal-intelligence (SIGINT) aircraft intercepted communications traffic over the entire front and to and from command centres in North Vietnam.

While the world was watching the drama unfolding at Khe Sanh, however, NVA and VC regulars were also drifting into Saigon, Hue, and most of South Vietnam's cities. They came in twos and threes, disguised as refugees, peasants, workers, and ARVN soldiers on holiday leave. In Saigon, roughly the equivalent of five battalions of NVA/VC gradually infiltrated the city without anyone informing or any of the countless security police taking undue notice. Weapons came separately in flower carts, jury-rigged coffins, and trucks apparently filled with vegetables and rice. There was also a VC network in Saigon and the other major cities which had long stockpiled stores of arms and ammunition drawn from hit-and-run raids or bought openly on the black-market. It was also no secret that VC drifted in and out of the cities to see relatives and on general leave from their units. Viet Cong who were captured during the pre-Tet build up were mistaken for regular holiday-makers or deserters. In the general pattern of New Year merry-making, the VC's secret

Below VC use the devastated streets of Hue as a temporary fire-base.

151

army of infiltrators went completely unnoticed.

Tet had traditionally been a time of truce in the long war and both Hanoi and Saigon had made announcements that this year would be no different – although they disagreed about the duration. US Intelligence had gotten wind that something was brewing through captured documents and an overall analysis of recent events but Westmoreland's staff tended to disregard these generally vague reports. At the request of General Frederick Weyand, the US commander of the Saigon area, however, several battalions were pulled back from their positions near the Cambodian border. General Weyand put his troops on full alert but – due to a standing US policy of leaving the security of major cities to the ARVN – there were only a few hundred American troops on duty in Saigon itself the night before the attack began. Westmoreland later claimed to have anticipated Tet but the evidence suggests that he was not prepared for anything approaching the intensity of the attack that came and that he was still concentrating his attentions on the developing battle at Khe Sanh where he thought Giap would make his chief effort.

In the early morning hours of January 31st, the first day of the Vietnamese New Year, NLF/NVA troops and commandos attacked virtually every major town and city in South Vietnam as well as most of the important American bases and airfields. There were some earlier attacks around Pleiku, Quang Nam, and Darlac but these were largely misinterpreted as the enemy's main thrust by those who were expecting some activity during Tet. Almost everywhere the attacks came as a total suprise. Vast areas of Saigon and Hue suddenly found themselves "liberated" and parades of gun-waving NVA/VC marched through the streets proclaiming the revolution while their grimmer-minded comrades rounded up prepared lists of collaborators and government sympathizers for show trials and quick executions.

In Saigon, nineteen VC commandos blew their way through the outer walls of the US Embassy and overran the five MPs on duty in the early hours of that morning. Two MPs were killed immediately as the action-team tried to blast their way through the main Embassy doors with anti-tank rockets. They failed and found themselves pinned-down by the Marine guards who kept the VC in an intense fire-fight until a relief force of US

Below Marines battling with VC/NVA sniper fire behind a wall near the enemy-held Citadel in Hue.

101st Airborne landed by helicopter. By mid-morning, the battle had turned. All nineteen VC were killed, their bodies scattered around the Embassy courtyard. Five Americans and two Vietnamese civilians were among the other dead. The commandos had been dressed in civilian clothing and had rolled-up to the Embassy in an ancient truck. The security of the Embassy was not in serious danger after the first few minutes and the damage was slight but this attack on "American soil" captured the imagination of the media and the battle became symbolic of the Tet Offensive throughout the world.

Other NVA/VC squads attacked Saigon's Presidential Palace, the radio station, the headquarters of the ARVN Chiefs of Staff, and Westmoreland's own MACV compound as part of a 700-man raid on the Tan Son Nhut air-base. During the heavy fighting that followed, things became sufficiently worrying for Westmoreland to order his staff to find weapons and join in the defence of the compound. When the fighting at Tan Son Nhut was over, twenty-three Americans were dead, eighty-five were wounded and up to fifteen aircraft had suffered serious damage. Two NVA/VC battalions attacked the US air-base at Bien Hoa and crippled over twenty aircraft at a cost of nearly 170 casualties. Further fighting at Bien Hoa during the Tet Offensive would take the NVA/VC death total in Saigon to nearly 1200.

Other VC units made stands in the French cemetery and the Pho Tho race track. The mainly Chinese suburb of Cholon became virtually a NVA/VC operations base and, as it later turned out, had been the main staging area for the attacks in Saigon and its immediate area. President Thieu declared martial law on January 31st but it would take over a week of intense fighting to clear-up the various pockets of resistance scattered around Saigon. Sections of the city were reduced to rubble in heavy street by street fighting. Tanks, helicopter gunships, and strike aircraft blasted parts of the city as entrenched guerrillas fought and then slipped off to fight somewhere else. The radio station, various industrial buildings, and a large block of low-cost public housing were levelled along with the homes of countless civilians who were forced to flee. The city dissolved into a chaos which took weeks to begin to put right.

The fighting within Saigon itself was pretty much over by February 5th but it carried on in Cholon until the last week of the

Below Marines jury-rig a machine-gun rest to return VC/NVA fire in Hue.

month. Cholon was strafed, bombed, and shelled but the NVA/VC held on and even mounted sporadic counter-offensives against US/ARVN positions within the city and against Tan Son Nhut airport. B-52 strikes against communist positions outside Saigon came within a few miles of the city. When the NVA/VC were finally driven out of Saigon's suburbs, they retreated into the surrounding government villages and fought there. US and ARVN artillery and strike-aircraft bombed and shelled these supposedly pacified villages before troops moved in to re-occupy them. The NVA/VC repeated this tactic again and again in a clear effort to make the Saigon Government destroy their own fortified villages and, by doing so, further alienate the rural population. A month after the Offensive began, US estimates put the number of civilian dead at some 15,000 and the number of new refugees at anything up to two million – and still the battles went on.

Elsewhere in South Vietnam, the success of the Tet Offensive was erratic. Many of the attacks on the provincial cities and US bases were easily beaten back within the first minutes or hours, but others involved bitter fighting. In the resort city of Dalat, the ARVN put up a spirited defence of the Vietnamese Military Academy against a determined VC battalion. Fighting raged over the Pasteur Institute – which changed hands several times – and the VC dug themselves in in the central market. Fighting in Dalat went on until mid-February and left over 200 VC dead. In cities like Ban Me Thuot, My Tho, Can Tho, Ben Tre, and Kontum, the VC entrenched themselves in the poorer sections and held out against repeated efforts to push them out. The biggest battle, however, occured at Hue.

The Buddhist crisis had left bitter feelings towards the Saigon Government in the ancient Vietnamese capital and, within a few hours of their attack, the disguised insurgents supported by some ten NVA/VC battalions had overrun all of the city except for the headquarters of the ARVN 3rd Division and the garrison of US advisors. The main NVA/VC goal was the Citadel, an ancient imperial palace covering some two square miles with high walls several feet thick. NVA troops assaulted the Citadel and ran up the VC flag on the early morning of January 31st but were unable to displace ARVN holding out in the northeast section. Having overrun the city and found considerable support among sections of Hue's populace, the NVA/VC began an immediate revolutionary "liberation" program. Thousands of prisoners were set free and thousands of "enemies of the state" – government officials, sympathizers, and Catholics were rounded up and many were shot out of hand on orders from the security section of the NLF which had sent in its action squad with a prepared hit-list. Most of the others simply vanished.

After Hue was finally recaptured at the end of February, South Vietnamese officials sifting through the rubble found mass graves with over 1200 corpses and – some time later – other mass burials in the provincial area. The total number of bodies unearthed came to around 2500 but the number of civilians estimated as missing after the Hue battle was nearly 6000. Many of the victims found were Catholics who sought sanctuary in a church but were taken out and later shot. Others were apparently being marched off for political "re-education" but were shot when American or ARVN units came too close.

Below The body of a VC lies in the streets of Saigon hardly noticed by the Vietnamese trying to get on with their daily business on the first day of the Tet Offensive.

Above VC corpses dragged to an outlying area of Danang where they will be picked up for eventual burial.

Top left The corpses of three NVA regulars lie in the streets near Saigon's Old French Cemetery. The area was quickly devastated by US/ARVN artillery fire and air-strikes in an effort to drive out the enemy during the Tet Offensive.

Left Ten VC bodies lie in the streets of the Saigon suburb of Cholon where they were dumped by ARVN rangers. Cholon was the staging area for the VC/NVA's Saigon operations during the Tet Offensive and was only cleared of the enemy after some of the fiercest fighting of the war.

The mass graves within Hue itself were largely of those who had been picked up and executed for various "enemy of the people" offenses. There is some doubt that the NVA/VC had planned *all* these executions beforehand but unquestionably it was the largest communist purge of the war.

US Marines and ARVN drove into the city and, after nearly two days of heavy fighting, secured the bank of the Perfume river opposite the Citadel. Hue was a sacred city to the Vietnamese and apart from the ancient Citadel held many other precious historical buildings. After much deliberation, it was reluctantly decided to shell and bomb NVA/VC positions. Resistance was heavy and sending the Marines into the city without air and artillery support would have meant an unacceptable cost in lives. To many, the battle for Hue reminded them of the bitter street-by-street fighting that occurred during World War II. The NVA had blown the main bridge across the Perfume River so US forces crossed in a fleet of assault craft under air and artillery cover which blasted away at the enemy-held Citadel. Its walls were so thick that few were killed but the covering fire made the enemy keep their heads down while the Marines and soldiers hit the bank below.

While the ARVN, with US support, fought its way through the streets of Hue block by block, the Marines prepared to assault the Citadel. On February 20th American assault teams went in through clouds of tear gas and the burning debris left over from air and artillery attacks. The NVA/VC were pushed into the southwestern corner of the Citadel and finally overwhelmed on February 23rd. Enemy resistance in Hue was finally reduced to isolated pockets and sniper teams. As the Citadel fell, NVA/VC units began retreating – some of them marching groups of soon-to-be-massacred prisoners before them – into the suburbs while their rear guards fought holding actions with the advancing ARVN. The fight for Hue ended by February 25th at a cost of 119 Americans and 363 ARVN dead compared to about sixteen times that number of NVA/VC dead.

The dramatic difference in fatalities makes the battle look a one-sided affair. But it wasn't! The difference in casualty figures came largely from the heavy use of artillery and aircraft back-up to devastate NVA/VC positions throughout Hue which reduced large sections of the city to body-laden piles of rubble. Had the commanders decided to preserve the ancient and revered city, US/ARVN casualties would have been much higher. American wounded during the battle for Hue came to just under a thousand compared to slightly over 1,200 ARVN. Nearly 120,000 citizens of Hue were homeless and, of the close to 6,000 civilian dead, many died in the bombing and shell-fire.

Contrary to many reports, large sections of Hue escaped relatively undamaged but after the battle they were forced to suffer days of looting by soldiers from the original ARVN garrison who had spent the previous weeks keeping their heads low. Their commander – who had also sat out the city's Buddhist rebellion against Ky – was later accused of having known about the coming attack for days beforehand. His defence was that he had allowed the NVA/VC battalions into Hue in order to spring a trap! In the villages outside Hue, the battle went on for another week or so as the retreating NVA/VC took over the villages just long enough for them to be destroyed by bombing and concentrated artillery shelling. Civilian deaths and refugees increased.

Far left top Marine snipers at Khe Sanh. During the long siege, Marine snipers engaged in long-running duels with NVA marksmen. At times, the respective sniper teams were relieving the boredom of the long wait as much as they were trying to harass the enemy. Note the special sniper-scopes fitted to the carrying handles of their M-16 rifles.

Left Two Marine helicopters approach the Khe Sanh airstrip passing the wreckage of a US chopper shot down by the NVA during the seventy-seven-day siege.

Far left below Summary execution of a Viet Cong Officer in the streets of Saigon. This is one of the most famous pictures to come out of the Vietnam war. The executioner is General Nguyen Ngoc Loan, then head of the South Vietnamese National Police. Loan's cold-blooded killing provoked a great deal of understandable outrage amongst anti-war elements in the United States and Europe but – unfortunately – VC/NVA atrocities did not receive the same publicity.

Left Going on leave at Khe Sanh. Marines run for a waiting helicopter under threat from NVA artillery and sniper fire. Some of the men are being flown out on re-assignment while the others were lucky enough to get R&R (rest and recreation) leave. Giap had hoped to make Khe Sanh another Dien Bien Phu but America's ability to re-supply the base by air helped defeat him.

On February 5th, the fighting died out in Saigon and the Marines prepared for their river assault on the Citadel in Hue. The electronic sensors around the besieged fire-base at Khe Sanh warned of enemy preparations to assault the entrenched positions on Hill 881, which was outside the main camp. Intensive artillery fire broke up the assembling NVA troops but a second planned attack on Hill 881 had gone unnoticed until the Marines found themselves fighting off waves of on-coming North Vietnamese regulars. For half an hour, the beleaguered Marines battled the NVA in hand-to-hand fighting – even trusting their flak jackets enough to use grenades at close quarters – until the artillery could be brought to bear on the hill and the attackers forced to withdraw.

Two days later, the Green Beret's camp at Lang Vei was attacked by an NVA assault force led by ten Soviet-built, PT-76 light, amphibious tanks. Despite a shortage of anti-tank ammunition three of the armored vehicles were put out of action before the NVA swarmed over the wire. Because of the very real likelihood of an ambush, no relief force was sent and the Lang Vei commander, Captain Frank Willoughby, ordered his men into the jungle, and called down air and artillery strikes directly onto the camp. Of the original force of twenty-four Special Forces and 900 Montagnard, only Willoughby and seventy-three others managed to struggle into Khe Sanh. The next day, NVA troops overran nearly half of an outer Marine position at Khe Sanh before being blasted back by artillery, aircraft, and armor.

Giap's ambition to win a massive victory against the Americans was thwarted by massive aerial bombardments of NVA positions. B-52s and strike aircraft dropped their loads with pin-point accuracy within a few hundred feet of Khe Sanh's perimeter. During the course of the battle, tons of bombs and napalm were dropped around Khe Sanh. Bad weather and increasing anti-aircraft fire inhibited the steady flow of incoming supplies but the vital cargo planes and helicopters kept coming despite losses. The fortified hills around Khe Sanh were supplied by Sea Knight Helicopters, frequently accompanied by fighter escorts. The battle settled down into a siege. The NVA concentrated on shelling the base and trying to stop the supply planes with anti-aircraft fire while digging in around the camp. Both sides employed teams of snipers to harass each other's movements.

The NVA launched further attacks on February 17th, 18th, and 29th but massed artillery and air-strikes broke the first up fairly easily while the second involved heavy fighting. In early April, relief forces reached the base. A 1st Cavalry helicopter assault force landed near Khe Sanh as American and ARVN forces hit NVA positions along Route-9. Khe Sanh was relieved on April 6th and, four days later, Lang Vei was re-occupied. Fighting continued around Khe Sanh for a time but Giap had long since given up any hope of overrunning the base. The drive to relieve Khe Sanh had gone smoothly and without heavy resistance. From this, many inferred that the whole siege of Khe Sanh had been a feint to cover preparations for the Tet Offensive

Right Wounded NVA regular is questioned by an ARVN paratrooper after he was captured during a sweep near the Old French Cemetery, Saigon.

Far right US Marine fuel dump at Khe Sanh burns out of control following an NVA artillery barrage.

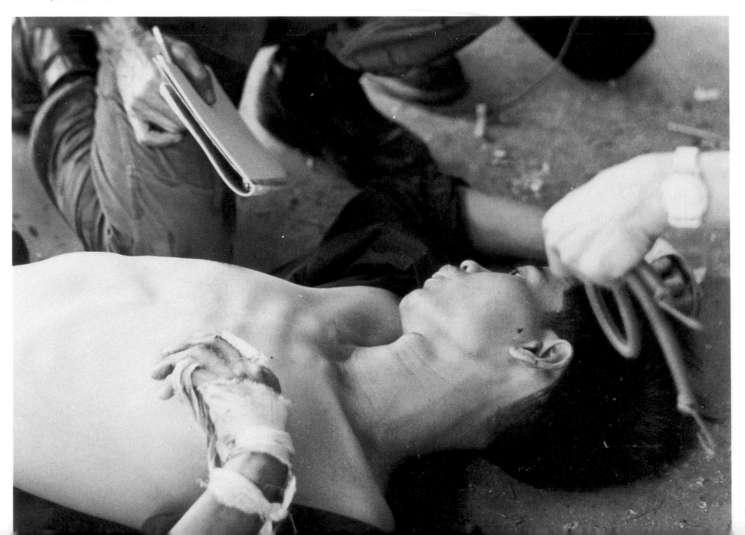

in the South. And to an extent, this was true but the evidence suggests that Giap's moves on Khe Sanh had a more deadly purpose than simply drawing American attentions away from the South at the critical time. By the middle of February, it was obvious that the battle for South Vietnam's cities was failing and that US airpower would deny the NVA another Dien Bien Phu. Seeing the inevitable, Giap seems to have began a slow wind down of the siege before the US counter-attack began.

The After-effects of Tet

The Tet Offensive and Khe Sanh may well have reminded Johnson and Westmoreland of the Duke of Wellington's dictum: "If there's anything more melancholy than a battle lost, it's a battle won". Giap had been frustrated at Khe Sanh and defeated in South Vietnam's cities. NVA/VC dead totaled some 45,000 and the number of prisoners nearly 7000. But the shockwave of the battle finished Johnson's willingness to carry on. Westmoreland was pressuring Washington for 206,000 troops to carry on the campaign in the South and to make a limited invasion of North Vietnam just above the DMZ. As the battle for Hue died out, Johnson asked Clark Clifford (who had recently replaced a disillusioned McNamara as Secretary of Defense) to find ways and means of meeting Westmoreland's request.

Clifford and an advisor group looked at the war to date and, among others, consulted CIA Director Richard Helms who presented the Agency's gloomy forecasts in great detail. On March 4th, Clifford told Johnson that the war was far from won

and that more men would make little difference. Johnson then turned to his chief group of informal advisors (which included among others, Generals Omar Bradley, Matthew Ridgway, and Maxwell Taylor; Cyrus Vance, Dean Acheson, and Henry Cabot Lodge). Johnson soon found that they too, like Clifford, had turned against the war. According to Thomas Powers, Johnson's "wise old men" had been told that recent CIA studies showed that the pacification programme was failing in forty of South Vietnam's forty-four provinces and that the NLF's manpower was actually twice the number that had been estimated previously. Not only had Tet shown that the optimism of the previous year had been an illusion but it now seemed that the enemy was far stronger than anybody had thought and that the long efforts to win Vietnamese "hearts and minds" had largely been a disaster.

If Tet wasn't a full-scale shock to the American public, it was at the very least, an awakening. The enemy that Johnson and the generals had described as moribund had shown itself to be very alive and, as yet, unbeaten. America and its ARVN ally had suffered over 4,300 killed in action, some 16,000 wounded and over 1,000 missing in action. The fact that the enemy suffered far more and had lost a major gamble mattered little because the war looked like a never-ending conflict without any definite, realistic objective. The scenes of desolation in Saigon, Hue, and other cities looked to be war without purpose or end. Perhaps the most quoted US officer of the time was the one who explained the destruction of about one-third of the provincial

capital of Ben Tre with unintended black humor: "It became necessary to destroy it," he said, "in order to save it". For many, this oft-quoted statement was not just a classic example of Pentagon double-think but also a symbol of the war's futility. Westmoreland became the parody "General Waste-more-land" of the anti-war movement.

Being against the war became more-or-less politically respectable for liberal elements. Robert Kennedy spoke of giving up the illusion of victory and Democratic Senator Eugene McCarthy challenged Johnson for the Presidential nomination on a peace platform. He was supported by thousands of students and young Americans opposed to the war. Vocal elements of the extreme right largely supported the war but condemned the Administration for not going all-out for victory. The JCS backed Westmoreland but convinced him to settle for half of the over 200,000 additional troops he wanted to take the initiative. The JCS then reported to the White House that the extra men were needed to get things back to normal following the battles of the Tet Offensive.

Johnson's dilemma was complete. He couldn't meet the generals' manpower requests without either depleting Europe of American troops – which was unacceptable – or without calling up the active reserves which would have been a political disaster. His most senior advisors had turned against the war and Johnson took another briefing from the CIA analyst whose gloomy reports had soured some of his most hawkish counsellors. A few days after this briefing, Johnson went on TV to announce a bombing halt of the North and America's willingness to meet with the North Vietnamese to seek a peace settlement. Johnson then said that he was not a candidate for re-election under any circumstances and would spend the rest of his term in a search for peace in Indochina.

One of those present at the special CIA briefing which convinced Johnson that a change of course was inevitable was General Creighton Abrams, Westmoreland's deputy commander. Shortly after Johnson's turnabout, Abrams replaced Westmoreland as head of US forces in Vietnam. Westmoreland came home to become Army Chief of Staff – a move many saw as a kick upstairs – but, whatever the reasons behind the changeover, Abrams went to Saigon with a mission. He was to institute a program of "Vietnamization"; in other words, to take all necessary measures to enable the ARVN to bear the main burden of the fighting and gradually return the chief role of American troops to that of advisors. Vietnamization had always been a feature of America's role in Vietnam but it had been on a back-burner since 1965 when it seemed that Saigon was incapable of doing the job. Now things were to be returned to what they were supposed to have been from the beginning. Vietnamization is usually credited to Nixon but it began in the wake of the Tet Offensive and Johnson's turnabout.

Giap's gamble had another side effect. When the Tet Offensive began, many US officials believed that the NLF had offered the Americans a golden opportunity by fighting a pitched battle where it could be defeated in open combat. In effect, the NLF was "leading with its chin" and the massive losses it suffered bear this out. The VC was not broken by the Tet Offensive but it was severely crippled by it and, from then on, the North took on the main burden of the war. Further fighting in 1968 and the increasing activity of the *Phoenix* Program further decimated the NLF's ranks and the role of the North grew even larger. The northern and southern parts of Vietnam had ancient cultural and social differences and while the communist cadres at the center of the NLF had managed largely to suppress these natural antagonisms, there still were basic differences in goals and approach. The NLF had gone into the Tet Offensive in the hope of giving a death-blow to the Saigon Government and, if it couldn't capture power directly, it could at least gain a coalition leading to ultimate authority. The NLF's dream vanished in the rubble of South Vietnam's cities and it would be Hanoi that conquered Saigon.

Above General Creighton W. Abrams. After the shock of the Tet Offensive, General Westmoreland was promoted to Army Chief of Staff and the overall command of MACV was given to Abrams. General Abrams became responsible for the increasing policy of Vietnamization. As the 1972 NVA offensive began to wear down in late June, General Abrams was replaced by General Frederick Weyand, one of the few top US commanders in Vietnam to have anticipated the Tet Offensive

Right A C-130D prepares for take-off after unloading its supplies – with the engines running – at Khe Sanh.

Above 105mm howitzer fires at NVA positions during the siege of Khe Sanh.

Left US fifty caliber machine-gun on the perimeter defences of Khe Sanh.

Above Burning out abandoned NVA trenches near the defences of Khe Sanh.

Right Rangers prepare to move in on VC positions in the outskirts of Saigon during the Tet Offensive.

Above The Danang airbase is hit by VC rocket fire in the first hours of the Tet Offensive. Virtually every important US base was attacked by the enemy in a coordinated effort during the Vietnamese New Year.

Left Vietnamese civilians flee as the ARVN Rangers charge VC holed up in their village.

Above South Vietnamese troops move up to reinforce the Marines at Khe Sanh while the 1st Cavalry pushes its way through on Route 9. The wreckage is that of aircraft lost to NVA fire.

Right "C" Battery, 1st Battalion, 13th Marines fires on NVA positions around Khe Sanh.

Above Members of the 38th ARVN Rangers fire into a VC-held building in the Saigon suburb of Cholon during the intense fighting that followed the Tet Offensive.

Above left KC-130 air-drops its vitally needed supplies to the besieged Marine garrison at Khe Sanh.

Right An ARVN Ranger sprints for cover through the corpse- and rubble-filled streets of Cholon, a suburb of Saigon that saw some of the most vicious fighting of the war.

Left ARVN Airborne check out a burnt-out gas station that was used by NVA/VC guerrillas as a temporary ammo dump during the battle near the Old French Cemetery, Saigon.

9 Nixon's War

The Wider Peace

The Presidential campaign of 1968 was one of the most bitter in recent American history. The Democrats nominated Johnson's Vice President, Hubert Humphrey, an old-time liberal. The Republicans nominated Richard Nixon who had not held political office since his defeat by Kennedy in the 1960 Presidential election. Humphrey's four years as Johnson's Vice-President and his vocal backing of Johnson's war policies had earned him the hatred of much of the anti-war movement, and the Democratic convention in Chicago was marred by scenes of rioting demonstrators and over-reacting police clubbing virtually anyone in sight. Nixon, on the other hand, had surprised a great many people by bouncing back from the political wilderness to get a second chance at the Presidency. Both men took much the same stand on the war and – despite a last-minute surge by Humphrey – Nixon won a close victory.

During the campaign Nixon made a brief guest appearance on the popular TV show *Rowan and Martin's Laugh-in* where he popped in and out quoting the program's famous one-liner, "Sock it to me!" These proved to be prophetic words. Five years later Nixon stood virtually alone as the Congress moved toward a Bill of Impeachment against him. Once heralded as bold and imaginative, his foreign policy was crippled and, by his own actions, the prestige and authority of the Presidency had declined on a scale unknown in modern times. In 1972, Nixon had won re-election by one of the biggest majorities in history, and just over two months later, the Vietnam cease-fire everybody had waited for since 1968 was finally agreed between Washington and Hanoi. Nixon's peace was flawed but workable. Under other circumstances, the Republic of South Vietnam might have been able to maintain a perilous independence, but in his haste to get an agreement, Kissinger made Hanoi some ill-considered concessions which boded trouble for the future. Even so, a vigorous American administration might have been able to hold Hanoi sufficiently at bay to keep the Saigon Government a viable proposition.

Just after the 1973 cease-fire, communist strength in the South consisted of some 170,000 NVA regulars plus about 30,000 hard-core VC. Opposing them were 300,000 front-line ARVN troops with something like half a million men in varying support roles. At the time of the cease-fire, NVA Chief of Staff General Van Tien Dung and Hanoi Central Committee member To Huu visited the main pockets of North Vietnamese troops scattered throughout the South. Their findings suggested that the NVA was too weak to try any new large-scale offensives for at least three years. In addition, the new-found detente between Washington and the two superpowers of the communist world, China and the USSR, meant that Hanoi was fighting to a large extent on its own. North Vietnam itself was devastated by US bombing and had suffered at least a million dead since Johnson first sent the Marines ashore at Danang. Full recovery was years away and, even today, North Vietnam seems austere and

Right The face of Detente. In the early Seventies, President Nixon and National Security Advisor (later Secretary of State) Henry Kissinger succeeded in building bridges with both Moscow and Peking. The Soviets and the Chinese needed increased economic and diplomatic ties with the West to salvage their own ailing economies and to use Washington as a foil against the other. In time, this resulted in pressure on Hanoi from the two communist super-powers to give Nixon a "peace with honour" in Vietnam. Here, Nixon poses with Soviet leader Leonid Brezhnev following a June 1973 meeting in Washington.

impoverished compared to the South.

Although there was considerable doubt about its ability to carry on the war without the back-up of American ground troops and airpower, the ARVN was equipped with some of the most modern military equipment in the US arsenal. NVA discipline was far better and the ARVN were likely to lose in any stand-up fight against them, but there were signs of an increasing demoralization in the North Vietnamese ranks. Despite all the question marks, South Vietnam's chances of a semi-independent survival were better than they had ever been and, if America hadn't won the war, it had at least achieved some semblance of the "honorable peace" which Nixon had been promising since he first began campaigning for the Presidency. The peace plan which emerged was the closest thing to success that he could have hoped for.

In many ways, the war that Nixon fought was bloodier and more total than Johnson's but the American public cared less

because—however slowly—the troops were coming home. Unlike his predecessor, Nixon was prepared to follow Curtis Lemay's advice and bomb North Vietnam back "into the stone-age" in order to get a workable peace. One of Nixon's first acts as President after taking office in January 1969 was to pass a message via Kissinger to Moscow that he would bomb Hanoi into rubble if their negotiators proved obstinate at the Paris Peace Table. At the same time, Nixon ordered an intensive, secret bombing of NVA/VC bases in Cambodia which up until then—apart from covert commando-style raiding parties—had been off-limits. For months, waves of bombers pounded communist-held villages and bases in eastern Cambodia without the White House making it public and without significant protest from either Moscow or Peking. Superpower detente was on the horizon.

Vietnam was becoming an obstacle and embarrassment in the changing pattern of international relations. Nixon and his

National Security Advisor Henry Kissinger had been slowly building bridges to Moscow and Peking aimed at relaxing tensions, increasing trade, and limiting strategic armaments. The Soviet Union and China were locked in mutual hostility and both saw an advantage in cultivating friendship with Washington as a partial counter to the other. Moscow, in particular, did its best to try to talk Washington out of bringing China into the superpower club; the Russians also became quite cooperative in using their influence on Hanoi to help Nixon resolve the war in a manner that he could live with politically. Because of its own increasing internal political stability and the need to counter Moscow, China slowly moved to building bridges with the West and both communist superpowers began to see advantages in finding a satisfactory solution to a war nobody but North Vietnam wanted any more. It wasn't a case of abandoning the struggle for South Vietnam so much as postponing it for a while. No one – least of all in Peking or Moscow – doubted that, once American

troops left Vietnam, they would not be back. Although US airpower might be a force to be reckoned with for a time, Russia and China were confident that South Vietnam would fall sooner or later. In the beginning, the war was advantageous because it weakened American power abroad and fueled discontent in the United States, but now it was becoming an impediment to greater political realities and – as Moscow wanted a trade package with America – it was necessary to help Nixon find his honorable peace. One of the great ironies of the early Seventies was seeing Nixon – once the prototype Cold-War Warrior – receiving warm welcomes in both Moscow and Peking at the same time as waves of US bombers continued to pound North Vietnam.

The anti-war movement actually grew under Nixon's Presidency but it was no longer as politically acceptable as it was in 1968. Nixon promised to end the war but honorably and this went a long way to satisfying mainstream America. The fact that

Far left top Nixon's historic 1972 meeting with China's Chairman Mao Tse-tung in Peking.

Far left below US troops battle with anti-war demonstrators outside the Pentagon in October 1967.

Above General Nguyen Van Thieu. Thieu became Washington's main hope for a stable government in South Vietnam but fought against Nixon's 1973 cease-fire until forced to go-along. Thieu abdicated power only a few days before the fall of Saigon in April 1975.

Left American students protest Nixon's 1970 invasions of Laos and Cambodia.

Right A CH-53 helicopter brings in supplies of water for US forces entrenched on Hill 119, twenty miles southwest of Danang.

Far right top Guiding in a Huey helicopter to evacuate members of the 1st Cavalry after operations in Phuoc Thanh Province in January 1971.

Far right below The dead of My Lai. In the wake of the Tet Offensive, some US troops on a search-and-destroy mission in VC territory shot the inhabitants of the village of My Lai in March 1968. When the story broke in 1969, the incident sent shockwaves through the American public. Many couldn't believe that US soldiers were capable of this kind of atrocity while others saw My Lai as an extreme example of the brutalizing effects of a never-ending war against an unseen enemy in an alien and far-away culture.

there were peace talks in progress and that Nixon was gradually cutting back on US troop commitments in Vietnam eased the fears of many doves, while his insistence on an honorable settlement appeased the hawks afraid of a sell-out. Nixon hadn't gotten America into the war and – despite explosions of protest over the invasion of Cambodia and the renewed bombing of North Vietnam – the general public tended to accept his efforts. Demonstrations against the Cambodian invasion ran from wide-spread rioting on US campuses – including Kent State, Ohio, where trigger-happy National Guardsmen shot four students dead – to a 100,000-strong protests march in Washington. Eleven months later, something like a half-million people converged on Washington to protest the war but, in the following year, Nixon was to win re-election with a massive majority over the liberal Democratic Senator George McGovern.

The early Seventies was a period of cautious optimism. The domestic turmoil of the Sixties appeared to be dying out while detente seemed to be offering a genuine thaw in the Cold War. The United States and the Soviet Union had signed the SALT I Treaty limiting strategic weapons and another agreement restricting anti-ballistic missiles. China had not only warmly welcomed Nixon to Peking but was also relaxing its previous

hard-line foreign policy. Peace was agonizingly slow in coming but coming it was. US casualties in the war were now fairly light, compared to what they had been. Nixon was never an overly popular President but – until Watergate began to take its toll – most Americans approved of what he was doing and didn't really care what happened in Vietnam as long as it didn't increase US casualties and eventually led to some sort of honorable peace.

Nothing illustrates this more than the 1969 revelations over the My Lai massacre. During post-Tet offensive operations in 1968, a company of American soldiers had wiped out a village while on a search-and-destroy patrol in VC-controlled territory. Over three hundred innocent Vietnamese – mainly women and children – were shot and buried in a ditch. While countless Americans were shocked and horrified at what happened, large segments of the population felt a grudging sympathy for the men as victims of what the pressures of a hated war could do to perfectly normal US servicemen. Many others adopted a more indifferent attitude; after all, killing Vietnamese in VC territory was pretty much what the war was all about, wasn't it? My Lai was just another part of a war nobody wanted and public sympathies were largely responsible for the fairly light punishments given to the men involved. Their actions were

seen more as a one-off mental aberration than as a calculated war crime against innocent civilians.

The Paris Peace talks had dragged on for years without any obvious result; in fact, the first few months of the conference had been spent arguing about the shape of the table at which the negotiators would sit. It was clear that the North Vietnamese were stalling and trying to win themselves a better deal in the hope that the anti-war movement would pressure Nixon into giving away too much too soon. To a point, this worked because Nixon was extraordinarily concerned about his public image. He wanted to appear tough but would often back down when his actions looked like generating too much controversy. By the time of the 1972 election, the elusive peace he had sought seemed to be at hand but Hanoi backed off once again. Nixon threatened a massive new bombing campaign and, when that produced no response, he launched the B-52s against Hanoi and Haiphong over the Christmas period.

The bombing worked. Hanoi agreed to talk again and the long-awaited cease-fire came into effect on January 28, 1973. Kissinger and Nixon genuinely believed that they had forged a lasting peace in Indochina and guaranteed the independence of South Vietman but they both knew that for it to work, it would be necessary to continue to support Saigon with massive military aid and maintain the threat of US airpower while Saigon built on its fragile authority. When they agreed to the cease-fire, the North Vietnamese saw little alternative. Nixon had been overwhelmingly re-elected and was fully prepared to bomb them back to the peace table. The Politburo in Hanoi, therefore, opted not for peace but to suspend the war for a time. Within the year, America had withdrawn her forces. Saigon stood virtually alone and victory was suddenly in sight.

Nixon was an insecure, almost paranoid man who hated criticism of any kind. He created his own team of covert agents and troubleshooters – the now infamous "plumbers" – to harass

Below A captured NVA officer under interrogation by members of the 5th ARVN Cavalry following an attack on Bien Hoa.

and spy on anyone who might conceivably give him trouble. His potential "enemies" included almost everybody who was not solidly behind him and certainly the whole of the Democratic Party. In the lead-up to the 1972 election, Nixon's unreasonable fears of losing led him to order a number of dirty tricks on likely Democratic contenders including the bugging of Democratic Party Headquarters in the Watergate buildings, Washington. Unfortunately for the President, his team of plumbers were a singularly inept collection of CIA cast-offs and general social misfits. They managed to get themselves caught breaking into the Watergate and what started as a "third-rate burglary" led to a growing scandal that came ever closer to the President.

On August 9, 1974, after being warned by a delegation of Senators headed by Barry Goldwater that he faced almost certain impeachment, Nixon became the first American President to resign. The Presidency he bequeathed to Vice-President Gerald Ford was a shadow of its former authority.

Congress, having pushed Nixon to the brink of impeachment, was feeling a power it had not known since the last century and it placed almost crippling restrictions on the President's authority to use troops abroad and upon US military aid to South Vietnam. The West was in the midst of an oil crisis and an economic recession so when the NVA began its renewed campaigns in South Vietnam, few ordinary Americans cared and the White House was more or less powerless to do anything about it. Whatever chance Nixon had won for South Vietnam on the battlefield had been thrown away in a bungled Washington break-in.

Vietnamization
The lynch-pin of Nixon's war plans was Vietnamization. By convincing the American public that he was bringing the troops home and turning the war over to the South Vietnamese, Nixon was able to escape much of the hostility which had been faced

Below An M-551 Armored Reconnaissance Airborne Assault Vehicle of the 25th Infantry Division patrols the muddy perimeter of helicopter landing zone *Hampton*.

by Johnson. During 1969, Nixon announced troop cutbacks of 25,000 on June 8th, another 25,000 on September 16th, and 50,000 in mid-December. Front line ARVN forces were given a wide variety of artillery and armor and these soldiers were issued with US Armalite M-16 rifles to replace the old M-1 Garrands and carbines they had been carrying up until then. Promising ARVN soldiers and non-commissioned officers were given the opportunity for advancement in the ranks for the first time and there was an effort to weed out inefficient commanders. High ranking officers often treated the war as a part-time job preferring to spend their weekends relaxing or looking after their business interests. Every effort was made to encourage professional attitudes in the ARVN officer corps.

It's curious that – apart from some elite units – the ARVN were not generally issued with the M-16 until 1968. Montagnard and Meo tribesmen working with the CIA and the Special Forces frequently carried M-16s which is an ideal weapon for slightly-built Asian soldiers. The M-16 is a 0.223 caliber, clip-fed, light-weight rifle with a selector switch for full or semi-automatic fire. The small bullet is backed by a large, crimped cartridge which gives a very high muzzle velocity with little recoil. The M-1, on the other hand, dates from World War II and is a fairly heavy 3.06 caliber, semi-automatic rifle with considerable recoil and an internal clip-loading mechanism which can be quite awkward to handle. Apart from a tendency to jam when it was first issued, the main problem with the M-16 in Vietnam was the comparative ease with which the light bullet could be deflected by foilage, with a corresponding loss of accuracy.

There was little new in the idea of Vietnamization. The French had tried it to an extent during the first Indochina war and it had been official US policy up until 1965 when Johnson agreed to let American troops take over the burden of the fighting. Johnson's decision was the direct result of the failure of America's earlier efforts at Vietnamization but now there was no choice but to try again. What was different about the new Vietnamization was the scale of the military aid offered and the fact that the Vietnamese were left in no doubt that US troops were going to be withdrawn and would not be coming back. Saigon had no choice but to go along and gradually assume responsibility for the war.

Eventually, Nixon intended to reduce American involvement in the fighting by the use of airpower or off-shore shelling from warships and minimal back-up of helicopter teams in ARVN ground operations. The fewer US casualties, the easier it would be for Nixon to seek the sort of Indochina settlement he wanted without excess pressure from anti-war factions in the United States. General Abrams was practically ordered to keep casualties low but he was helped by the fact that the VC – partly because of its heavy losses during the 1968 Tet Offensive – had reverted to the small hit-and-run raid and harrassing actions that had typified its efforts in the early 1960s. Abrams largely abandoned Westmoreland's large-scale "reconnaissance-in-force" drives into NVA/VC held territory in favor of smaller, highly coordinated attacks on the enemy's forces and supply lines. The only problem was locating the enemy and the strategy proved to be less than totally successful due to faulty intelligence and leaks which alerted the VC when an attack was being prepared. All too often a raid on an enemy concentration accomplished little as the NVA/VC were either not there in the

Right The most famous picture of the Vietnamese war. Children flee a misplaced napalm strike near Trang Bang. Phan Thim Kim Phuc (the girl at the center) suffered severe back burns but her life was saved by American doctors and her injuries were later treated by West German skin specialists. She is now living in Saigon and studying to be an English teacher.

Above Huey spraying jungle areas of the Mekong Delta with a chemical defoliant in mid-1969.

first place or had melted away before the attack began.

For the American troops, Vietnamization was a mixed blessing. On the one hand, the chances of getting killed were less but, on the other hand, the possibility of becoming a casualty in a war that everybody treated as already over, was hardly a motivation to fight. Alienation increased along with cannabis and hard-drug abuse. Rest and recuperation (R&R) leaves in Hong Kong and Thailand became a regular feature of a GI's Vietnam tour and the Pentagon went to great lengths to try and provide amusements, entertainments, and various amenities to keep up morale. For a time, Korean prostitutes were imported to compete with the bar-girls of Saigon as – at least outside the major cities – the VC recruited widely from local ladies of the night, turning them into intelligence agents and, occasionally, assassins.

Avoiding combat whenever possible became widespread and eager officers who were anxious for combat sometimes found themselves in danger from their own men. "Fragging" (from "fragmentation grenade") became a catch phrase for killing an officer or non-com and passing the death off as a combat casualty. One of the side benefits of the war for the Pentagon was the chance to give young career officers some

combat experience, but many who tried to take advantage of the opportunity were forced to lead sullen, uncooperative draftees and disillusioned professional troops who threatened to be as much danger to their commanders as they were to the enemy. Brutality became fairly widespread. There were numerous incidents of rape and of GIs collecting VC heads or ears out of simple boredom.

It is a common misconception that the American troops didn't fight well in Vietnam. The truth is that when locked into head-to-head combat with the NVA/VC, the vast majority of US soldiers and Marines fought with a courage, discipline, and professionalism that not only surprised the enemy but soundly defeated him nearly every time. It was the endless waiting and the small, often fruitless, but nevertheless risky patrols that generated indifference, hostility, and alienation. Nobody wanted to get killed for nothing.

Even in Johnson's day, there was growing criticism of what looked to be an overly generous dishing out of medals simply as morale boosters and for the propaganda value at home. It wasn't that the medals weren't earned but rather that the higher ones such as the Congressional Medal of Honor were occasionally awarded for acts of heroism that would perhaps

not have qualified in earlier wars. One Special Forces non-com on a "pathfinder" patrol scouting out a landing zone for a helicopter assault force, suddenly found himself surrounded by hidden VC. He managed to shoot his way out and to alert the incoming helicopters. "They told me I was a hero and had saved the mission," he said. "They gave me the Military Cross but all I did was panic and manage to save my butt. They were shooting at me so what was I supposed to do but shoot back?" On another patrol, the same non-com and his squad stayed the night in a Vietnamese village. "During the night, I happened to catch sight of a mortar hidden under some stuff in the hut I was sleeping in," he said, "but I didn't even bother to report it as the family I was staying with were friendly and seemed like decent people. Everybody was sick of the war and why should I bother to get them into trouble?

"Everything got to be a bit of a sick joke. Sometimes our convoys paid some sort of road taxes to local officials but, half the time, it was the VC and we all knew it. Another time we gave a lift to what we thought were some ARVN but we found out later that they were VC. Nobody said anything because we would just have made trouble for ourselves. Most of us just wanted to get home alive and didn't give much of a damn about the ARVN or

Above A helicopter patrols a free-fire zone looking for VC/NVA with special equipment for "people sniffing" – infra-red detectors and sensors detecting the smallest sound.

Left Men of the Royal Australian Regiment on ambush patrol in the Nui Thi Vai Hills.

Right Trooper of the Royal Australian
Regiment helps guide in a helicopter.

Left ARVN helicopter assault force lands some 15 miles inside Laos during Operation *Lam Son*.

the VC. If nobody gave us any trouble, we didn't see any reason to give them any." This sort of cynicism was present almost from the beginning but was greatly intensified by the process of Vietnamization. The war was now officially Vietnam's to fight. Let them get on with it.

Operations by the US 9th Division in 1969 swept the northern parts of the Mekong Delta as part of a massive clean-up campaign known as the "Accelerated Pacification Program". In the central highlands, similar operations by the Marines, the American Division, and South Korean troops reduced VC activity in the area to a minimum. Enemy corps were defeated and VC-held villages were destroyed, their populations joining the large numbers of homeless refugees. In September, the Delta became the responsibility of the ARVN with back-up from US air-power. Whole areas once under VC domination now came under Government control for the first time as insurgent activity dropped to a minimum. The VCI ceased to exist or fled to Cambodia or went deeply underground to await better days. Caught between the Army's sweeps, and Operation *Phoenix's* attacks, the VC – already trying to recover from the Tet Offensive's losses – found itself on the retreat in many of the areas it had formerly controlled.

At the same time, hit-and-run raids from NVA/VC sanctuaries in Laos and Cambodia increased and several US

operations north of Saigon, and near Danang, were aimed at smashing these invaders. One of 1969's most controversial battles occurred in the A Shau Valley close to the Laotian border. In May, the 101st Airborne attacked entrenched NVA/VC on Hill 937 – or at it was nicknamed, "Hamburger Hill" – for six days. It took nine separate assaults before the enemy was finally overrun but – after all the effort – the troops were soon withdrawn. The whole battle seemed a pointless waste of life and the hill of no strategic value whatsoever. The NVA/VC had dug in seemingly just to lure the Americans into a battle for the sake of having a battle, and the US commanders seem to have taken up the challenge just because the enemy was there. This sort of combat was useful to the NVA/VC who were trying to weaken American resolve but pointless for a Washington trying to minimize casualties and convince the US public that the war was being wound-down and that lives were not being squandered needlessly.

Laos and Cambodia

The problem of NVA/VC sanctuaries in Laos and Cambodia had been an irritant to the US commanders from the very beginning. Westmoreland had wanted to attack them directly but he was always overruled by the White House or the Secretary of Defence. By 1969, however, the build-up of NVA/VC

Above Burning a hole in the foliage. Four 50-gallon drums of JP-4 fuel were placed by a "Mad Dog" helicopter cargo flight and ignited by a second helicopter gun-ship firing its mini-guns.

in Laos and Cambodia had reached major proportions as the enemy abandoned its policy of trying to defeat the US Army in direct confrontations. There was also the question of supplies reaching the enemy through the Cambodian port of Sihanoukville – the so-called Sihanoukville trail. The military had long maintained that this was a major NVA/VC supply route but the idea was (incorrectly) rejected by the CIA. Eastern Cambodia was also supposed to contain the enemy's political and military command headquarters known as the Central Office for South Vietnam or COSVN. From his first days in office, Nixon was determined not to let these major bases flourish unchallenged and he approved a secret bombing campaign that was to prove a long prelude to invasion a year later.

Officially both Cambodia and Laos were neutral and had been so since the last days of French rule in Indochina, but it was often neutrality in name only. From the mid-1950s, Laos was a battleground between three warring factions: the communist Pathet Lao supported by North Vietnam, China, and the USSR; neutralist forces led by the country's premier, Prince Souvanna Phouma; and, third, a US-backed Laotian Army led by General Phoumi Nosavan. Fighting – chiefly around the Plaine des Jarres – saw shifting changes of fortune on all sides as each battled to capture control of the fragile coalition government. In December 1959, the pro-Western faction gained the upper hand and Washington looked the winner in the battle-by-proxy for Laos. Just under a year later, however, a young army captain, Kong Lee, in command of an army parachute battalion, seized the capital, Vientiane, in a semi-coup. He accused the US of rampant, old-fashioned colonialism and demanded the government's return to a neutralist stance.

The possibility of a major confrontation between the Soviet Union and the United States over Laos looked increasingly likely as both sides stepped up their military aid to the embattled country's various factions. The Royal Laotian Army moved against Lee's forces in Vientiane and, due mainly to a long-running artillery duel, over 1,500 civilians were killed in a battle that devastated large parts of the city. Lee finally retreated and soon joined forces with the Pathet Lao near the Plaine des Jarres. In May 1962, Nosavan moved the US supported troops against the Pathet Lao near the North

Vietnamese border but a relief mission by the NVA shattered his army and he was forced to accept a new neutralist, coalition government which included communist elements. For a time, it was the possibility of a major war in Laos that captured US headlines rather than Vietnam.

Neither the Soviet Union nor America wanted to go to war over Laos and, in May 1961, they agreed to make the country truly neutral. Nosavan's 1962 campaign against the Pathet Lao was a more-or-less independent move and his defeat assured the country's neutralist government. North Vietnam's chief concern was to secure the Laotian portions of the Ho Chi Minh Trail, and having the country officially declared neutral suited Hanoi's purposes. Hanoi continued to fund the Pathet Lao as an arm of North Vietnamese policy aimed both at an eventual communist takeover of Laos and as back-up force which could help secure the Trail's vital communication lines for a war in the South. Although practical politics had led everybody to accept a neutral Laos, the CIA and the North Vietnamese did not intend to let matters rest.

The covert war in Laos dates from this time. The CIA backed the Meo tribesmen while the North Vietnamese used the Kha tribe and the Pathet Lao, although Hanoi was forced to send in regular troops in order to secure the Ho Chi Minh trail. The drug trade made a curious background to this proxy war. Opium cultivation is practically a national cash crop in Laos and among the Meo tribes. Because of its close involvement with the Meo, the CIA found itself with a large say in the local drug traffic. Cargo shipments leaving Laos aboard Air America (the Agency's front airline at the time) reportedly often included raw opium. Local CIA operatives also seem to have made deliberate efforts to influence the market as a means of dominating large parts of the regional rural economy. In Vietnam, the VC rapidly moved into the heroin trade both as a source of income and to encourage drug abuse among the American forces. It is typical of the tortuous complexity of the Vietnam war that at least some of the hard drugs reaching the GIs were indirectly supplied by the CIA.

Cambodia was granted full independence by the French in late 1954 under the leadership of King Norodom Sihanouk who — if nothing else — was a genuine nationalist. In his earlier political

Above US Forward Air Controller (FAC) flying out of Pleiku. FACs were Air Force officers assigned to 01E "Bird-Dog" aircraft patrolling over the Vietnamese countryside in a search for VC/NVA forces as targets for air-strikes. The role was a liaison co-ordinator between the ground forces and the Air Force.

struggles with the French, Sihanouk had become a willing puppet of the Japanese and, after being deposed as head of state in a 1970 coup, danced to Peking's tune in a vain effort to get himself back into power. Sihanouk abdicated in 1955 to head a semi-socialist political coalition but became Head of State again in June 1960. Cambodia left SEATO in 1956 and Sihanouk tried a precarious balancing act between East and West in an effort to keep his country out of the wars that were raging over the rest of Indochina. On balance, his policies showed a distinct hostility toward the West and a corresponding lean toward the communist block. In 1963, Cambodia ended its aid ties with Washington and, in May 1965, it broke off diplomatic relations with the United States altogether in protest over American bombing raids on NVA/VC positions in eastern parts of the country.

Like Laos, Cambodia was riddled with various right-wing, neutralist, and communist factions who were soon funded and exploited by the CIA and the NVA/VC in preparation for a covert war. The communist insurgents – soon known as the Khmer Rouge – established intimate links with the VC and with North Vietnamese agents; the CIA concentrated on a number of right-wing factions and, in particular, the Khmer Seri. A section of the Cambodian Army headed by Defence Minister and – after 1966 – Prime Minister Marshall Lon Nol proved ideal allies and overthrew Sihanouk in a March 1970 coup. Khmer Rouge guerrilla activity (particularly in the province of Battambang) during the early 1960s led Sihanouk to quash the insurgents with a ruthless efficiency but he did little or nothing to try to stop the increasing use of Cambodia's eastern areas by the NVA/VC as the war heated up after 1965. While Sihanouk's meagre army may have been able to do little about the NVA/VC sanctuaries, the so-called Sihanoukville Trail was another matter. Ships docking at the Port of Sihanoukville were unloading vast amounts of military supplies destined for the NVA/VC. Loaded aboard trucks and other local transport, convoys of arms passed through the Cambodian countryside until they reached the NVA/VC bases along the Vietnamese border. Had Sihanouk wished to practice the precious neutrality that he tried so hard to project in public, it would have been fairly easy for him to cut this supply line. Instead he seems to have encouraged it and it is probably only the Pentagon-CIA quarrel on the relative importance of this route that prevented direct US intervention in Cambodia at some point before the 1970 invasion.

After Johnson committed American troops to fight the Vietnam war, covert operations in Cambodia increased. Missions using Cambodian mercenaries, local tribesmen, and specially trained South Vietnamese were aimed at harassing NVA/VC communications and supply lines along the Ho Chi Minh Trail and at kidnapping individuals for questioning. But these were spoiling and intelligence gathering operations and never reached the scale of the secret war in Laos. The NVA/VC's massive build-up in the border areas of both Laos and Cambodia became an increasing irritation and Nixon launched his secret bombing campaign in early 1969. But even this was not enough to break up the enemy's growing dependence on its sanctuaries in supposedly neutral territory and Nixon began to take a closer look at long-standing Pentagon plans for a major US invasion.

One of the main attractions of a Cambodian border

crossing to Nixon was the idea of capturing COSVN. Like Johnson, Nixon tended to see strategic issues in rather simple terms and taking the enemy's high-command looked irresistible to him. It would also be a brilliant public relations exercise. Nixon and some leading elements of the military saw COSVN as a sort of NVA/VC Pentagon in the wilds of Cambodia which, if taken, would chop the head off communist insurgency in Indochina. Others – and the CIA in particular – pointed out that the leading communist political and military cadre moved from place to place as necessity demanded and weren't based in some sort of Cambodian office-block, but Nixon couldn't be shaken and he used the elimination of COSVN as an important justification when he announced the US invasion of Cambodia to the American public. When COSVN proved to be an illusion, and it was obvious that the NVA/VC commanders had slipped away, Nixon was reportedly far from amused and felt that he had been made to look foolish.

During March 1970, Cambodian mobs attacked the North Vietnamese Embassy and the headquarters of the Provisional Revolutionary Government of Vietnam (a political branch of the NLF) in the capital, Phnom Penh. Elsewhere mobs attacked Vietnamese residing in the Cambodian countryside. The demonstrations had been largely stirred up by the pro-Western Prime Minister, Lon Nol, and many of the rioters were Cambodian troops in civilian dress. On March 13th, Sihanouk left Cambodia for visits to the USSR and China but – five days later – was informed that he had been deposed in a quick coup. Faced with a rightist takeover in Cambodia, the NVA quickly moved in to drive Lon Nol's troops away from the base areas along the Vietnamese border. Nixon responded rapidly to the deteriorating situation and gave the go-ahead for an ARVN foray across the border.

On April 14th, the ARVN drove into Cambodia, catching the NVA partly by surprise, while the US command prepared for a major offensive. Following massive bombardments from waves of B-52s, some 15,000 US and ARVN troops invaded Cambodia on May 1st. The attacks were directed against three areas of eastern Cambodia known to have heavy concentrations of NVA/VC bases and supply depots: the "Parrot's Beak", the "Fish Hook", and the "Bulge" – nicknames given by military intelligence and taken from the general geographical shape of each area. The Parrot's Beak lay to the west of Saigon and the Fish Hook to the northwest. At first, NVA/VC resistance was light and US/ARVN forces driving on the Cambodian town of Mimot in the northwestern part of the Parrot's Beak reached their objective within three days and captured large amounts of communist supplies. Further north in the Fish Hook was the town of Snoul which US forces reached on May 7th after some heavy fighting.

Near Snoul, US troops found what became tagged "The City": a vast maze of tunnels, bunkers, and enemy store-rooms. The retreating NVA/VC had abandoned The City and, with it, over a million rounds of ammunition, some twenty tons of plastic explosives, hundreds of weapons, and over 60,000 pounds of rice. Many believed that COSVN had been over-run although Saigon described The City only as a major NVA/VC staging area and supply base. COSVN and The City were probably pretty much the same thing but the enemy cadre had long since fled somewhere else. At other locations in the Fish

Above Clouds of dust envelop ARVN troops as they prepare for an airlift into Laos during Operation *Lam Som.* The kick-off point is the old Marine base at Khe Sanh, scene of a 77-day siege in 1968.

Left US military advisor Captain George Kish helps evacuees towards a waiting helicopter during the fighting at Kontum in April 1972.

185

Above A CH-47A Chinook unloads an assault team on a mountain ridge during Operation *White Wing*.

Top right Vietnamese strategic hamlet in the Mekong Delta in 1970.

Right Troops of the 1st Infantry Division move up on VC positions during a search-and-destroy sweep of the Xa Cam area in early 1966.

Hook, hundreds of tons of enemy ammunition and other supplies were captured as US forces overran previously untouched base camps. Operations in the Parrot's Beak actually began on April 29th, when the ARVN moved in prematurely, but their incursion was backed up by a second US drive into the Se Sam Valley on May 4th. Results were disappointing compared to the enemy materials captured in the Fish Hook but several thousand NVA/VC were reported killed.

Nixon's Cambodian adventure aroused a storm of public and Congressional protest at home. Nixon quickly announced that US objectives were limited to wiping out the NVA/VC sanctuaries in the border area and he promised a quick withdrawal. The President claimed the invasion to be one of the war's most successful operations, and in many ways it was. As much as fifty per cent of the enemy's supplies had been captured and his casualties were high. But the political effects in Washington were more far-reaching. Angered by what seemed to be a deliberate widening of the conflict, anti-war elements in Congress succeeded in getting enough support to repeal the Gulf of Tonkin Resolution on June 24th and, as the last US troops crossed back into Vietnam on June 30th, the Senate passed the Cooper-Church Amendment which put a block on any further

American military ventures in Cambodia or aid to Lon Nol without Congressional consent. The last ARVN units left the Parrot's Beak on July 22nd and Lon Nol effectively stood alone in the face of a growing tide of Khmer Rouge insurgency actively encouraged by Hanoi and Peking.

Having suffered a reverse in Cambodia, Hanoi began a rapid re-supply of forces and material to the South. American attention immediately concentrated on NVA positions and communication lines in Laos. Operation *Lam Son-719* was scheduled for late January and early February 1971 and was aimed at the NVA staging area and supply base at Tchepone in Laos where success would choke off the Ho Chi Minh Trail. The main feature of the operation was that it was to be the ARVN's show. Apart from air support, American participation in Lam Son was to be restricted to a drive on January 31st from Quang Tri to the old, now abandoned, Marine Base at Khe Sanh. Khe Sanh would then be converted into the chief staging area for the ARVN drive into Laos itself which was scheduled for February 8th. Reaching Tchepone, the ARVN would consolidate their positions, destroy enemy supply depots, and establish fire-bases which could be used in future operations against the Ho Chi Minh Trail and NVA communications.

Above Two members of A Company, 1st Battalion, 14th Infantry make a wary approach to a VC bunker during Operation *Wayne Thrust* in January 1970.

Above NVA regulars battle the ARVN in the Quang Tri area. Note the US M-16 rifles beside the casualties lying on the ground.

Despite intelligence reports indicating the presence of over 20,000 NVA regulars in the area and clear indications that Hanoi would bitterly contest ARVN moves against the northern positions of the Ho Chi Minh Trail, the South Vietnamese leaders seem to have expected a sort of one-sided walkover on the lines of Cambodia. Things went pretty much as planned until some four days after the jump-off, when the ARVN infantry and armor driving west from Khc Sanh to Tchepone began encountering increasing NVA ambushes and harassing attacks. Three days later, the ARVN drive had ground to a halt and the NVA had begun attacking the supply routes feeding the advancing South Vietnamese. The NVA moved in on recently established ARVN fire-bases and, by February 22nd, two of them — Ranger Base South and Ranger Base North — were surrounded by rings of troops and anti-aircraft batteries ready to prevent re-supply or relief. The ARVN rangers had to fight their way out with heavy casualties on both sides. A few days after that, NVA regulars with tank support enveloped an elite ARVN airborne unit at Base Objective-31 and, in repeated attacks, killed several hundred

ARVN soldiers, and forced the defenders to abandon the position. After deciding that the moves in Laos were not a feint to draw the NVA away before launching an attack across the DMZ, Hanoi ordered three divisions south to encircle and trap the ARVN in Laos. General Hoang Xuan Lam, the ARVN commander, was now faced with being cut off by the oncoming monsoon now only a couple of weeks away, but decided to have a final try at Tchepone. American helicopters put the 1st ARVN Infantry Division down in three separate landing zones in the Tchepone area and — with clearing weather — B-52s began bombing enemy positions around the town.

In the largest airborne assault of the war, 120 helicopters flew two ARVN battalions from Khe Sanh to the outskirts of Tchepone but, when the troops entered the town, they found that the enemy had slipped away. NVA material captured or destroyed included over 100 tanks, seventy-five heavy guns, several hundred tons of ammunition, and about 25,000 pounds of rice. The ARVN withdrawal began on schedule on March 10th, but soon verged on disaster after Giap's counter offensive

began two days later. ARVN positions were hit with artillery and rocket barrages and then NVA infantry and armor moved in. Within two days, the ARVN front was collapsing and US helicopters had to stage an emergency rescue.

Helicopters coming in to the landing zones flew through a wall of anti-aircraft and small arms fire and – touching down – were met by swarms of panicked ARVN soldiers clamoring to get aboard. Helicopters lifted off dangerously overloaded and occasionally had to fire into the crowd to keep more and more ARVN from trying to fight their way aboard. On March 22nd, ARVN Marines at fire-base Alpha were attacked by the NVA and, after some four hours of intense fighting, US helicopters once again had to fly in to evacuate the defenders before they were completely overrun. It was the last battle of Operation *Lam Son*-719. Officially all ARVN had been withdrawn from Laos and official statements from Saigon described the operation as a complete success. Unofficially, however, many ARVN had simply vanished into the Laotian countryside and the prospects for Vietnamization were less than promising.

The ARVN had employed their best commanders and their best troops including Rangers, Marines, and the elite Airborne Division, which, up to then, had served as a battle-arm of the Saigon Government in its quarrels with Buddhists, students, and other dissidents. The ARVN fought well and often with great courage. The main objective had been reached albeit in a last-ditch effort that proved disappointing. Something like 10,000 NVA had died in combat with the ARVN and a similar number were killed by US air-strikes. The ARVN, on the other hand, suffered nearly 4,000 killed and just over 5,000 wounded. Giap had been willing to accept large casualties in order to annihilate the ARVN invasion forces and, had it not been for the American rescue mission, he would almost certainly have succeeded.

In May 1971, the ARVN made a second invasion of Laos into the Ashau Valley but – after a month of inconclusive fighting – got nowhere. Another ARVN drive into the Parrot's Beak of Cambodia was mauled by the NVA near Snoul. As *Lam Son* drew to a close, the NVA took the offensive in the Central

Above North Vietnamese POW captures in the last stages of the 1972 offensive.

189

Highlands and south of the DMZ. Khe Sanh was abandoned once again during April and, by summer, traffic down the Ho Chi Minh Trail had increased to levels far above those of earlier in the year. Desertion from ARVN units jumped by about fifty per cent during 1971 to some 12,000 a month and there was a growing bitterness over Vietnamization. To many Vietnamese, Vietnamization simply meant an American willingness to fight to the last ARVN.

Although Washington wouldn't admit it publicly, the ARVN's ability to fight the war on its own was now in considerable doubt. Many believe that Nixon's chief purpose in the Cambodian and Laotian operations was to send Hanoi a signal suggesting that – unless a successful peace agreement could be reached – he would fight a wider war. Such a war could have included (as some South Vietnamese officials had been loudly and pointedly calling for) limited ARVN invasions north of the DMZ backed-up by massive US air-strikes. US troop withdrawals were continuing along the lines called for by Vietnamization and by the end of 1971, American forces in Vietnam stood at under 160,000 compared with just over 339,000 the previous year. Nixon made clear that he was not prepared to reintroduce any of these into Indochina.

Kissinger's efforts to build detente with the Soviet Union were beginning to pay dividends and his highly secret approaches to Peking had paid off in an invitation for Nixon to visit China in what was probably the most dramatic diplomatic event of the early Seventies. For their own reasons, both giants of the communist world wanted better relations with Washington and this gave Nixon a freedom of action in Vietnam that Johnson would never have dreamed of. Earlier fears that

Left VC prisoners captured in the Fish Hook region of Cambodia await transit to a South Vietnamese base for interrogation.

Below Members of the 5th ARVN Cavalry aid civilians fleeing from an NVA attack on Bien Hoa in March 1969.

mining the ports of North Vietnam, intensive bombing in the areas of Hanoi and Haiphong, or even a limited invasion north of the DMZ would bring in Chinese troops, no longer applied. As long as Washington did nothing that threatened to topple the regime in Hanoi itself, Moscow and Peking, other than the obligatory outburst of anti-American propaganda, were likely to turn a blind eye to whatever Nixon did in Indochina.

The 1972 NVA Offensive

The thaw in East-West relations led Kissinger to believe that the North Vietnamese would be willing to relax their conditions for a cease-fire. Until the summer of 1971, Hanoi's chief negotiator, Le Duc Tho, had steadfastly refused to consider any withdrawal of NVA forces already in the South (or in the neighboring eastern provinces of Laos and Cambodia) unless the US agreed first to the unconditional removal of South Vietnam's President Thieu. Thieu, who had been returned to office in a one man election in October, was not, needless to say, prepared to go and in any case at that time he enjoyed what was more-or-less Washington's full backing.

Despite Thieu's obvious faults, democracy in South Vietnam was one of the main planks in Nixon's Indochina policy. He sought not only peace with honor, but also the establishment in Saigon of a non-communist, democratic government which at least resembled the Republic it claimed to be. Thieu's government was clearly corrupt and – despite a growing appearance of legitimacy – was highly unpopular with large segments of the Vietnamese population. Hanoi and the NLF had a candidate list of more acceptable Presidents which included "Big" Minh who, since being thrown out of the ruling military junta after the anti-Diem coup, had been playing a role of semi-neutrality, as an elder statesman waiting for something to do. Washington, however, was opposed to any sort of coalition or even neutralist government which shared power with the NLF. This would smack of defeat and be unacceptable to America's right-wing politicians and public. Thieu shared these opinions and occasionally took a harder line against such a settlement than either Nixon or Kissinger.

Left The destroyer *USS Everett F. Larson* fires a salvo from two of her five-inch guns on NVA positions south of the DMZ.

Left and far left The guided-missile, light cruiser *USS Oklahoma City* uses her six-inch guns in support of ARVN ground operations against the NVA south of the DMZ. Between April and May 1972, *USS Oklahoma City* fired close to 6,000 rounds at NVA positions on the shore.

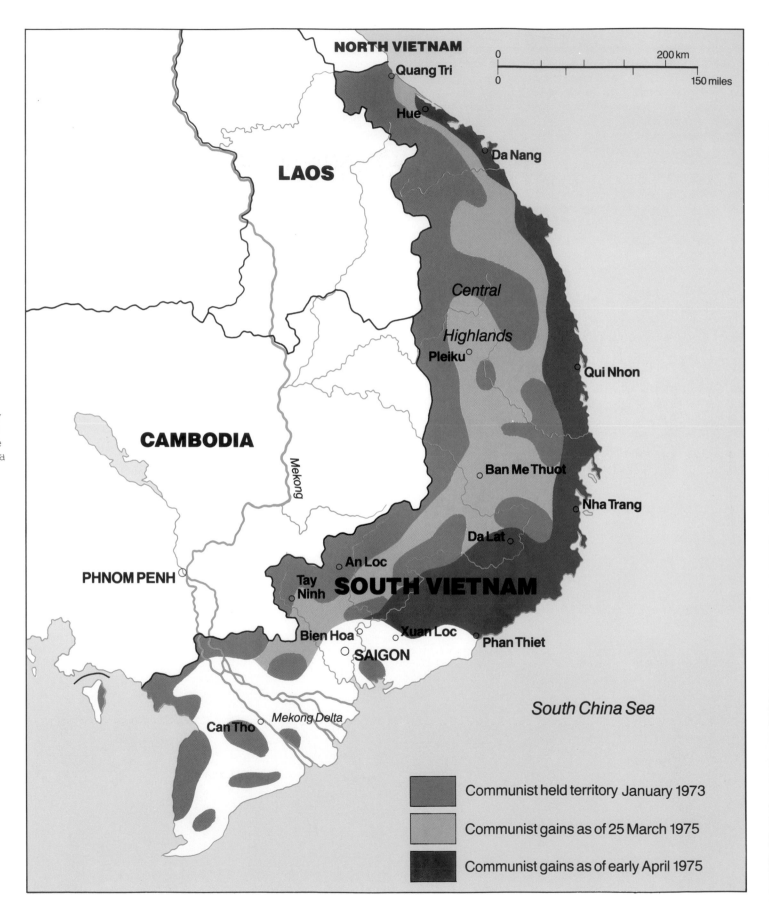

Right The fall of South Vietnam, January 1973–April 1975. As of the January 1973 cease-fire, the VC/NVA held about one third of the country but controlled only a small percentage of the population.

NORTH VIETNAM

Quang Tri

Hue

Da Nang

LAOS

Central

Highlands

Pleiku

Qui Nhon

CAMBODIA

Mekong

Ban Me Thuot

Nha Trang

Da Lat

An Loc

PHNOM PENH

Tay Ninh

SOUTH VIETNAM

Bien Hoa

Xuan Loc

SAIGON

Phan Thiet

South China Sea

Can Tho

Mekong Delta

Communist held territory January 1973

Communist gains as of 25 March 1975

Communist gains as of early April 1975

Towards the end of 1971, Kissinger softened on his insistence that NVA troops be withdrawn from the South in the hope of a breakthrough in the peace talks. America's new-found detente with the USSR and China, he thought, could well include a new spirit of cooperation from Hanoi. But the North Vietnamese saw Kissinger's move more as a desperation gambit arising from the recent ARVN debacles in the land war. The failures and weaknesses of Vietnamization were obvious in Hanoi as was Nixon's political need to get a settlement in time for the forthcoming 1972 election.

Instead of striking a bargain, Hanoi opted for a military solution. The NVA had received massive supplies of the most modern Soviet weaponry including tanks, long-range guns, and surface-to-air (SAM) missiles. A massive offensive, Hanoi reasoned, would have three distinct results; it would destroy the ARVN once and for all; it would force Washington into a quick settlement on terms favorable to North Vietnam; and, finally, a successful offensive would leave the NVA in control of large areas of the South from which the final conquest could be prepared after the Americans had gone away. Once again, Hanoi miscalculated.

Giap planned an offensive on three main fronts and enormous amounts of equipment were moved down the Ho Chi Minh Trail to the edge of the DMZ. The first prong of the attack would drive across the DMZ towards Dong Ha and Quang Tri and on to Hue. In the middle prong of the attack NVA/VC forces would move across from Cambodia and make a push on An Loc, Loc Ninh, and Quan Loi; Highway-13 which linked the region with Saigon would be secured at the same time. The third front would drive into the Central Highlands aimed at capturing Pleiku, Kontum, and Dak To as well as the roadways linking the highlands with the coast. Success would not only give the NVA control of the highlands but would effectively cut South Vietnam in two. Elsewhere smaller attacks were planned as spoiling

Below North Vietnamese infantry move across a river during their 1972 invasion of the South. The invasion was defeated only after bitter fighting throughout South Vietnam and the intensive application of US airpower in support of the ARVN.

Above North Vietnamese supply vehicles move down the Ho Chi Minh Trail. Although the camouflage wouldn't be likely to fool a patrolling US fixed-wing gun-ship or low-flying aircraft, it might deceive a high-flying reconnaissance aircraft.

operations or to cut off ARVN reinforcements from the main battlefields.

To a large extent, the 1972 NVA offensive caught the US by surprise. Reconnaissance flights noted considerable activity in North Vietnamese supply depots, the construction of new roads and fuel pipe-lines leading to the DMZ, and a build-up of forces in Cambodia, the highlands near Pleiku, and the DMZ itself. But despite such warnings, Kissinger, until it was too late, apparently refused to believe that Hanoi was going to try for a full-scale military solution rather than a diplomatic settlement. If there was to be major NVA activity, US intelligence thought it would come in the Central Highlands but – unlike President Thieu and his General Staff – did not predict a drive across the DMZ. NVA build-ups in the highlands and the DMZ were bombed in mid-February but both the Tet New Year and Nixon's historic visit to China passed without serious NVA/VC provocations. US troop withdrawals continued. By the end of March, American

forces in Vietnam totalled 95,000 and, more significantly, US Air Force personnel numbered only 20,000 compared to some 60,000 at the high point of American involvement.

Giap's offensive began in the early morning hours of Good Friday, March 30th, with a massive artillery barrage along South Vietnam's northern border and, within a few hours, up to 40,000 troops and 200 tanks moved across the DMZ. The northernmost ARVN fire-bases fell quickly and Dong Ha was overrun on April 28th. A lingering monsoon hampered American airpower which was being rapidly reinforced with men and planes from US bases around the world. For the first time, Giap employed massive concentrations of armor – mainly Soviet-built T-34 and T-54 tanks – in its traditional military role. Previous NVA tactics had included a heavy emphasis on camouflage, night movement, and entrenchment to counter US airpower, but now Giap's forces were attempting a full war of movement in their drive on Quang Tri.

Left NVA artillerymen man their Soviet-built guns. The Russian 130mm gun made its first major appearance in Vietnam during the 1972 invasion and – with a range of seventeen miles – it was particularly effective.

Below Refugees fleeing towards Danang from Hue and Quang Tri as the NVA moves south. The exodus began at Quang Tri but panic quickly spread to Hue and the roads of South Vietnam's northernmost areas became flooded with frightened civilians disrupting what ARVN military planning remained.

They were helped by the addition of Soviet SAM missiles which came south for the first time and by abundant anti-aircraft weapons including new 85mm and 100mm Russian guns. Another new addition to the NVA's now abundant arsenal was the portable Soviet SA-7 *Strela* surface-to-air missile. Designed to be carried by a man and fired rather like a rifle, the missile was equipped with an infra-red homing device which, locking on to the heat from an aircraft's engines, would track it until it made contact. SAM missiles work by the same principle but this was the first time US pilots had faced the man-carried version. The SA-7 was a particular danger to helicopters and slow-flying aircraft at lower altitudes.

Another Soviet weapon which Giap brought south was the AT-3 anti-tank wire-guided missile. Like the SA-7, the AT-3 was designed to be carried by an infantryman who selects a target and fires the missile at it. Instead of an infra-red homing device, however, the missile is guided to its target by the infantryman who sends course-correcting signals down wires trailing from its tail. The AT-3 and the SA-7 were the first examples of a new generation of weapons known as precision-guided munitions (PGM) which had been under development for some time in both the USSR and the USA. They are distinguished by guidance technology assuring a high degree of accuracy and, consequently, a high probability of killing what they're fired at. An expression used to describe PGM is: "If you can see it, you can kill it."

During air-strikes on the invading NVA and over the skies of North Vietnam, US aircraft would be trying out their own PGM – bombs which locked-on to their targets by means of a small TV camera or onto a laser beam illuminating the aim-point. Having

Left and below The US B-52 bomber. Designed as a strategic nuclear bomber in the late Fifties, the B-52 – when converted – made an excellent delivery vehicle for conventional bombs in Vietnam. When the B-52s were sent over North Vietnam in 1972, the older models, which lacked the most up-to-date electronic countermeasures equipment, were seriously threatened by communist anti-aircraft and SAM missile fire. The B-52 is still in service and remains the back-bone of the nuclear delivery fleet. It is only now being partly replaced by the B-1 strategic bomber.

Above North Vietnamese anti-aircraft crew watch for US bombers near Hanoi.

locked onto the laser beam, the bomb simply follows it down to strike the targets with a pin-point accuracy previously unknown in gravity weapons which are just dropped on a best-guess trajectory. When they were introduced into Vietnam, laser and TV-guided bombs proved devastatingly effective and no more so than in the fighting of 1972. PGM were used against NVA tanks in the South and to hit targets in North Vietnam which had either eluded destruction up to then or were considered too close to civilian facilities to warrant the risk of using less accurate weapons.

Vietnam was the first test-run of PGM under actual combat conditions for both East and West but a year later, the new weapons were to get a second try-out in the 1973 Arab-Israeli war. Within the first days of the Mid East blood-letting, the effects of PGM were so dramatic that few doubted that the face of modern warfare had changed forever. In the years since Vietnam, PGM techonology and the related fields of electronic countermeasures, surveillance, and intelligence have advanced to the point that the weapons of only a decade ago seem primitive by comparison. Soon we will reach the point where robot drones overfly battlefields to send back pictures to commanders dozens or even hundreds of miles away where targets will be selected and attacked by a diverse range of semi-intelligent PGM. The drones themselves will illuminate targets for laser-guided artillery shells or rockets.

The unique use of helicopters in Vietnam has already been mentioned but they found a new role during the 1972 offensive. American UH-1B helicopters were fitted out with US TOW (tube-launched, optically-tracked, wire-guided) anti-tank missiles and sent in against NVA armor. Sighting a tank or NVA truck, the helicopter would swoop down to close range, launch the missile, and fly off before enemy fire could bring it down. On May 26th, an NVA attack was on the verge of over-running the embattled ARVN defenders at Kontum but TOW-armed helicopters took out ten tanks and two machine-gun positions to turn the tide at almost the last minute. This anti-armor role is now a permanent fixture of helicopter operations and the latest generation of "fire-and-forget" tank-killing missiles do not even require an operator to steer them to the target after launch; once launched, the warhead's guidance system locks on to its victim and homes in by itself.

Another innovation of the Vietnam war was the fixed-wing gunship. US Air Force AC-119s, AC-130 Hercules, and AC-47s (the famous Dakota troop-transport) were fitted with side-firing 7.62mm, 20mm, or 40mm weapons. The 7.62mm weapons were multi-barrel, gatling-design-type machine-guns capable of firing thousands of rounds per minute. With exotic names such as "Puff-the-Magic-Dragon", Dakotas with three multi-barrel machine-guns firing through the door and two side windows would fly in tight circles devastating the ground below in a hail of

This page Soviet-built SAM missiles in North Vietnam. The battle between SAM missiles and US electronic countermeasures was the beginning of what is now one of the most vital parts of modern technological warfare.

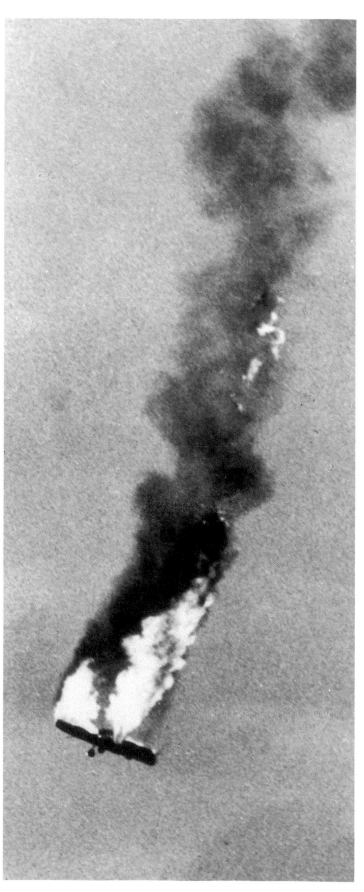

This page North Vietnamese anti-aircraft batteries score hits on US aircraft over Hanoi in 1972.

bullets. During the 1972 offensive, fixed-wing gun-ships would patrol over contested areas for many hours at a time. Spotting likely targets or informed of the enemy's whereabouts by ground radio, the gun-ship would riddle the position. The technique proved invaluable in breaking up NVA/VC attacks during the bitter fighting for cities like Pleiku, An Loc, and Kontum.

Before the 1972 offensive, the vast majority of fixed-wing gunship missions were flown out of Thailand to harass traffic on the Ho Chi Minh Trail in Laos and Cambodia. The planes were fitted with a sophisticated optical night-sighting equipment and infra-red detectors to sense-out truck engines and — in more open areas — body heat. A recent addition to the arsenal was the AC-130 armed with a 105 mm howitzer which — unlike planes carrying the smaller 20mm and 40mm guns — was capable of destroying heavy armor and fortifications. When the NVA launched its Easter attacks, part of the gunship fleet was moved from Thailand to South Vietnam where the planes played a vital role in the defence of the Central Highlands and Binh Long Province. Fixed-wing gunships are fairly vulnerable to surface-to-air missiles and several were damaged or downed during the 1972 offensive. Unlike many of the military innovations of the Vietnam War, the fixed-wing gunship's future role may be somewhat limited.

By the beginning of May, NVA pressure on Quang Tri had reached critical proportions and the ARVN began falling back in what was to become a disorderly rout. Orders were issued to evacuate American personnel and the ARVN commanders (with a couple of notable exceptions) began their own withdrawal. Within hours, Highway-1 leading south to Hue was filled with retreating ARVN soldiers and countless abandoned vehicles. Thieu rushed ARVN reinforcements to Hue which was on the verge of collapse as a secondary panic set in among the defenders and the civilian population. US and ARVN airplanes sought out and attacked bridges, heavy guns, and tanks with ruthless efficiency. Some 285 NVA tanks were destroyed in the battles around Quang Tri and Hue between April 1st and August 15th. Laser-guided bombs were used with great effect but the majority of the kills were still from tactical aircraft carrying old-fashioned gravity bombs.

A defence line was rapidly drawn up along the south bank of My Chanh River north of Hue. On May 20th, NVA tanks and troops crossed the My Chanh and breached the defences but, after days of heavy fighting, were forced back. On May 25th, waves of NVA infantry again breached the defences but the ARVN held the line and, following intense hand-to-hand fighting along the whole front, pushed the enemy back across the river after four days. Late June saw more than 20,000 ARVN launch a counter-offensive across the My Chanh. Backed by massive US B-52 and tactical air-strikes and off-shore naval bombardments, the ARVN fought their way to the suburbs of Quang Tri in the second week of July. By the end of the month, most of Quang Tri was back in ARVN hands but several NVA held out in one entrenched area until mid-September.

In the Central Highlands, two NVA divisions moved in from Cambodia and Laos to attack Dak To, Tan Canh, and Kontum. Highway-14 between Kontum and Pleiku, and Highway-19 between Pleiku and the coast were cut to isolate the beleaguered cities and bases of the highlands. Rocket fire closed

Left North Vietnamese pilots get a pre-takeoff briefing.

Below North Vietnam Mig fighters on patrol.

the Dak To airbase and the NVA soon overran a number of fire-bases in the area. Despite fierce resistance and running battles between US gun-ships and NVA tanks, Dak To fell on April 24th. Refugees fled towards Kontum but many were killed by the NVA or rounded -up and driven into the wire of attacked fire-bases as the North Vietnamese moved in behind. There was other fighting at various villages and fire-bases as the NVA moved on Kontum. At Polei Kleng, a Hercules gunship – with some back-up by tactical aircraft – managed to hold off a full NVA regiment, killing several hundred North Vietnamese in the process.

Polei Kleng finally fell on May 9th, but a number of other fire-bases managed to hold out. On May 14th, NVA infantry and tanks hit Kontum but were finally dispersed by a combination of ground-fire, tactical air-strikes, and TOW-armed helicopters. A

second, stronger attack the next day came closer to success but – despite some bad weather early on – was finally broken by the same combination of firepower. For weeks, the NVA besieged and attacked Kontum with waves of infantry and armor supported by endless artillery and rocket barrages; the enemy concentrations in turn were pounded day and night by tactical aircraft, massed B-52s, and a variety of gunships. The NVA abandoned the attack in the beginning of June but held out in the surrounding area for several weeks more. NVA entrenched positions along Highway-14 were completely cleared by the end of June to re-open the supply route to Pleiku. NVA/VC attacks in neighboring Binh Dinh Province had tremendous success at the beginning and managed to block Highway-1 running along the coast from Saigon all the way to the north. The ARVN counter-offensive commenced in July of 1972 and the whole

Below An A-4F Skyhawk prepares for launch from the attack carrier *USS Hancock.*

area cleared by the end of the summer.

The battle for An Loc began on April 2nd, with the NVA shelling Lac Long and other fire-bases in Tay Ninh Province. Two days later, the ARVN were forced to withdraw to the provincial capital where they dug in. The NVA then moved east into Bihn Long Province to join up with 5th VC Division which had slipped across the Cambodian border. The city of Loc Ninh was battered by waves of communist infantry which finally overwhelmed the defences on April 7th as the defenders – protected by overflying gunships – hacked their way through the jungle to reach safety at An Loc. At the same time, the NVA overran the nearby Quan Loi airfield and cut Highway-13 running south to Chon Thanh and Saigon. Reinforcements were rushed to An Loc as the NVA began moving in armor for a final push on the city. The first attack came on April 13th but was broken up chiefly by anti-tank rockets carried by the ARVN defenders or fired by US and South Vietnamese helicopters.

The next day, NVA/VC infantry and armor battled into the city but the attack was finally repulsed by highly coordinated air and ground fire which destroyed the attacking armor and battered concentrations of troops whenever they assembled together for massed assaults. The battle settled down to a long-running siege with NVA/VC artillery steadily shelling the hapless city into piles of rubble filled with untreated wounded. At the same time, the NVA/VC fought off an ARVN relief column trying to fight its way through on Highway-13. Supplies were dropped in by air as US and ARVN airpower continuously pounded communist positions. Following a massive artillery barrage, the NVA/VC launched a third mass attack on June 11th led by up to fifty Soviet tanks. For two days the battle raged as

Below A US Navy F-8J Crusader makes its approach for landing aboard the attack carrier *USS Bon Homme Richard.*

concentrated NVA anti-aircraft fire tried to cripple the allied air effort. Despite heavy losses, the attackers were slowly beaten back as B-52s bombed the surrounding area. Shelling and attacks continued sporadically through June but the momentum had gone out of the communist offensive. By the middle of June, An Loc had been reinforced with fresh troops and the battle was effectively over.

Once again, Giap had failed to win an all-out offensive and the army he withdrew had been battered to the point where no further major military efforts could be expected from it for some time. NVA casualties could be replaced from the North but equipment losses were another matter. As always when the Soviets supplied material, there were strings. Moscow wanted to let Nixon get his honorable peace as an aid to detente and the Russians were not prepared to actively encourage any more large-scale offensives for the immediate future. Despite the debacle at Quang Tri, the ARVN had fought well and battled the NVA to a standstill at An Loc and Kontum. To a point, Vietnamization seemed to be working and Saigon had a fighting chance to keep the NVA and VC at bay on its own.

But the VC – if no longer a direct military threat – was still a formidable power in the South and 1972 saw the position of non-communist forces in Laos and Cambodia deteriorate rapidly. Despite the ARVN's ability to fight with courage, discipline, and efficiency on its home soil, it was US airpower which broke Giap's 1972 offensive. No one – least of all the generals and Politburo members in Hanoi, Moscow, and Peking – doubted that without the American air umbrella Giap would have won the day. The question now was how long American air cover would stay. Nixon was still set on taking America out of Indochina and, as Giap's offensive began to wear down during May and June, there were definite signs of a major breakthrough in the Paris Peace Talks that put the war into its final days.

Just before visiting Moscow, Nixon announced a resumption of bombing raids on North Vietnam above the 20th parallel (the first such missions since Johnson's 1968 bombing halt). This act outraged the American anti-war movement but had the tacit understanding of the Russians. In Moscow, Kissinger offered to stop the bombing if Hanoi would drop its insistence on the removal of Thieu as a precondition to peace. In mid-June, US Intelligence in South Vietnam had passed on Kissinger's message to Hanoi with a favorable recommendation and, shortly afterwards, Peking forwarded similar advice. In short-term communist planning a reasonable peace was now advantageous but – in the long-term – the question was how to disengage America's commitment to support Saigon's war with military aid and the backing of the world's most powerful Air Force. As it turned out, the communists needn't have worried. Nixon practically did the job for them when he took the Presidency into the greatest swamp of domestic political scandal that the country had known since the 19th century.

The Air War

When Johnson gave the go-ahead for Operation *Rolling Thunder* and sent US airpower into the skies of North Vietnam, it was a very limited affair. The JCS had wanted a twelve-week campaign designed to destroy North Vietnam's lines of communication (LOC) plus certain specifically military targets such as fuel and ammunition dumps. Priority targets were the

Left US Air Force A-1H Skyraiders on a mission to bomb VC positions in the South. Piston aircraft in the age of the jet, Skyraiders were highly effective, particularly in close support of ground troops.

Right US Navy Phantom IIs operating off the attack carrier *USS Coral Sea* hit North Vietnam during the early days of the 1972 NVA Offensive.

140-mile railway linking Hanoi with southwestern China, the eighty-mile rail line running between Hanoi and southeastern China, the forty-five-mile railway connecting Hanoi and Haiphong, and the 165-mile rail-link running south from Hanoi to Thanh Hoa, Vinh, and on to the DMZ. The idea was to cut off external sources of supply coming down from China and to cripple Hanoi's ability to ship war materials to the South.

Apart from ground-support operations, airpower has three historic functions. The first is to destroy an enemy's ability to make war through the methodical bombardment of his vital industries, lines of supply, communications facilities, fuel and ammo depots, air-fields, naval bases, command headquarters, and any or all other targets supporting his ability to field and maintain an effective military machine. The second is to win air superiority by destroying, counteracting, or otherwise eliminating the enemy's ability to defend himself. Third and most controversial is breaking the enemy's will to fight. To a certain extent, this is the same function as the first but the important difference is that – fully implemented – it adds the deliberate bombing of civilian areas as part of a terror campaign aimed at destroying the general population's willingness to support the government's war.

Wars are fought for political objectives. In World War II, the goal was the unconditional surrender of Germany and Japan. As a consequence, enemy cities such as Hamburg, Dresden, and Tokyo were deliberately turned into blazing infernos while Nagasaki and Hiroshima vanished in flashes of nuclear light. But America's war with Hanoi had the extremely limited objective of

Left A North Vietnamese convoy hit by a Navy strike force off the carrier *USS Constellation* north of An Loc during the 1972 NVA offensive in the South.

Below A Walleye TV-guided bomb. The Walleye was one of the first of a new generation of Precision Guided Munitions offering an accuracy previously unheard of. In the case of the Walleye, the pilot locks the target onto a TV picture transmitted by a camera in the bomb's nose. Once released, any deviations in the bomb's glide-path are corrected to line up with the pre-programmed target.

dissuading the North Vietnamese leaders from supporting the war in the South but at the same time preserving the wider peace with China and the Soviet Union. Thus Johnson went to war in small steps and constantly faced the problem of how far each step should go. In the beginning he vetoed the JSC's twelve-week bombing campaign because it seemed too much like an all-out war which could well provoke a Chinese intervention.

Operation *Rolling Thunder* was restricted to military and LOC targets south of the 20th parallel. It was decided not to attack Hanoi's rail links with China nor to bomb even indisputably military installations above this point because of the political risk. Bombing North Vietnam's rail lines to the South and the Ho Chi Minh Trail was both an effort to inhibit the flow of supplies to the NLF and—even more—a warning to Hanoi that things could get worse if its leaders failed to cooperate. As McCone and others warned, Operation *Rolling Thunder* was far too mild and Hanoi began to cooperate only when Nixon began to make things a great deal worse and showed that he was prepared to go further.

Operation *Rolling Thunder* began on March 2nd, 1965 when US fighter-bombers destroyed the North Vietnamese ammunition storage facilities at Xom Bang while South Vietnamese planes hit the naval base at Quang Khe. NVA anti-aircraft batteries downed four US planes in what was to be a long battle for air supremacy. Two days later, US Air Force planes attacked what was to prove to be the most elusive target of Johnson's war—the Thanh Hoa Bridge spanning the Song Ma River. Known as the "Dragon's Jaw", the bridge was opened by Ho Chi Minh in 1964 to repace an earlier, French-built structure destroyed by the Viet Minh in 1945. It was 540-feet long by 56-feet wide and was supported by a reinforced, sixteen-foot diameter concrete structure. A rail line ran through the center with concrete roadways on either side.

By the end of May 1965, Operation *Rolling Thunder's* basic target list had been hit including twenty-six bridges. Only the Dragon's Jaw still stood, the survivor of four separate US Air Force strikes and hundreds of bombs and rockets. Sortie after sortie flew through a hail of flak to drop their bomb loads with precision accuracy but the bombs just weren't powerful enough

Below A flight of US Air Force A-1H Skyraiders holds formation on a bombing sortie.

A US Air Force A-37 heads for North Vietnam during Operation *Linebacker* in 1972.

to bring the mammoth structure down. The roadways and approaches were made impassable but the North Vietnamese began their repairs virtually the minute the planes had turned for home. From June to the following May, the Dragon's Jaw became the chief responsibility of the Navy's carrier-based air-arm. In two dozen strikes over that year, Navy attack planes dropped nearly 130 tons of bombs and rockets on the Thanh Hoa Bridge but—despite repeated devastation—it continued to stand as a sort of battered symbol of North Vietnam's determination to carry on.

In May, a specially equipped Air Force Hercules dropped four, 5000-pound, shaped-charge weapons in the waters near the Dragon's Jaw. The bombs were specially designed to demolish bridges but hardly scratched the Dragon's Jaw. By March 1967, several more hundred tons of bombs had been expended on the Thanh Hoa Bridge but caused only repairable damage. The Navy then tried three new Walleye TV-guided,

glide bombs which all hit with phenomenal accuracy but again failed to send the Dragon's Jaw collapsing into the river. Before Johnson called a halt to the bombing of North Vietnam in 1968, the Dragon's Jaw had survived over a hundred further strikes and thousands of pounds of bombs.

B-52s began bombing North Vietnam at the end of January 1966 but were restricted to stretches of the Ho Chi Minh Trail and the Mu Gia Pass in particular. Converted from their original strategic nuclear role, the B-52 can carry up to eighty-four 750-pound bombs and a cell of three aircraft can devastate an area three kilometers long by something like a kilometer wide. When used against enemy troop concentrations in the South, the B-52s had the advantage of flying so high that the NVA/VC had no idea they were in danger until the bombs began falling. But against the Ho Chi Minh Trail, the B-52 was a bit of a waste of fuel and munitions. Unlike the fixed-wing gun-ships, the B-52 could not seek out enemy movement to

attack. It dropped its bombs and – if lucky – hit NVA supply columns who just happened to be underneath but otherwise devastated little but empty ground. These bombardments made the Trail unusable but the NVA's engineering battalions would quickly cut an alternative pathway or bring in the bulldozers and shovel-teams to make the Trail passable again. At first, B-52 missions were flown out of Guam but were switched to Thailand when the CIA discovered that Russian trawlers were monitoring the missions leaving Guam and warning Hanoi of incoming attacks.

In the first few months of 1967, the bombing was extended to selected targets within the restricted zone and the prohibited zone, extending thirty and ten square miles from the center of Hanoi respectively. On August 11th, the US Air Force went after what became the second most popular target in North Vietnam, the French-built Paul Doumer Bridge across the Red River in the suburbs of Hanoi. Refuelling over Laos, three wings of F-105

"Thunderchief" fighter-bombers, fighter escorts, and "Wild Weasels" (aircraft especially equipped to attack SAM batteries and anti-aircraft installations) flew out of Thailand, turned into North Vietnam and flew into the Hanoi area to attack the bridge. Unlike the Dragon's Jaw, the Doumer Bridge came down with the first attack but, up to Johnson's 1968 bombing halt, it took over 175 further strikes to keep undoing North Vietnamese repair efforts.

North Vietnamese fighters made their first appearance in the April 4th 1965 strike on the Dragon's Jaw when four Migs dove out of the sun to down two F-105s heading for the bridge. It was to be some time though before the enemy fighters did much more than follow and harass attacking US aircraft. By early 1966, the Mig interceptors were worrisome enough for Headquarters to try a trap. A strike force headed into North Vietnam in the usual pattern but, instead of the anticipated F-105s, the strike force actually contained an escorted formation

Below The US F-5 fighter-bomber. The F-5 became the main strike aircraft of the South Vietnamese Air Force.

Left A US Air Force F-4 Phantom. The Phantom was probably the Vietnam war's most all-round aircraft. It was used as a Mig-killer in the air campaign against the North, as a strike-aircraft against ground targets, in specialized reconnaissance roles, and as a "Wild Weasel" fighter-bomber equipped with electronic gadgetry and radar-seeking missiles to take on SAM batteries.

of F-4 Phantoms outfitted for an air-superiority role. As the flight approached, NVA radar showed what they thought was an F-105 strike-force and the Migs which rose up to take the bait suddenly found themselves in a full-fledged dog-fight. Seven Migs were downed for no American losses. In 1967, the President and Pentagon added military airfields to the list of allowed targets and nearly fifty Migs were caught on the ground.

By the summer of 1965, US pilots found themselves under attack from Soviet-built SAM missiles. Tactics for avoiding a SAM include sudden and erratic maneuvers and steep dives or climbs to send the missile off-course. Violent maneuvers confuse the SAM operator who is tracking the aircraft and signalling course changes to the missile or cause its guidance

system to lose the heat signals from the plane's engines. Climbing towards the sun and then veering away suddenly can make the missile's heat-seeking sensors chase away harmlessly into the sky. Another partial answer was an electronic counter-measures (ECM) pod fitted beneath attacking aircraft which broadcast jamming and spoofing signals to confuse NVA radars. Special ECM-equipped American aircraft would overfly North Vietnam to detect and jam NVA radars and warn attacking US planes of SAM launches, anti-aircraft radar activity, or of Migs taking-off from distant airfields.

Another tactic was having lead planes release streams of chaff—bundles of metallic strips which reflect hostile radar signals and mark the attacking aircraft in hundreds of false

Below Navy F-4 Phantom prepares for take-off on a bombing mission to North Vietnam.

images on the detector screens. This was especially useful when flights of B-52s were sent against military targets in North Vietnam in 1972. F-105Fs were equipped with special radar detection equipment and Shrike radiation-seeking missiles. SAM or anti-aircraft radars tracking US planes would be detected by the Wild Weasel which would swoop in to fire a Shrike (or later, the more advanced Standard Arm) which locked onto the signal and homed-in on its source to destroy the installation. The missiles were liable to miss if the signal was shut down and the NVA responded by reducing the broadcast times of SAM radars. This increased the value of electronic counter measures and – from its first trial runs in Vietnam – ECM is now one of the world's most important military technologies.

By the time Giap launched his 1972 offensive, the budding detente between Washington and the two Communist super-powers had reduced the risk of a wider war and Nixon could order military actions against North Vietnam which Johnson would never have dared. Haiphong and other, less important ports were mined after May 8th and Nixon ordered a new air campaign against North Vietnam for the first time since 1968. Known as *Linebacker I*, Nixon's air strikes were still highly limited in their objectives but, unlike Johnson's harassing operations, were directly aimed at crippling Hanoi's ability to make war in the South. For the first time, US planes were given permission to cut North Vietnam's rail links with China and – combined with the mining of the ports – disrupt the flow of supplies into North

Vietnam as well as their movement to the South.

In general, there was a thirty-mile strip running along North Vietnam's border with China that was off-limits to US aircraft but even here certain important railway bridges were targeted with the new laser-guided bombs. The precision accuracy of these weapons also enabled strikes on military or industrial targets within or adjacent to civilian areas. Previously these had been prohibited because inaccurate bombing would produce large numbers of innocent casualties and hostile world opinion. Local commanders were given a wider latitude in determining missions, targets, and engagements than Johnson had ever allowed. Previously prohibited major airfields were added to the target list as were hydroelectric plants, oil storage depots, and important industrial facilities in the middle of Hanoi, Haiphong, and other cities.

Thirteen rail bridges linking North Vietnam and China were destroyed in US bombing raids as well as four on the route from Hanoi to Haiphong. The southern rail lines were attacked once again and a number of bridges were brought down. One of these was the elusive Dragon's Jaw. On April 27th, Air Force Phantoms flew through intense flak and SAM fire to hit the Dragon's Jaw with five laser-guided bombs but, despite heavy damage, the bridge stayed up. On May 13th, the Dragon's Jaw was hit by some twenty-five laser-guided and nearly fifty conventional bombs to finally break apart and fall into the river. A further thirteen Air Force and Navy strikes were sent against the Dragon's Jaw to counter ambitious NVA repair efforts. The Doumer Bridge (repaired during the long bombing halt) was downed in laser-guided bomb strikes on May 10th and 11th with a final knock-out punch on September 10th.

By August, Hanoi knew that North Vietnam stood virtually alone against the onslaught of American airpower. Giap's offensive had failed, a battered ARVN army had stayed intact, and now Nixon was almost certain to be re-elected. Russia and China were calling for a settlement and were unlikely to contest Nixon's war apart from anti-American propaganda. On September 10th, the Russians informed Kissinger of Hanoi's

willingness to reach an agreement on the lines of America's proposals of nearly a year earlier. A settlement was scheduled for signing at the end of October and *Linebacker* was called off in preparation for peace. Thieu, however, resisted the terms of the agreement and Nixon began to have second thoughts about whether the agreement was tough enough to satisfy hawkish Americans. Further talks ground to a stalemate and, on December 15th, Nixon gave an ultimatum promising renewed bombing if Hanoi wasn't willing to negotiate seriously.

For twelve days beginning on December 18th, North Vietnam was bombed without respite save for a short Christmas break. Nearly 730 B-52 and over 1000 fighter-bomber missions were flown in an all-out war on Hanoi's military capabilities including raids over Hanoi and Haiphong. Rail-yards, industrial facilities, military airfields, SAM sites, radar installations, and virtually every target of any importance was attacked by waves of fighter-bombers or flights of B-52s dropping over 20,000 tons of bombs. *Linebacker II* was not unrestricted aerial warfare but it came quite close to a total effort to destroy North Vietnam's military capability. Numerous civilians died and non-military targets such as hospitals were destroyed, but – despite the many allegations – *Linebacker II* was not a campaign of full-fledged terror bombing. Had it wished to do so, the US Air Force could easily have carpet-bombed Hanoi into oblivion with wave after wave of B-52s flying in cells of three.

Nonetheless, Vietnam had sustained unparalleled devastation and it was obvious that Nixon was prepared to carry on. Both Moscow and Peking were becoming impatient with Hanoi's stubborn refusal to reach an agreement which to them at least seemed to be more an advantageous truce than a defeat. At last, Hanoi agreed to talk again and Nixon stopped the bombing on December 30th. A week later, Kissinger and Le Duc Tho met in Paris to iron out the last obstacles to peace. On January 23rd the two negotiators initialled an agreement for a formal signing on the 27th. On January 28th, 1973, an uneasy cease-fire came to Vietnam and America's longest war ended.

Left North Vietnamese anti-aircraft guns near Hanoi during Operation *Rolling Thunder.*

Below An Air Force F-111 armed with cluster bombs. The F-111 fighter-bomber was used principally in low-level, night strikes on SAM sites and air fields. The F-111 was equipped with a terrain-following radar which allowed it to fly at extremely low altitudes at night or in bad weather. The F-111s would hit targets just ahead of the main strike force. When the main cluster-bomb-cannister was released, a number of smaller sub-munitions were scattered outwards to devastate a wide area.

Right A 1st Air Commando Squadron A-1E Skyraider armed with napalm bombs en route to Viet Cong targets in 1966.

Above An attack force is launched from the flight deck of the *USS America* in the Gulf of Tonkin.

Left F-4 Phantom drops a laser-guided bomb. The laser-aimed weapon was the second of the new PGMs introduced into the Indochina war. The target is illuminated by a laser beam. When the bomb is released, a laser-sensor in the nose follows the beam to the target and signals glide corrections to its steering mechanism. The bomb's main weakness is bad weather which interferes with the laser beam.

Left The F-105 Thunderchief could carry more fire-power than other fighter-bomber of its time. Armaments included a 20mm gatling-type Vulcan cannon mounted in the nose. Other F-105s were specially equipped for "wild weasel" anti-SAM roles. On the outer portion of the wing, this F-105 is carrying a Shrike radar-seeking missile; on the inside of the wing is another radiation-seeking missile, the Standard Arm.

Below The bombing of the Dragon's Jaw. Aircraft from the attack carrier *USS Oriskany* hit the Thanh Hoa Bridge with pin-point accuracy in November 1967. But the gigantic bridge survived this and numerous other attacks until – hit by laser-guided bombs in 1972 – it was finally brought down.

10 The Bitter End

After Nixon's Peace

Nixon's peace was greeted with a general sigh of relief but was not looked upon as a triumph of diplomacy. To the doves, the war had gone on far too long while the hawks were sceptical of exactly what had been won. Both Washington and Hanoi claimed victory but it was obvious that the cease-fire was just a stop-gap on which a lasting peace had yet to be built. Nixon claimed that the independence of South Vietnam had been assured but its future was still very much in doubt and he made it clear that the main burden of protecting that independence now lay with Saigon. In mid-March 1973, the MACV was shut down and US TV programmes highlighted the last few American forces boarding a plane at nearby Tan Son Nhut airport for the flight home. US airpower remained behind in neighboring Thailand and off-shore on the carriers of the Pacific Fleet, but American ground forces had gone for good.

With the cease-fire came the return of America's prisoners of war. Many downed Air Force and Navy pilots had languished in NVA prison camps or in the "Hanoi Hilton" since 1965 and – spearheaded by a vocal POW wives' lobby in the United States – had been a persistent political issue through nearly eight years of war and the seemingly endless negotiations. In November 1970, Nixon had tried for a dramatic coup when he ordered a Special Forces commando raid on the Son Tay POW camp some twenty miles from Hanoi to rescue sixty-one US prisoners reportedly being held there. The raid went off like clockwork,

Left US POWs in Hanoi wait for their names to be called before boarding a US Starlifter cargo aircraft which will take them on the first leg of their journey home.

Below Memphis Tennessee welcomes the Navy's Lt James Bailey after his release from a North Vietnamese POW camp.

and the commandos killed well over 100 NVA soldiers, but the prisoners had been moved because of flooding in the area. Ironically, the flooding was apparently due to a secret US project involving seeding the clouds over North Vietnam to produce damagingly high levels of rainfall.

Hanoi returned over 500 American prisoners but Pentagon figures showed some 3300 others missing or unaccounted for. Years later nearly 800 were still classed as unaccounted for and there are reports even now of Americans imprisoned in the backwaters of Vietnam. Close to 27,000 NVA/VC were released in exchange for the American and South Vietnamese prisoners, but Thieu did his best to hold onto the NLF cadres and agents like Tai who would simply go back to work, subverting his government. The exact number of prisoners who stayed in Thieu's jails is uncertain but it was certainly well above the official figure of 30,000. Many had little or no connection with the NLF but had been guilty of opposing Thieu in other ways. Like Tran Ngoc Chau, some were communists only in the spacious dossiers drawn up to justify locking them away.

It was a messy peace. When Hanoi began talking again in the fall of 1971, Nixon and Kissinger were so anxious to end the long-running deadlock that the final agreement left open nearly as many questions as it settled. NVA troops in South Vietnam, for example, were allowed to stay in place and the country effectively became a patchwork split into areas of communist and Saigon Government control. In many cases, control was fluid and there was a great deal of jockeying about by both sides to extend their respective areas of influence. The communists held about a third of the South Vietnamese countryside but Saigon controlled the built-up areas and well over ninety per cent of the population. Although Kissinger later claimed he had reached a tacit understanding with Le Duc Tho on their withdrawal, NVA/VC troops also stayed on in Laos and Cambodia where they continued to threaten South Vietnam.

When Thieu first heard the proposed peace terms, he was immediately and totally opposed to the idea of NVA troops staying in the South. He remained steadfast and soon became the only obstacle to a settlement with Hanoi. Nixon and Kissinger became so frustrated that they threatened to sign a separate peace with Hanoi if he didn't quickly change his mind. As a further inducement to cooperation, Thieu was promised massive aid packages and was led to believe that Washington

Below Former POW Lt Colonel Robert L. Stirm is re-united with his family at Travis Airforce Base, California. The picture won a Pulitzer Prize for Associated Press photographer Sal Veder.

Left Men of the NVA's 3rd Company, Khe Sanh Infantry Brigade move up to the front in South Vietnam. The picture dates from late December 1974 when Hanoi was committed only to limited probes and drives in the South aimed at testing Washington's resolve and weakening Saigon's defences. A spy in Thieu's inner circle passed top-secret military information to the NVA and the battles of the new year turned into a rapid and total victory.

Below A few of the 6,000 South Vietnamese refugees who fled the fighting around Dau Tieng in March 1975.

Above NVA regulars run up the flag after over-running an ARVN base near Saigon.

Right ARVN mortar team fires at the NVA.

would use American airpower to counter any future communist aggression. These were not false promises but they proved exceedingly rash. Neither Nixon nor Kissinger had any intention of letting Hanoi move south to make a mockery of their hard-won peace with honor, and when it was clear that the NVA was staying in its neighboring sanctuaries, Nixon sent the B-52s against communist positions in Cambodia again.

But the increasing turmoil of Watergate boosted Congressional opposition to any involvement in Indochina and soon Thieu was left on his own; Congress tied the administration's hands by pushing through Bills which prohibited any use of American forces in the area without legislative approval. By working through the Soviets, Kissinger managed to get Hanoi to withdraw some of its forces from the Laotian and Cambodian sanctuaries but, at the end of July, the Congress passed legislation which gave itself the final say on any future uses of the American military in Vietnam, Cambodia, or Laos. In November the Congress went much further and – despite Nixon's opposition – passed the War Powers Act which put severe limitations on the President as Commander-in-Chief. From that time, the President may not use American troops abroad for more than sixty days without first getting the prior approval of Congress.

Needless to say, Hanoi was watching these events with great interest, but the NVA was still relatively weak compared to the ARVN and neither Moscow nor Peking was yet prepared to encourage further North Vietnamese adventurism in the South. Communist tactics reverted to the tried and true guerrilla raid and spoiling hit-and-run attacks aimed at causing the maximum amount of disruption while avoiding major battles. For his part,

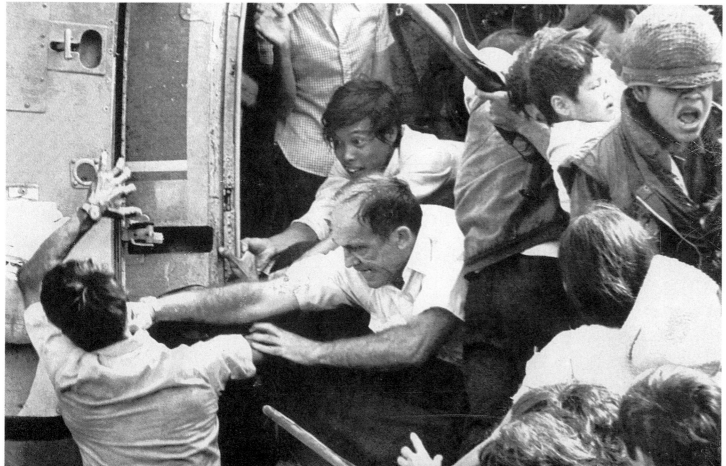

This page Fighting for space aboard an evacuation plane at Nha Trang in early April. The collapse of the ARVN forces led to panic and quick evacuation of South Vietnam's cities in face of the rapidly advancing NVA. Time after time, the evacuations were done at the last minute and with little preparation. The evacuations themselves were done with skill and courage but the poor preparation meant that hundreds – if not thousands – of South Vietnamese who should have been taken out were lost to the on-coming communist troops. In a number of cases, CIA officials abandoned top-secret papers without destroying them. These included lists of long-serving South Vietnamese agents and contacts – a find for which the NVA was no doubt extremely grateful.

Top right Communist troops overrun Tan Son Nhut Airport, Saigon. When NVA fire closed the airport, US officials had no choice but to complete the last minute evacuation of Saigon by helicopter.

Bottom right Communist forces move into Tan Son Nhut Airport. Note the unscratched helicopters. The amount of US military equipment – much of it quite advanced – that fell intact into communist hands has been valued at hundreds of million dollars despite dedicated American efforts to destroy or evacuate as much as possible.

Below Ngyen Trung Kien – who later became a well-known actress – poses for a bit of communist publicity during the last minutes of the NVA drive on Saigon.

Thieu ordered clean-up raids on NVA/VC pockets in the Delta, around Saigon, and along the Cambodian border. In early November, the NVA attacked three ARVN fire-bases north of Saigon in a sort of test-run both to discredit Thieu and to probe Washington's reactions. On April 12th 1974, Saigon announced the fall of Tong Le Chan to an NVA attack but Thieu had apparently ordered its beleaguered ARVN garrison to withdraw quietly the night before so he could publicize North Vietnamese aggression for the benefit of US policy makers.

At the same time, NVA troops moved against ARVN operations near Saigon and laid seige to several isolated towns and villages. By the time Nixon resigned the Presidency on August 9th, the Congress had put a limit of one billion dollars on military aid to Saigon and over 25,000 ARVN and 100,000 NVA had died in battle. Although the new President Gerald Ford assured Saigon of American support, Hanoi believed that such support was likely to prove illusory. Caution eventually prevailed, however, and the NVA were ordered to prepare a number of offensives for 1975 that would effectively test American responses. Rather than full-scale attacks, the NVA would launch what amounted to probes in selected military and economically vulnerable areas of the South. If these operations showed signs of success, the pressure would be increased, but

if they proved too risky they could be quickly abandoned. The Politburo was determined to "liberate" the South but it was not prepared to go too far too soon and risk the return of the B-52s. Hanoi expected a final victory sometime in 1976 at the earliest and was as surprised as anyone else when South Vietnam began collapsing almost from the moment of the first NVA attack in 1975.

The Fall of Saigon and Phnom Penh
Of North Vietnam's most famous leaders, Ho Chi Minh had died in September 1969 and Giap was incurably ill. The image of "Uncle" Ho as a kindly old man who loved talking to children and quiet reflection (an image that was partly true despite its deliberate cultivation for propaganda purposes) had become a national rallying point and Giap had an awesome reputation as one of the chief architects of guerilla warfare. But the conqueror to whom Saigon would ultimately fall, was a man most people had never heard of, fifty-eight year old General Van Tien Dung. Like Ho Chi Minh, Dung had a peasant background and received training in the Soviet Union. Dung had done most of the day-to-day planning and logistics for Giap's great offensives (including Dien Bien Phu) and, in the late 1950s, formulated much of Hanoi's approach to the escalating guerrilla war in the

South. In late 1974, Dung received an unexpected bonus which gave him the key to Saigon.

Thieu and his generals had been looking at the pattern of NVA activity throughout the country in an attempt to predict where the next NVA offensive was going to fall and to disperse ARVN's dwindling resources accordingly. Congressional cuts in US military aid to Saigon had caused considerable difficulties (but not nearly so many as Thieu pretended) and the ARVN net had to be spread fairly thin. In the end, Thieu predicted a major NVA attack on Tay Ninh northwest of Saigon with only moderate activity in the north of the country and in the highlands. A spy close to Thieu sent this information on to Hanoi and they promptly decided to launch the NVA against Phuoc Long Province. Not surprisingly, this was the area Saigon had chosen not to reinforce and where Thieu did not expect the main blow of the offensive to fall.

On January 1st 1975, the NVA, having already overrun several small towns and ARVN outposts in Phuoc Long Province, opened its assault on the local capital, Phuoc Binh, with a massive artillery barrage. A week later, the city fell. In Hanoi, this success caused another revision of NVA strategy. The offensives of 1975 would not now be aimed at a final victory in 1976 but, if circumstances permitted, in 1975. The next target

Far right top The US merchant ship *Pioneer Contender* loaded with South Vietnamese refugees.

Far right below Evacuation of refugees at Xuan Loc in face of the advancing NVA.

Right Vietnamese refugees wait on board the US merchant ship *Green Port* to go by barge to the island of Phu Quoc in early April 1975.

was to be Ban Me Thuot in the western highlands but with a feint in the northern highland area to pin down the ARVN forces there and prevent Saigon from sending reinforcements until it was too late. Travelling down the Ho Chi Minh Trail, Dung came south to take direct command of the attack on Ban Me Thuot himself; in reply, Thieu began weakening his defences north of Hue by withdrawing the Airborne Division to reinforce the Saigon area.

The NVA attack on Ban Me Thuot began on March 10th after Dung had secretly built up his forces around the city and, in the previous week, captured several ARVN outposts guarding the main roadways. Partly because the South Vietnamese Air Force had managed to bomb some ARVN positions, and partly because of the NVA's numerical superiority, the city fell the next day. Thieu now came to a difficult and — as things turned out — fatal decision. Faced with defeats in the highlands, growing NVA pressure throughout South Vietnam, and an American Congress which clearly was not going to come to his aid, Thieu decided to abandon the northwestern highlands and parts of the north altogether in order to concentrate his defences around the major cities and the Delta, the country's rice-bowl. Thieu called his strategy "light on the top, heavy on the bottom". Having resisted the idea of giving the communists any additional territory for years, Thieu was now reversing himself and electing to become the head of a small, defensible, and economically viable country.

Quang Tri, Kontum, and Pleiku were to be abandoned so troops could be moved south to shore up the defences around Saigon and to prepare for a counter-offensive against Ban Me Thuot. Based on Dung's on-the-spot assessment of the situation, Hanoi approved an increased offensive in the highlands to exploit the deteriorating ARVN position. As the ARVN began withdrawing from Pleiku and Kontum, thousands of civilians joined in to create a helpless, confused, and panicked mob. The same thing happened when the ARVN began leaving Quang Tri. Streams of frightened civilians poured south into Hue where they started a secondary panic and, within hours, a flood of refugees was strung out along the road to Danang. When Dung realized that Pleiku and Kontum were being abandoned, he sent two regiments on an intercept path to cut the route south and encircle the now disorganized ARVN. Few of these soldiers ever reached safety as the NVA cut the column to pieces.

The NVA moved on to block Highway-1 south of Hue and began massing an attack from all directions. Similar moves around Danang reduced Saigon's hold in the north to the small enclaves around Hue and Danang and upwards of two million people found themselves refugees. At Hue and further south at Quang Ngai, every available commercial vessel, press-ganged fishing boats, and the South Vietnamese Navy were evacuating

Right Air Vice Marshal Nguyen Cao Ky *(front right)* – leader of the Republic of South Vietnam before he was eclipsed by Thieu – arrives aboard the *USS Midway* to begin a life of exile in the West.

Right The wives and families of South Vietnamese Air Force personnel arrive aboard the amphibious command ship *USS Blue Ridge* on April 29th.

mobs of ARVN and local civilians clamoring to escape the on-coming NVA. Hue and Quang Ngai fell on March 25th and pressure on Tay Ninh and Danang was increasing daily. The day before the fall of Hue, the Politburo in Hanoi voted to go for an all-out offensive aimed at taking Saigon by early May and Dung prepared to annihilate what was left of the ARVN in the north and in the highlands.

Danang fell on Easter Sunday. Before the NVA moved in, South Vietnamese and American personnel began what started as a reasonably orderly evacuation but which, by the time it was finished, had turned into a rout that beggars description. Planes leaving Danang airport were filled to the brim as ARVN soldiers, refugees, and government officials fought for the smallest space. On the beaches, the same scenes were repeated as occasional NVA rockets and artillery rounds burst among the milling crowds. Thousands were saved but countless others were left behind to face the NVA or try to walk their way to safety.

Dung had an unintentional ally in the panicking ocean of refugees. They clogged the roadways making it virtually impossible for the ARVN to move and the NVA took full advantage of this by deliberately firing at crowds of fleeing civilians to herd them into the cities or against what was left of South Vietnamese defence positions. Panic increased everywhere and most of the ARVN forces simply began dissolving into a rampaging mob of looters or frightened individuals desperately trying to catch a ride out. Nha Trang was overrun by April 2nd as local American diplomatic, CIA, and military advisors carried out another chaotic evacuation. The same day, Dung began turning the majority of his forces south

to prepare for a final assault on Saigon. The entire northern and central parts of the country had fallen. Thieu's forces drew up a new defence line running from Tay Ninh in the west to Phan Rang on the eastern coast. In Hanoi, the NVA's phenomenal successes caused the Politburo to move up the timetable once again. Saigon was now targeted to fall in April.

The NVA had some 300,000 troops in the South and these were reinforced by additional troops gathering for the final push on Saigon. They had plentiful supplies of Soviet-made equipment including tanks and mobile SAM launchers.

By contrast, the disasters in the highlands and in the north had reduced ARVN numbers to less than 100,000 effective troops and their equipment losses had been staggering. Approximately half of Saigon's aircraft and helicopters had either been destroyed or abandoned to the advancing NVA. Total equipment losses came to at least a billion dollars and demoralization was widespread. A few American officials did their best to get new supplies of weaponry and equipment for Thieu's battered army but, whatever the administration wanted, there was no chance of getting the one thing that just might have held the NVA off – a massive commitment of US airpower at the last minute.

To back up their military triumphs, Hanoi and the VC (under the name of the Provisional Revolutionary Government) began a diplomatic offensive designed mainly to sow further confusion in Washington and Saigon. In Algeria, the VC's Madame Nguyen Thi Binh announced the NLF's willingness to negotiate a settlement with General Duong Van "Big" Minh if he were to replace Thieu as President. In the last weeks of Saigon

there were a variety of proposals for setting up an independent South Vietnam along the territorial lines of the old French colony of Cochinchina through a political agreement with Hanoi. These proposals never had a chance to come to fruition despite the desperate optimism of US Ambassador Graham Martin and other Americans who refused to see that the collapse of Saigon was now only a matter of time. Right to the end the communists did nothing to discourage these beliefs as a counter to the (extremely remote) possibility of American intervention.

Intelligence quickly revealed that Hanoi had absolutely no intention of accepting any sort of interim political settlement but Martin and, to a point, Kissinger, steadfastly avoided the obvious truth. May 19th was the anniversary of Ho Chi Minh's birthday and the Politburo made it the absolute deadline for the conquest of Saigon. The idea of salvaging some sort of smaller Republic of South Vietnam out of the ashes of the old was a cruel self-deception and the refusal to see Saigon's coming collapse caused the blinkered officials to delay evacuation plans until almost the last minute. Consequently, when the collapse did come, the desperate rush to get out of Saigon provided not only an extremely distasteful image of America's withdrawal but also caused the abandonment of thousands of Vietnamese who – due to their links with the US – should never have been left to the mercies of the NVA.

Part of the problem was that Madame Binh's offers of a negotiated settlement had convinced the French of her sincerity. Seeing a role for French diplomacy in the last days of Saigon, Paris began a series of futile efforts designed to make Hanoi settle for a political agreement which the Soviets publicly encouraged with vague and non-committal statements. The removal of Thieu was put forward as a precondition but Kissinger wasn't at all interested until Cambodia's Lon Nol decided on a self-imposed exile. When military disaster, the fragmenting political situation, and American pressure pushed Thieu into resigning on April 21st, he blamed the mire of Watergate for destroying US resolve and South Vietnam's defeat. When "Big" Minh assumed power and began talking about negotiations, the communists hardened their line and it became clear to all but a few eternal optimists that there would be no agreement short of unconditional surrender.

Nothing characterized the NVA's last offensive more than the role of the respective superpowers. In the preceding months, Soviet military supplies had increased dramatically. Detente had soured somewhat after Nixon's resignation and, as the South began reeling under the first NVA blows, the Russians thought the opportunity was too good to pass by. Kissinger, on the other hand, was determined to do what he could to save the Saigon government more for what its fall would do to America's image abroad than anything else. If America were to let an ally fall, its commitments around the world could not help but suffer and other countries relying on US power might begin to re-think their long-term interests. Based on the recommendations of a military fact-finding mission, Kissinger called for a quick transfusion of US aid to the tune of $722-million to prop up the collapsing Saigon Government.

While direct US military intervention remained an impossibility, the South Vietnamese were given a lethal range of US weapons to boost their crippled Air Force's firepower. One was a "Daisy Cutter" first developed to clear dense jungle and

Far left top A boat from the *USS Blue Ridge* moves in to pick up the pilot of a ditched South Vietnamese helicopter. Fifteen helicopters landed refugees on the *Blue Ridge* during the evacuation and – because of the lack of space on deck – had to be ditched in the sea afterwards.

Far left below Making space for another in-coming refugee helicopter aboard the *USS Blue Ridge*.

Left Raising the flag on the *Mayaguez*. Just after the fall of Saigon, the Cambodian Khmer Rouge captured the US merchant ship *Mayaguez*. President Ford ordered the Marines in and, after a short battle, the *Mayaguez* was back in American hands and her imprisoned crew was set free.

overgrowth as emergency helicopters landing areas. Dropped from an aircraft, the 15,000-pound bomb detonates a few feet over the ground to blast everything over a radius of some 100 yards. Other weapons provided were at least two types of cluster bombs. One type had seen much service in Vietnam. It was simply a large canister containing a number of small fragmentation bombs. When dropped by an attacking aircraft, the canister splits apart to saturate a wide area with its exploding sub-munitions.

The other works on the same principle but the sub-munitions contain a liquid which, released into the air, forms a highly volatile cloud. As each bomblet releases its liquid, a number of small clouds are formed over a large area which then coalesce into a single, large cloud. Along with the liquid, the bomblets release timed detonators which ignite the cloud in a blast which creates a downward force of as much as several hundred pounds per square inch. Although vulnerable to such things as weather and wind, these weapon-types (known generally as "fuel-air munitions") form some of the most potent military explosives known. They can be used generally for the rapid clearing of mine-fields and in attacks on entrenched positions.

During attacks on NVA positions at Xuan Loc just thirty miles north-east of Saigon, the South Vietnamese used an American-converted C-130 transport plane to drop at least one fuel-air cluster bomb on the headquarters of the NVA 341st Division. Over 250 North Vietnamese died in one of the few known uses of a fuel-air munition in anger. Further attacks with Daisy Cutters, fragmentation cluster munitions, and conventional gravity bombs provoked the NVA into increasing the shelling of the Bien Hoa Air base which was rapidly made unusable and the South Vietnamese Air Force was effectively finished. Again Vietnam was a proving ground for weapons development. The fuel-air munition is now a promising area of military research. One intriguing possibility is the fuel-air "land-mine" which could be far more devastating that the weapon used at Xuan Loc. Helicopters would spray a large area with the liquid which settles into the ground where it remains active for a day or so; if and when enemy troops enter the area, remote-controlled detonation would explode the ground itself.

Unofficially, US aircraft participated in the battle for Saigon on at least one occasion. Frank Snepp mentions a strike on mobile NVA SAM batteries by US aircraft and there may well have been others. In the final days, anti-aircraft guns and

Below Communist troops move into Saigon.

missiles became exceedingly worrying to US officials planning an emergency evacuation that could only be carried out by planes and helicopters after the NVA cut all roads into Saigon. The attack related by Snepp occurred in the Xuan Loc area and probably consisted of a flight of F-105Fs operating out of Thailand. Needless to say, the attack was highly secret and carried out without the knowledge of even local US personnel. At the time, President Ford was busily assuring Congress that American forces would not be taking part in the fighting and had no wish to be caught out.

Xuan Loc was the ARVN's last real battle. When Thieu had planned his "light-on-the-top-heavy-on-the-bottom" strategy, he had hoped to run his defence line from Tay Ninh to Nha Trang on the coast, but NVA breakthroughs in the Dalat area made that impossible from the start. The new Saigon defence line ran to Phan Thiet and Xuan Loc became a pivotal position. Despite intense artillery and rocket fire, the ARVN 18th Division held Xuan Loc against wave after wave of NVA troops. The unexpectedly stiff resistance caused Dung to put back the date for the final push on Saigon for a week or two to build up further forces. Renaming the drive on Saigon the "Ho Chi Minh Campaign", Dung began encircling the embattled town to put

pressure on Bien Hoa and to cut the roads out of Saigon. The defences at Xuan Loc began crumbling on April 21st when what was left of the ARVN 18th Division was withdrawn by helicopter. A few hundred of its soldiers stayed behind to cover the aircraft before being overrun. NVA troops moving down the coast encircled Phan Rang which fell as the ARVN began abandoning An Loc.

The fall of An Loc opened the door to Saigon and made certain that Thieu would be removed from office in a last desperate bid to find some sort of negotiated settlement with the North. At the same time, Dung settled on the 27th as the date for the NVA's initial attacks on Saigon's suburbs and the 29th for the push into the city itself. Artillery and SAM missiles were laboriously positioned where they could cover the city and Tan Son Nhut airport. The SAM missiles were an increasing concern to the Americans now airlifting South Vietnamese out of Tan Son Nhut and preparing for a mass evacuation of US personnel, but there is no evidence that the NVA intended to risk Washington's military intervention by attacking the aircraft.

Cambodia fell to the Khmer Rouge on April 17th. As the communist forces began digging in around Phnom Penh and closed the airport with heavy shelling on April 12th three US

Below NVA tanks and infantry attack the Presidential Palace in Saigon in the last minutes of Vietnam's thirty-year war.

CH-53 helicopters flew in under fighter escort to land a 250 Marine team at the American Embassy's landing pad. Further helicopters followed and within a few hours eighty-two Americans, 159 Cambodians and thirty-five various other nationalities were peacefully evacuated. Technically, President Ford had committed US forces to an operation in Indochina without the prior approval of Congress but he justified the step as protecting American lives in accordance with his authority as Commander-in-Chief.

The same arguments were to recur over the evacuation of Saigon. Ford's request to use American forces to cover the Saigon withdrawal met with Congressional suspicion and many Senators and Representatives were hostile to the idea of evacuating Vietnamese, but Ford went ahead and did it anyway. As the NVA moved towards Saigon, US officials were deluged by Vietnamese seeking visas or permission to be taken out. Americans living in South Vietnam brought their Vietnamese dependents, girl friends, and close acquaintances for immigration. Conscientious CIA operatives and military advisors organized a number of secret evacuations of Vietnamese high on the communists' wanted list, those possessing sensitive information, and others who were simply being repaid for their long-term loyalty to America's long effort in Vietnam.

Something like $50,000 in bribes was paid to South Vietnamese immigration officials at Tan Son Nhut airport to let selected refugees pass without the proper papers before NVA shelling closed the field on April 29th. Sadly, less conscientious Americans in the State Department, CIA, and the military ignored or abandoned countless Vietnamese whose US affiliations assured them a dark future under the communists and whose loyalty had earned them something better. As South

Left A North Vietnamese tank enters the Presidential Palace gates in Saigon.

Below ARVN Guards Officer surrenders the Presidential Palace.

Vietnam began to crumble, there were a number of incidents where panicking or otherwise inefficient CIA officers failed to destroy their lists of South Vietnamese agents in what must be one of the most disgraceful episodes in the Agency's history. It was matched only by those Congressmen, State Department officials, and others who were opposed to any mass rescue of the Vietnamese.

On April 29th, Dung's advance tanks began moving into Saigon and the US emergency airlift began. When it was finished the next day, seventy helicopters had flown 630 sorties to lift 7053 people to aircraft carriers waiting off-shore. Nearly thirty per cent of these had been lifted out of the American Embassy as Marines held off a vast mob of Vietnamese struggling to get near the landing pads. Only hours before, Saigon radio had begun broadcasting Bing Crosby's "White Christmas", the pre-arranged signal for the city's Americans and favoured Vietnamese to begin making their way through the crowded streets to pre-selected pick-up points.

The helicopter evacuation was a last ditch choice. Washington had been hoping to conduct a more orderly evacuation from Tan Son Nhut but panicking mobs, NVA artillery, and communist commandos made that impossible. The airlift was a remarkable achievement in logistics but the images of the last crowded helicopter taking off seconds before it was engulfed by an on-rushing mob which had finally broken through into the Embassy compound left only distaste. River barges carried away another 6000 Vietnamese and, for the whole month of April, something like 52,000 people had been evacuated from a beleaguered Saigon. Several thousand others managed to reach safety on their own over the same period and in the weeks afterward. Two years later, a total of some 65,000 Vietnamese had managed to get themselves out of the country. Shortly before 8.00 AM local time, the last US helicopter lifted off from the US Embassy as the first NVA tanks began to take up positions around the Presidential Palace and the streets of Saigon.

What followed in Vietnam makes grim reading. Up to a quarter-million politically "risky" Vietnamese, former ARVN officers, policemen, and officials of the Saigon Government were sent to harsh and remote "re-education" camps which, in many cases, were little more than sentences of hard labour. Over 1.5 million citizens of South Vietnam's cities were forced to move into the countryside in a program of economic reform, which quickly led to privation and disease. Soviet aid to Vietnam was cut back and – despite promising negotiations between Kissinger and Hanoi – a proposed renewal of US aid never materialized to any extent. Vietnam is still in desperate economic difficulties and there is little chance of significant

Below Communist victory parade through the streets of Saigon (now re-named Ho Chi Minh City) on May 15th, 1975.

Following pages The Khmer Rouge's road to communism. When the Khmer Rouge overran Phnom Penh, they forced the population into the countryside to build a rural socialism. Starvation and mass murder became the order of the day. How many actually died will never be known for certain.

This page Government troops in Cambodia make their last stand against the Khmer Rouge in the outskirts of Phnom Penh. The city fell on April 17th and entered a Cambodian dark age that sent the country to the verge of extinction.

Right Pol Pot, leader of the Khmer Rouge and – for a time – Prime Minister of Cambodia/Kampuchea. With the Khmer Rouge's efforts to build a sort of bronze-age communism in the Cambodian countryside, Pol Pot succeeded in making himself one of the 20th Century's most notorious mass murderers.

Far right Vietnamese anti-aircraft battery points skyward along the Cambodian border.

244

improvement in the near future.

If Vietnam received a taste of communist austerity and thought control, what happened in Cambodia was a nightmare. Almost from the first moment the Khmer Rouge entered Phnom Penh, they began a purge of unimaginable proportions. Cambodia's cities were cleared as the Khmer Rouge leader, Pol Pot, declared the "year zero" and drove the populations of the cities into the countryside to build a sort of peasant-based communism that Marx and Lenin had never heard of. Anybody showing the slightest "bourgeois" background, attitude, profession, or sympathy faced death by stabbing, shooting, clubbing, or lingering starvation. How many died is hard to say but what occurred was genocide on a scale unknown since Hitler's death camps, and a mass starvation which brought the country to the verge of extinction.

Friction between communist Cambodia (re-named Kampuchea) and now united Vietnam began almost immediately after the fall of Saigon. By late 1977, border skirmishing had evolved into a full-scale Vietnamese invasion. Further Vietnamese offensives occurred over the following months and, in late 1978, battle-hardened Vietnamese troops began a drive that overran Cambodia within a month. Pol Pot's Khmer Rouge troops were forced back into the jungles where – supported by Peking – they wage a continuous guerrilla war with the Soviet-linked Vietnamese.

Hanoi's long struggle to root out the Khmer Rouge guerrillas with largely conventional military forces has led some to call Cambodia "Vietnam's Vietnam" and there have been a series of long-running accusations that the Vietnamese have been using various Soviet-supplied chemical "yellow rain" weapons in an effort to defeat the insurgents once and for all. Because of its war in Cambodia and its continuing feud with China, Vietnam – in spite of crippling economic difficulties – maintains one of the world's largest armies. It is ironic that it is using this army to fight the sort of war that the Americans tried to fight in Vietnam itself.

America entered the Vietnam war to defeat VC insurgency so perhaps the greatest irony of all is the fate of the NLF. When the NVA moved into Saigon, South Vietnam became governed from Hanoi. Within just over a year, the country was proclaimed united but the power still lay in the North. A few leading figures in the NLF received minor or ceremonial positions in the new Vietnam but that was about all. The movement which had become the model of a people's war and inspired countless imitators throughout the world simply ceased to exist in a country governed by practical politics and communist dogma. Of the thousands in the West who had loudly shouted their support for the VC's "libertarian" struggle during the war, few noticed when it was callously cast away into political oblivion.

Far right Rear Admiral Felix Ballenger (right), commanding officer, National Naval Medical Center, escorts ex-POW Lt Commander Wendell Alcorn and his family upon their arrival at the hospital.

This page Vietnam's Vietnam. Since the late 1970s, the Vietnamese Army (the fourth largest in the world) has been fighting a long-running war in Cambodia. American military equipment captured during the fall of the South in 1975 has proved most useful in Vietnam's new Indochina war. The pictures show Vietnamese artillerymen firing a US-made field gun on Cambodian positions.

247

Following pages The Vietnam War Memorial listing the names of the fallen, Washington DC.

Left Marshal Lon Nol of Cambodia visits the front against the Khmer Rouge in March 1975. Arriving in a Rolls-Royce, Lon Nol had little to feel happy about. His administration was to last only a few more weeks before he was forced to go on a long "good will trip" out of the country.

Far left Cambodian government troops hold off the advancing Khmer Rouge at Prek Pnouu, fifteen miles from Phnom Penh on the Mekong River. Note the Soviet AK-47 Kalashnikov 7.62mm rifle, probably the world's most successful military carbine. Countless numbers have appeared among revolutionary movements and terrorist bands everywhere.

JACK D LANELLI

WILLIAM H EBERHARDT · ALVIN C FORNEY · GEORGE GUTIERREZ Jr · MICHAEL G HOVER · CARL MANGOLD
JERRY LEE ROBERTS · LOUIS D ROYSTON Jr · NELSON E WILSON · LESTER O BIEHL Jr · DOUGLAS L FOLEY
DAVID E GILL · MERRILL L LANTRY · DALE L TOOLOOSE · JOSEPH L TSCHAMBERS · GEORGE A ZELINKO
TONY GENEVEVO ABEYTA · GEORGE W BURKHEART · FRANCES F NOVELLO · THOMAS H BOTTS
JAMES A BRANCH · EUGENE M JEWELL · WILLIE E H HONAKER · LAWRENCE E JACKSON · WILLIAM J LA CROA
LEE ROY JAMES · RICHARD C MARSHALL · EDWARD B SHAW · MICHAEL T BADSING · ALLAN R FISCHBACH
LARRY A LINDSEY · RICHARD B FITZGIBBON · FRANK A HENISS · EARL C WILLOUGHBY · ORLANDO O DEAN
CHARLES B GOODWIN · GEOFFREY E GREEN · ROBERT D RUDOLPH · BARNEY E BOYER · LEONARD J DADA
THOMAS E CZZOWITZ · HARRY A HIPKE · JAMES W MAHLER · PAUL J MARQUEZ · ROBERT W REAGAN
ERICH SIMKAITIS · LARRY R TAYLOR · LEO A BAUER · CHARLES M IOPA · GLEN E KING · HENRY J ZEICHERT
ANDREW J HINDERMAN · PAUL W MANSIR · JOSEPH E MUIR · GEORGE S BALAZY · GERALD GREEN
WILLIAM A MITCHELL II · JOE R MOSSMAN · JAMES W STEPHENS · DONALD L BENNETT
ROBERT O FRANKLIN · FRANK R SAXON · NEIL B TAYLOR · BERNARD
DAVID D CASE · WILLIAM J HENRY · KENNETH R IRELAN · SAM IVEY · DONALD H MEY
PARKS · EDUARDO CAMARENA-SALAZAR · DEAN A KLENDA · GEORGE A NEST · ROBERT BL
A L PARKS · HAROLD A BIRD · FRANK BOYNTON · LEROY HICKS · HERBERT D FEE
DAVID E BENSON · EDWARD H FOX · ERNEST K GERHARDT · GEORGE E BLODGETT · L
NNIE W FAIRCLOTH · EDGAR L PETERSON Jr · ROBERT E RAINS · PAUL E OTTE
ERNEST L MILLER · FRED R TICE · THOMAS TOLLIVER · JOHN P
DALE · ROYNALD E TAYLOR · JERRY D UNDERWOOD · LEONARD R S PIERCE
ECK · GAR L HAWKINS · DUANE W MARTIN · RICHARD E WINGATE · GARY
SHOOK Jr · DAVID A MORGAN · EUGENE J CLARK · R
FORTUNATO FERNANDEZ · FRANK COSME ALCANTAR
THOMPSON Jr · MURRAY · DANIEL THADD

Above A unit of the Vietnamese army holding Kampuchean prisoners in August 1978. This was on Vietnamese territory, but it wasn't long before the tables were turned. Note the American-made troop carrier: the star has simply been repainted yellow, the color of the star on the Vietnamese flag.

Right Hue in 1982. Vietnam's young men have time to take an interest in motorcycles.

Left Phnom Penh, April 1975: Khmer Rouge guerrillas patrolling the Kampuchean capital during the first days of communist power. Less than three years later these fighters were at war with Vietnam.

Below The continuing tragedy of Indochina. This is not Mai Lai in 1968 but the village of My Duc in March 1978 and the fruits of the long-running war between the now united Vietnam and Khmer Rouge of Cambodia.

Right War veteran togged up in the combat gear and camouflage paint of a decade ago: now he's wearing it at the Veterans' Parade held in New York in May 1985. But beneath the face paint his expression carries other, indelible marks of the war.

Left Vietnam, May 1985. A mourner visits the memorial of an incident in 1968. For those who cannot read the message, the red symbol on the stone graphically conveys the fate of those commemorated.

Below One of the tens of thousands attending the May 1985 Veterans' Parade in New York. In front of him are the names of some of those who didn't make it to the parade. How can anyone adequately describe the savagery of the experience that is still uppermost in his mind, ten years after he saw it?

MIKE BAILEY   PAUL JAMES MIKE BODE   BOB ZELL
DAN WALTENER   Buddy JACOBI   JERRY BRANTLEY   NICK ROUSH
    JOE POST   KEN HARRISON   DAVE GOSSEL
TOM BROWN   TOM RUDLAND ROBERT GLOVER   MANUEL G
    BILL MASIC

Right Phan Thim Kim Phuc in December 1982. Ten years previously, she was the girl in the photo she holds up, showing how bravely she smiled only weeks after she was severely burned by an American napalm strike. Her traumatic escape from a fiery death is shown on pages 176-7.

Below Vietnam at peace: Paul Henter, a US veteran of the Vietnam war, is one of the many volunteers engaged in reconstruction of the country. He is helping to provide new accommodation for this homeless family.

Above Patriotism in the tropical sunshine as Vietnam holds its 10-year celebrations commemorating the communist victories of April 1975. The Dodge truck is at least ten years old, and still not replaced.

Left The war that won't go away: in March 1985 Vietnamese regular troops, after years of fighting against Kampuchean resistance, pushed across the border in Thailand and met the Royal Thai Army. Many of them were taken prisoner, like these two who were photographed at the border village of Aranyaprathet.

257

Peace in Vietnam The US tank came to this spot before any of these children were born. Now they use it as a climbing frame in their games: in future, it will be their task to evaluate the true meaning of Southeast Asia's bitterest war.

Abbreviations

ARVN	Army of the Republic of Vietnam	NATO	North Atlantic Treaty Organization
CIA	Central Intelligence Agency	NLF	National Liberation Front – the Viet Cong
CORDS	Civilian Operations and Rural Development Support	NSA	National Security Agency
COSVN	Central Office for South Vietnam	NSC	National Security Council
DIA	Defense Information Agency	NVA	North Vietnamese Army
DMZ	De-Militarized Zone	OSS	Office of Strategic Services. The World War II
ECM	Electronic Counter Measures		forerunner to the CIA
GI	Slang for an American foot soldier; literally,	PGM	Precision Guided Munitions
	Government Issue	POW	Prisoner of War
ICP	Indochinese Communist Party	PRP	People's Revolutionary Party
ICEX	Intelligence Coordination and Exploitation	RAF	Royal Air Force
	Program	R & R	Rest and Recreation
JCS	Joint Chiefs of Staff	SALT	Strategic Arms Limitation Talks
KGB	Komitet Gosundarstvennoye Bezopastnosti. The	SAM	Surface to Air Missile
	Russian State Security Organization	SAS	(British) Special Air Service
LLDB	Luc Luong Dac Biet. An intelligence gathering	SEATO	South East Asia Treaty Organization
	operation carried out by the Special Forces against	SIGINT	Signal Intelligence
	the VCI and NLF	TOW	Tube-launched, Optically-tracked, Wire-guided.
LOC	Lines of Communication		A newly developed anti-tank missile
LZ	Landing Zone; usually for helicopter operations	USAF	United States Air Force
MAAG	Military Aid and Assistance Group	VC	Viet Cong
MACV	Military Assistance Command, Vietnam	VCI	Viet Cong Infrastructure

Biographies of Major Participants

DEAN ACHESON. American Secretary of State under President Truman. Urged Truman to supply aid to the French in Indochina; was later to urge President Johnson to seek a negotiated settlement.

GEORGES d'ARGENLIEU. French High Commissioner to Indochina in the years immediately after World War II. Tried to re-establish French rule in her former colony.

BAO DAI. The last emperor of Vietnam. Ruled as a puppet emperor under the French, the Japanese, and then the French again. Was defeated by Diem in the 1955 referendum which established the Republic of South Vietnam.

GEORGES BIDAULT. French Foreign Minister during the Geneva Conference of 1954. Took a hard line against the Viet Minh which contributed to the downfall of his government.

CHRISTIAN de CASTRIES. French commander at Dien Bien Phu.

CHIANG KAI-SHEK. Chinese general and statesman. Ruled China briefly until deposed by the communists under Mao Tse-tung.

CHOU EN-LAI. Chinese Foreign Minister. Ensured that Hanoi had a friendly neighbor to the North.

CLARK CLIFFORD. McNamara's successor as Secretary of Defense. Tried to dissuade President Johnson from further escalations of the war.

WILLIAM COLBY. CIA operative in charge of Operation Phoenix and later Director of the Agency.

Major PETER DEWEY. The first American to die in Vietnam. Accidentally killed by the Viet Minh who may have thought he was French.

JOHN FOSTER DULLES. American Secretary of State under Eisenhower. Devout anti-communist. Favored continued American support for the French and later for the anti-Communist (but corrupt) President Diem.

DUONG VAN ("BIG") MINH. Took over from Diem in a coup in 1963 but was himself deposed shortly after. Was in charge of the Saigon government when it surrendered to the North in April 1975.

DWIGHT D. EISENHOWER. American President, 1953-61. Permitted American support of the French to continue; committed the first American advisers to Vietnam in support of Diem's regime.

GERALD FORD. American President 1974-76. Granted Nixon a full pardon after his resignation as President.

General DOUGLAS GRACEY. Commander of the British force that, under the Potsdam agreement, was to disarm the Japanese in South Vietnam. He favored a return to French rule and his favoritism triggered early clashes (1945) between the Viet Minh and the French.

ALEXANDER HAIG. American negotiator during the final cease-fire talks in 1972. Later, Secretary of State under Reagan.

HO CHI MINH. One of the numerous aliases of Nguyen Tat Thanh, President of North Vietnam from 1945 to his death in 1969. Ho Chi Minh means roughly, "He who brings light."

RICHARD HELMS. Director of the CIA who doubted that intensifying the bombing would deter the North Vietnamese. His advice was largely ignored by President Nixon.

LYNDON JOHNSON. President of the US, 1963-68. More than any other single American perhaps, Johnson was responsible for the slow escalation into war.

JOHN KENNEDY. American President, 1960-63. Intensified American involvement by sending additional American advisers to support President Diem's government. Assassinated in 1963, three weeks after Diem's assassination.

HENRY KISSINGER. Nixon's National Security Adviser and, Later, Secretary of State. He was the main architect of the Paris Peace Talks which ended in the 1973 ceasefire, but has also been criticized for endorsing the secret bombing of Cambodia.

Colonel EDWARD LANSDALE Working under CIA auspices, Lansdale threw the weight of Agency support behind Diem. It is doubtful that Diem would have become President without this support.

General de LATTRE de TASSIGNY. French military commander in Vietnam, 1950-51. By using airpower and napalm he was able to inflict heavy losses on the Viet Minh.

General PHILIPPE LECLERC. France's first military commander in Vietnam after World War II. Earned much approbation by favoring a diplomatic rather than military solution to the Vietnam problem.

LE DUC THO. North Vietnam's principal negotiator at the Paris Peace Talks and a founder of the Indo-chinese Communist Party.

LON NOL. Prime Minister of Cambodia who overthrew Prince Norodom Sihanouk. Pro-western, he went into voluntary exile in 1975.

MAO TSE-TUNG. Leader of Communist China from 1949 to his death in 1976. Supplied arms to North Vietnam.

PIERRE MENDES-FRANCE. French Prime Minister strongly opposed to French involvement in Vietnam. As much as any one man, he was responsible for French concessions at the 1954 Geneva Conference.

JOHN McCONE. A Director of the CIA, vociferously opposed to overt American commitment in Vietnam. His warnings were largely ignored by President Johnson until it was too late.

ROBERT McNAMARA. Secretary of Defense under Kennedy and Johnson. Hawkish at the beginning, McNamara's disillusion with the war led to his resignation in 1968 to become President of the World Bank.

General HENRI NAVARRE. French military commander in Vietnam who rather ill-advisedly lured the Viet Minh into a fight at a place called Dien Bien Phu.

NGO DINH DIEM. Diem was President of South Vietnam from 1955 until his murder in 1963. His government was marked by corruption, inefficiency, anti-communism, and a strong pro-Catholic bias.

NGO DINH NHU. Diem's younger brother. A Machiavellian figure who grew increasingy unstable as the excesses of his brother's regime grew.

NGO DINH NHU, MADAME. Nhu's wife. An outspoken and manipulative woman who caused her brother-in-law much embarrassment. She was nicknamed "Dragon Lady" by western correspondents.

NGO DINH THUC. Diem's oldest brother and Archbishop of Hue. His insensitive handling of minority rights led to the Buddhist Revolt of 1963 which ultimately brought about his brother's downfall.

NGUYEN CAO KY. Colorful fighter pilot who became Prime Minister of South Vietnam after a coup in 1965.

NGUYEN KHANH. The first of Saigon's generals to pick up the pieces after the downfall of Diem. Ruled as Prime Minister for a year.

NGUYEN TAT THANH. Ho Chi Minh's real name (q.v.).

NGUYEN VAN TAI. An important Hanoi agent captured by the ARVN. When the North Vietnamese at last invaded Saigon, he met a particularly unpleasant end. See Chapter VI for details.

NGUYEN VAN THIEU. Prime Minister of South Vietnam, 1967-73.

NORODOM SIHANOUK. Prince and later King of Cambodia. Overthrown by Lon Nol in 1970.

POL POT. Apparently demented leader of the Cambodian Communist Party who is responsible for the death of as many as two million of his countrymen after the communist takeover in 1975.

DEAN RUSK. Secretary of State under Kennedy and Johnson. A hawk, he consistently argued in favor of a stronger American commitment to Vietnam.

General RAOUL SALAN. French military commander in Vietnam between de Lattre and Navarre. He later became infamous as the leader of the OAS, a terrorist organization which fought against de Gaulle in the streets of Paris and Algiers.

SOUVANNA PHOUMA. Prince of Laos ultimately deposed by the communists in 1975.

MAXWELL TAYLOR. Chairman of the JCS and ambassador to South Vietnam. Taylor enjoyed the close confidence of President Kennedy.

HARRY TRUMAN. American President, 1945-53. His decision to support the French efforts in Vietnam was the first step down the slippery slope of American involvement.

General ETIENNE VALLUY. French military commander in Vietnam between Le Clerc and de Lattre.

VAN TIEN DUNG. The man responsible for the day-to-day planning of most of Giap's great offensives, including Dien Bien Phu. In 1975, he was the general who led the final offensive on Saigon.

VO NGUYEN GIAP. One of the world's foremost guerrilla fighters, Giap led the North's military organization from the early 1940s onward.

General WILLIAM WESTMORELAND. American field commander in Vietnam from 1964 to 1968.

Index

PICTURE CREDITS